W9-BKP-637

WITHDRAWN

WITHDRAWN

*The
Triumph
of
Jim
Crow*

The
Triumph
of Jim Crow

TENNESSEE RACE RELATIONS
IN THE 1880s

Joseph H. Cartwright

320.976
C 329t

THE UNIVERSITY OF TENNESSEE PRESS

$13.95

6/24/77

27,890

Publication of this book was assisted by
the Tennessee Historical Commission and by the American
Council of Learned Societies under a grant
from the Andrew W. Mellon Foundation.

Copyright © 1976 by The University of Tennessee
Press/Knoxville. All rights reserved. Manufactured in
the United States of America.

Library of Congress Cataloging in Publication Data

Cartwright, Joseph H   1939-
    The triumph of Jim Crow.

    Bibliography: p.
    Includes index.
    1. Negroes—Tennessee—History. 2. Negroes—Politics
and suffrage. 3. Tennessee—Politics and government—
1865–1950. 4. Tennessee—Race question.
I. Title.
E185.93.T3C37   320.9′768′05   76-2009
ISBN 0-87049-192-X

To Pamela, Keith, and Jeffrey

Preface

Recent studies of Negroes in southern politics immediately after reconstruction and the restoration of white conservative rule have uncovered a thriving black political life.[1] Indeed, the most penetrating historian of the postreconstruction South, C. Vann Woodward, has sharply challenged the picture of a monolithic white community using its reclaimed power in the 1870s to clamp on blacks political shackles that would remain fastened until the second reconstruction of the 1960s.[2] Instead, Woodward, and others, have depicted the era between reconstruction and the turn of the century as one delicately poised between a reactionary white supremacist ethic and a trend toward biracial political activity and flexibility in interracial contacts.

Presently, most studies of blacks in the politics of this era survey the extent of black participation and the status of blacks in the political system on the one hand and chronicle the variety of white responses on the other. Consequently, while we have learned much about the offices blacks held and white attitudes about blacks, much remains obscure about the process and character of interaction between whites and blacks in politics, the

[1]The best state studies are those of George B. Tindall, *South Carolina Negroes, 1877–1900* (Columbia: Univ. of South Carolina Press, 1952); Vernon L. Wharton, *The Negro in Mississippi, 1865–1890* (Chapel Hill: Univ. of North Carolina Press, 1947); Frenise A. Logan, *The Negro in North Carolina, 1876–1894* (Chapel Hill: Univ. of North Carolina Press, 1964); Charles E. Wynes, *Race Relations in Virginia, 1870–1902* (Charlottesville: Univ. of Virginia Press, 1961); Margaret Law Callcott, *The Negro in Maryland Politics, 1870–1912* (Baltimore: Johns Hopkins Univ. Press, 1969); Lawrence D. Rice, *The Negro in Texas, 1874–1900* (Baton Rouge: Louisiana State Univ. Press, 1971).

[2]*The Strange Career of Jim Crow* (2d rev. ed.; New York: Oxford Univ. Press, 1966), 31–109.

internal struggle within both black and white communities over racial policies and strategy, and the reasons for the transition in race relations during these years.

This is the first intensive examination of the brief flowering of Negro influence in Tennessee politics after reconstruction; during the 1880s Negroes attained more political power than they had previously exercised in the state. By the end of the eighties, however, restrictive voting legislation, economic coercion, physical intimidation, and corruption in the electoral process virtually silenced the voices of blacks in Tennessee politics for more than fifty years. To mistake these changes, and others that occurred during the decade, as simply so much rhetoric, masking the fundamental similarity of things, is to risk falling prey to what Professor Woodward has sensitively described as "a want of feeling for the seriousness of human strivings, for the tragic theme in history."[3]

Although much of this study parallels what has been written about race relations in other states, I have endeavored to add a new dimension by examining intensively a relatively short time span in order to discern the intricacies of racial questions, the changes in dialogue between blacks and whites, and the way in which members of each race responded politically to the problems they perceived. Focusing on one decade, however transitional, doubtless involves a risk of exaggerating change and overemphasizing the intensity of conflict. Nevertheless, I think the possible rewards outweigh the disadvantages.

By concentrating on white attitudes about blacks, studies of race relations have often confined blacks to a secondary and passive role. Indeed, there is a dearth of primary sources from which the internal life of the black community can be construed; consequently, much of this information about blacks has been gleaned from sources written or compiled by whites. Read carefully, however, these sources yield a substantial amount of information about black attitudes and activities. Fortunately, several

[3]*American Counterpoint: Slavery and Racism in the North-South Dialogue* (Boston: Little, Brown, 1971), 280.

national black newspapers maintained correspondents in Tennessee throughout the 1880s, and the perspectives they supply is essential to augment the paucity of black manuscript materials and newspapers within the state.

Acknowledgments

For their generous assistance in locating sources and supplying
guidance in the use of facilities I am indebted to the staffs of the
Joint University Libraries, the Fisk University Library, and the
Nashville Public Library, all in Nashville; the Lawson-McGhee
Library, Knoxville; the Chattanooga Public Library; the Murray
State University Library, Murray, Kentucky; and, especially, the
Tennessee State Library and Archives, Nashville. The Committee on Institutional Studies and Research of Murray State Univer-
sity provided two grants that aided immensely in the completion of
this study. I am grateful, also, to the Tennessee Historical Com-
mission, the American Council of Learned Societies, and the
Andrew W. Mellon Foundation for their support of publication.
The Tennessee Historical Society gave permission to publish a
revised version of my article, "Black Legislators in Tennessee in
the 1880s: A Case Study in Black Political Leadership," *Tennessee
Historical Quarterly* (Fall 1973).

Two friends and colleagues—David S. Payne of Northern
Kentucky State College and Kenneth H. Wolf of Murray State
University—gave of their time to read the manuscript at one or
another stage of its development and offered valuable suggestions
for its improvement. I wish to thank both Professor Dewey W.
Grantham of Vanderbilt University for his constructive criticism
of the manuscript and Professor Henry Lee Swint of Vanderbilt
University for his encouragement during the initial stages of my
interest in the subject. Peg Moffett deserves a special thank-you
for expertly typing several revisions of the work. I also appreciate
the encouraging critique of the manuscript by Professor Joel R.
Williamson of the University of North Carolina at Chapel Hill.

My principal debt, however, is to Professor V. Jacque Voegeli of Vanderbilt University who spent many hours thoroughly criticizing the manuscript in its dissertation form and making innumerable analytical observations and suggestions for improvement in style and synthesis. His timely encouragement, unflagging support, and high scholarly standards have been extraordinary sources of intellectual stimulation; in every way he has served as a model of professional conscientiousness.

Finally, I would like formally to express my gratitude to my wife, Pamela, for her numerous personal sacrifices, her untiring patience, her unremitting faith in the author, and, most of all, for providing an ever-peaceful haven in a turbulent world.

Contents

*The
Triumph
of
Jim
Crow*

PRELUDE

The Entrance of Blacks into Tennessee Politics

The pattern of race relations that emerged in Tennessee in the wake of the Civil War was preconditioned by life in a slave society. When Tennessee entered the Union in 1796, slavery was an expanding institution. It spread so swiftly after the opening of the western part of the state in the 1820s that by 1860 approximately one-fourth of Tennessee's total population were slaves. Distributed unevenly across the state, they ranged, in 1856, from slightly over 8 percent of the population in East Tennessee to about 33 percent in Middle Tennessee and about 60 percent in West Tennessee.[1] The free black population in the state remained relatively small, although it, too, grew steadily from almost 3,000 in 1820 to 7,300 in 1860.[2]

Like other southern states, Tennessee gradually developed an extensive legal code to supervise the "peculiar institution." This code grew increasingly restrictive on both master and slave as slavery gained greater economic importance, as the abolitionist movement gained momentum in the free states, and as the fear of slave insurrection increased.[3]

Public opposition to slavery within the state, extensive before the 1820s, fell victim to the growing sectional discord in the nation and to the inability of antislavery leaders to present an alternative acceptable to most whites.[4] Delegates to a state constitutional convention held in 1834, for example, debated some thirty petitions which asked for the abolition of slavery in Tennessee, but the

[1]Chase C. Mooney, *Slavery in Tennessee* (Bloomington: Indiana Univ. Press, 1957), 101–102; Caleb P. Patterson, *The Negro in Tennessee, 1790–1865* (Austin: Univ. of Texas Press, 1922), 63.

[2]Patterson, *Negro in Tennessee*, 212.   [3]*Ibid.*, 8.   [4]*Ibid.*, 64–85.

vast majority of those who took part in the debates inordinately feared the emergence of a large class of free blacks in the state and could not visualize a biracial society based on freedom. Although the debates over slavery in the convention revealed widespread concern about the violence and tension which attended the institution, and even its defenders argued only that it was a necessary evil, to the vast majority of whites, law and order, economic progress, and white supremacy seemed best secured through the perpetuation of slavery.[5]

Under the antebellum color-caste system, the status of free Negroes in Tennessee steadily deteriorated. The state legislature, in 1831, barred the immigration of free blacks into the state, prohibited manumission unless provisions were made for removing the freedmen from the state, and, in 1854, required transportation of emancipated slaves to West Africa.[6] The constitutional convention of 1834 produced a further restriction by withdrawing the legal right to vote which free blacks previously had held in Tennessee.[7] Community mores often played an even more important role than the law in keeping free Negroes subordinate. By the eve of the Civil War their freedom in Tennessee was circumscribed by a system of registration, sharp limitations on their civil rights, occupational restrictions, and the constant pressure of the exclusion policy adopted in 1831.[8]

Within the broad framework of this legal and extralegal caste system, however, signs of interracial intimacy appeared. Shrewdly capitalizing upon white paternalism and indifference, blacks often managed to gain some measure of control over their own lives. Although black ingenuity and assertiveness were over-

[5]Chase C. Mooney, "The Question of Slavery and the Free Negro in the Tennessee Constitutional Convention of 1834," *Journal of Southern History* 12 (Nov. 1946), 487–509 (hereinafter cited as *Jour. Southern Hist.*).

[6]James Merton England, "The Free Negro in Ante-Bellum Tennessee" (Ph.D. diss., Vanderbilt Univ., 1941), 56, 69–72, 184, 189, 190, 193–94, 197, 290.

[7]Mooney, "Constitutional Convention of 1834," 80–82, 503–6; Patterson, *Negro in Tennessee*, assigns special importance to the political influence free blacks exercised in bringing about a change in white attitudes toward their status; see pp. 167–68.

[8]England, "Free Negro in Tennessee," 184, 189–94, 197, 290.

shadowed by the coercive power of whites, blacks helped shape the everyday conditions under which they lived; even in slavery they were not passive instruments of the white man's will. Moreover, public officials only sporadically enforced the legal codes pertaining to free Negroes and slaves, and the state legislature occasionally granted exceptions to the emancipation and emigration laws.[9]

The turmoil of Civil War severely shook the legal underpinnings of the caste system in Tennessee. Racial adjustment, consequently, became a central issue of postwar life. In a myriad of conflicting and volatile ways, it impinged upon practically every public question.[10]

The legal status of Negroes in the state swiftly changed during presidential reconstruction in Tennessee. The existence of a beleaguered but staunch minority of white loyalists in the state facilitated the restoration of civilian government. Tennessee Unionists, however, were divided by Lincoln's emancipation policy and by the continuation of antebellum political feuds.[11] Early in

[9]England draws the conclusion that there were "numerous indicators of intimacy in social relations between whites and free Negroes." *Ibid.*, 214–17, 298–99. See also Mooney, *Slavery in Tennessee*, 20. For an analysis of the varied ways in which slaves participated in the definition of antebellum race relations, see Eugene D. Genovese, "Rebelliousness and Docility in the Negro Slave: A Critique of the Elkins Thesis," *Civil War History* 13 (Dec. 1967), 293–314; Ulrich B. Phillips, *American Negro Slavery* (1918; rpt. Baton Rouge: Louisiana State Univ. Press, 1966), 327–28; and John W. Blassingame, *The Slave Community: Plantation Life in the Ante-Bellum South* (New York: Oxford Univ. Press, 1972), 184–216, and *passim.*

[10]For examples of the ways in which slavery was disrupted by the fighting, see B. A. Botkin, ed., *Lay My Burden Down: A Folk History of Slavery* (Chicago: Univ. of Chicago Press, 1945), 204–28; James M. McPherson, *The Negro's Civil War: How American Negroes Felt and Acted during the War for the Union* (New York: Knopf, 1965), 55–68; Bell Irvin Wiley, *Southern Negroes, 1861–1865* (New Haven: Yale Univ. Press, 1938), 3–23, 181–229.

[11]A discussion of Unionist sentiment in Tennessee is found in Verton M. Queener, "East Tennessee Sentiment and the Secession Movement, November, 1860–June, 1861" East Tennessee Historical Society's *Publications*, No. 20 (1948), 59–83 (hereinafter cited as ETHS *Publications*); J. Reuben Sheeler, "The Development of Unionism in East Tennessee," *Journal of Negro History* 29 (Apr. 1944), 166–203 (hereinafter cited as *Jour. Negro Hist.*); James Welch Patton, *Unionism and Reconstruction in Tennessee, 1860–1869* (Chapel Hill: Univ. of North Carolina Press, 1934), 3–123.

1862, Andrew Johnson, an uncompromising loyalist who had retained his United States Senate seat, was appointed military governor of Tennessee. A supporter of Lincoln's policies, Johnson met stiff opposition among Tennessee Unionists, most of whom opposed the Emancipation Proclamation and the President's insistence upon the abolition of slavery as a condition of reunion. Further divisions came in the presidential election of 1864 when Republicans in the state, under the label of the Union party, prescribed a loyalty oath that disqualified supporters of the Democratic candidate, George B. McClellan. Following the reelection of Lincoln, Union party supporters set in motion the full restoration of civil government by calling an *ad hoc* convention which met in January 1865 in Nashville.[12]

The convention, dominated by Unionist party leaders, assumed the authority to institute a statewide referendum on constitutional amendments repudiating secession, abolishing slavery, and prescribing the qualifications for voters.[13] After these were approved, a state election held in March resulted in the selection of William G. Brownlow as governor and a firmly Unionist General Assembly.[14] When it convened in April 1865, the General Assembly ratified the Thirteenth Amendment and passed a voting law that disfranchised former Confederates.[15] In addition, the legislature adjusted the state's obsolete slave code to postwar conditions. The legislators, most of whom were native Tennesseans and former slaveholders, drew upon the only experience they had had with free blacks and relied upon the antebellum laws pertaining to

---

[12]Eric L. McKitrick, *Andrew Johnson and Reconstruction* (Chicago: Univ. of Chicago Press, 1960), 126–28; Patton, *Unionism and Reconstruction*, 43–48.

[13]Patton, *Unionism and Reconstruction*, 30–49; Thomas B. Alexander, "Political Reconstruction in Tennessee," in *Radicalism, Racism, and Party Realignment*, ed. Richard O. Curry (Baltimore: Johns Hopkins Univ. Press, 1970), 40–45.

[14]Patton, *Unionism and Reconstruction*, 124–25, 49–50. For an analysis of the composition of the 1865 General Assembly, see Thomas B. Alexander, *Political Reconstruction in Tennessee* (Nashville: Vanderbilt Univ. Press, 1950), 69–71.

[15]Alexander, *Political Reconstruction*, 74–75; Alrutheus Ambush Taylor, *The Negro in Tennessee, 1865–1880* (Washington, D.C.: Associated Pubs., 1941), 4–5; Patton, *Unionism and Reconstruction*, 101–2.

"free persons of color" to define the Negroes' new legal status. The Tennessee version of the "black codes" required that contracts between whites and blacks be witnessed by whites, allowed Negroes to testify only in court cases involving blacks, and provided that blacks who were jailed could be bound out to those whites who offered to pay their fines for the shortest term of service.[16]

Three political factions quickly emerged within Unionist ranks. The Conservatives had arisen in opposition to emancipation and Lincoln's continuation of the war; they implacably denied the legitimacy of the Brownlow government and hoped for its early demise. A larger element conceded the legitimacy of the Brownlow government but opposed the extension of rights to Negroes and the disfranchisement of ex-Confederates. A group of Radical Unionists, on the other hand, enthusiastically endorsed the Brownlow government and its measures.[17]

Emboldened by President Andrew Johnson's moderate reconstruction policies, enemies of the Brownlow administration forged victories in the first state elections held under the new franchise law; they won five of eight congressional seats in the fall and the following spring gained control of several county governments. In defiance of the laws, some former Confederates even managed to win local offices.[18] Tennessee Radicals, convinced that there was a conspiracy afoot to replace the Brownlow regime with a Conservative government, pushed a stiffer disfranchisement measure through the legislature in April 1866.[19] The new voting law disfranchised all who had voluntarily supported the Confederacy and set up a voter-registration system that limited the franchise to those who could prove that they had held unquestioned Unionist sentiments during the war. Moreover, the crucial process of voter registration was taken out of the hands of county officials, many of whom were Conservatives, and placed under the ultimate control

[16]Taylor, *Negro in Tennessee*, 7; Alexander, *Political Reconstruction*, 69–71.
[17]Alexander, "Political Reconstruction," 52–53.
[18]Patton, *Unionism and Reconstruction*, 110–112; Alexander, *Political Reconstruction*, 86, 91, 98, 102, 105.
[19]Alexander, *Political Reconstruction*, 105–10.

of the governor, who was empowered to appoint commissioners of registration for each county.[20]

This policy of stern political reprisals against former Confederates and their sympathizers occurred alongside a moderate improvement in the legal status of Negroes. The Radical legislature, under Brownlow's prodding, repealed Tennessee's short-lived black code in the spring of 1866 and gave Negroes the right to testify in court against whites. This step was not altogether a humanitarian gesture, since it also answered the desire of most whites to rid the state of the unpopular Freedmen's Bureau courts.[21] Even this slight advancement for blacks, however, mustered a majority in the legislature only after a provision was attached emphatically stating that the law still prohibited Negroes from serving on juries or from attending white schools.[22]

To pave the way for the readmission of Tennessee into the Union, the long extra session of the 1866 state legislature reluctantly granted Negroes additional rights—to make contracts, to sue and be sued, to inherit property, to be protected in person and property, and to be subject to the same punishments and penalties for lawbreaking as whites. Blacks who were physically or mentally handicapped, economically destitute, or serving as apprentices were to be wards of the state on the same footing as whites. Again, the legislature attempted to calm white racial fears by stipulating that state law excluded blacks from jury service and from attending white schools.[23]

Events moved swiftly in the spring of 1866 as Congress deliberated over the course of action that offered the best hope for safeguarding the fruits of military victory. The first congressional prescription for reconstruction, the Fourteenth Amendment, emerged in June. Governor Brownlow, hoping that swift ratification of the amendment would result in the speedy readmission of

[20]*Ibid.*, 110; Taylor, *Negro in Tennessee*, 19.
[21]Robert H. White, ed., *Messages of the Governors of Tennessee* (8 vols.; Nashville: Tennessee Historical Commission, 1952–), V, 466–67 (hereinafter cited as *Messages*).
[22]Taylor, *Negro in Tennessee*, 16–17.
[23]*Ibid.*, 17–18.

8

Tennessee to the Union, called yet another special session of the state legislature in July. In that tumultuous session, Radicals overrode the fierce Conservative opposition and secured ratification, clearing the way for Tennessee's restoration to the Union, despite the objections of some congressional Radicals who thought the state should have been required to enfranchise Negroes.[24] While most other southern states adopted stringent black codes, rejected the Fourteenth Amendment, and elected former Confederates to Congress, native Radical Republicans engineered Tennessee's compliance with the early demands of congressional reconstruction. In Washington, however, congressional Radicals moved toward a more stringent reconstruction program for the other former Confederate states—one based on martial law and black enfranchisement.[25]

In a message to another special session of the Tennessee legislature in November 1866, Governor Brownlow reflected on the unsettled national and local conditions. At the time he spoke it still was not altogether certain that the Radicals in Congress would succeed in controlling reconstruction. Brownlow's insistence upon invoking stiffer penalties against former Confederates and their sympathizers cost him support in his own party. The steady departure of those who had reservations about the wisdom of a rigorous policy of white disfranchisement, albeit aimed at "rebels," and the simultaneous advancement in the legal status of Negroes caused a decline in Radical strength throughout Brownlow's administration.[26] Aware of the waning fortunes of Radicals in Tennessee and buffeted by the determined opposition of Conservatives, Brownlow decided upon a bold move to strengthen his political power. He announced that the time was "proper and right" for Tennessee to enfranchise Negroes. Such a step, he said, should be viewed as a natural extension of the spirit of the Fourteenth Amendment.[27]

[24]Alexander, *Political Reconstruction*, 110–11, 119–21; Taylor, *Negro in Tennessee*, 22.

[25]W. R. Brock, *An American Crisis: Congress and Reconstruction, 1865–1867* (New York: Harper, 1966), 168–203.

[26]Alexander, *Political Reconstruction*, 91–92, 101–10.   [27]*Ibid.*, 124–30.

Like many Radicals in Washington, Brownlow articulated ambivalent views on the question of Negro suffrage. In a legislative message in October 1865, he declared himself in favor of selective Negro voting but argued that it would be "bad policy, as well as wrong in principle, to open the ballot-box to the uninformed and exceedingly stupid slaves of the Southern cotton, rice and sugar fields." Brownlow feared that "the great majority of them could be influenced by leading secessionists to vote against the Government." If ex-Confederates had their voting privileges reinstated, however, he supported complete Negro enfranchisement.[28] Finally, while attending a southern loyalists' convention in Philadelphia in September 1866, Brownlow fully endorsed Negro suffrage "to weigh the balance against rebelism," and because he thought that suffrage "proper and just."[29]

Brownlow doubtless feared that a victory by President Johnson over the congressional Radicals might overturn disfranchisement of ex-Confederates in Tennessee. He was also aware of increasing violations of the disfranchisement law, of rising Conservative strength within the state, of the dismal failure of an immigration policy designed to attract sufficient Europeans and Northerners to buttress Radical control, and of the need to keep Tennessee in step with the growing sentiment in Congress for Negro suffrage. Brownlow now said that Negroes had demonstrated "a greater aptitude for learning and intelligence than was expected."[30] Thus, it seems, the governor's decision to seize the initiative in pushing for Negro enfranchisement represented an amalgam of local political expediency, growing pressure from Congress, and humanitarianism—probably in that order of influence.

Blacks themselves had persistently demanded the right to vote. In January 1865 a group of Nashville Negroes petitioned the state

[28]White, *Messages*, V, 460, 462, 465–66.

[29]Taylor, *Negro in Tennessee*, 23; E. Merton Coulter, *William G. Brownlow: Fighting Parson of the Southern Highlands* (Chapel Hill: Univ. of North Carolina Press, 1937; rpt. Knoxville: Univ of Tennessee Press, 1971), 320.

[30]White, *Messages*, V, 531, 532; Alexander, *Political Reconstruction*, 124; Patton, *Unionism and Reconstruction*, 127; Nashville *Dispatch*, June 2, 1865, quoted in Taylor, *Negro in Tennessee*, 8.

government for voting rights on the grounds that the ballot was necessary for the effective discharge of the responsibilities and burdens of citizenship. Black men had earned the right to vote, they further argued, by fighting for the Union.[31] During the first session of the legislature in April, a group of East Tennessee Negroes also petitioned for the right to vote.[32] When no action was taken on these proposals, black leaders called the State Convention of Colored Citizens of Tennessee, which met on August 7 in the African Methodist Episcopal Church in Nashville.[33] Delegates were instructed to fight for political and civil equality on the grounds that they had earned their rights through their long years of slavery, their participation in the war, and their loyalty to the Union. The convention sent resolutions to the state legislature and to President Johnson insisting that Negroes ought to have the right to vote in all elections before Tennessee should be readmitted to the Union.[34] Following the readmission of the state to the Union in 1866, black leaders met in a second state convention in Nashville, organized the State Equal Rights League, and again demanded full political rights.[35]

When Brownlow addressed the state legislature in November 1866, he had compelling reason, therefore, to disregard his "prejudices of caste" and to suggest cautiously that "the time had come when it is proper and right to confer the ballot upon the colored man."[36] After insistent prodding by Brownlow, and in the face of a black enfranchisement provision in the First Reconstruction Act, the Tennessee legislature reluctantly adopted manhood suffrage on February 5, 1867, becoming the second state outside New England—Wisconsin was first—to extend the vote to Negroes.[37] Once again, the new suffrage measure prohibited Negro officeholding and jury service.

[31]Nashville *Daily Times*, Jan. 18, 1865, as in Taylor, *Negro in Tennessee*, 2.
[32]Nashville *Daily Press*, Apr. 15, 1865, quoted in Patton, *Unionism and Reconstruction*, 94.
[33]Nashville *Dispatch*, June 2, 1865, quoted in Taylor, *Negro in Tennessee*, 8.
[34]Nashville *Daily Press and Times*, Aug. 9–10, 12, 1865, quoted in *ibid.*, 9.
[35]Taylor, *Negro in Tennessee*, 20–21.
[36]White, *Messages*, V, 532.
[37]Alexander, "Political Reconstruction," 62–63. In 1866 the Wisconsin su-

For two years after their enfranchisement in 1867, the 40,000 Negroes who had been added to the electorate contributed substantially to maintaining Radical power in Tennessee. The vast majority of black voters associated with the white-controlled Union Leagues, which acted as a grassroots organizational arm of the Radical party.[38] Early in 1868 the legislature, under Brownlow's direction, moved to strengthen Negro ties to the party by repealing the legislation excluding blacks from holding office or sitting on juries and by passing a law designed to protect black voters from economic intimidation.[39]

Bereft of whatever faint hopes they may have had about attracting many black voters, Conservatives initiated a campaign of intimidation aimed at destroying black political power in its embryonic stages. The Conservative party's state convention in 1868 focused attention on the Radical race policy, warning that efforts "to deprive the white men of America of their rightful position of superiority and supremacy," would invite "a war of the races."[40] The political activities of the Ku Klux Klan in the presidential and congressional elections of 1868 in Tennessee reflected the grim determination of Conservatives to secure control over the state government. Many Conservatives viewed the Klan as a necessary political expedient justified by the Radical disfranchisement policy, the high taxes of Brownlow's administration, and the threat black voting posed to white supremacy.[41]

---

preme court ruled Negro suffrage constitutional on the basis of an 1849 law. Referenda on Negro suffrage were defeated in Kansas, Ohio, and Minnesota in 1867; in Michigan and Missouri in 1868; and in New York in 1869. The voters of Iowa and Minnesota passed referenda permitting Negroes to vote in 1868. See Gilbert Thomas Stephenson, *Race Distinctions in American Law* (New York: Appleton, 1910), 285–86; William Gillette, *The Right to Vote: Politics and the Passage of the Fifteenth Amendment* (Baltimore: Johns Hopkins Univ. Press, 1965), 25–27.

[38]Alexander, *Political Reconstruction*, 141–62; Weymouth T. Jordan, "The Negro in Tennessee during Reconstruction" (M.A. thesis, Vanderbilt Univ., 1934), 128–30; Patton, *Unionism and Reconstruction*, 139; Paul D. Phillips, "A History of the Freedmen's Bureau in Tennessee" (Ph.D. diss., Vanderbilt Univ., 1964), 268, 293–302.

[39]Taylor, *Negro in Tennessee*, 56–57.

[40]*Ibid.*, 58–59.

[41]*Ibid.*, 60–61; Alexander, *Political Reconstruction*, 176–98.

Collectively, Klan violence, a decline in Union League activities, widespread economic coercion, the conversion of some blacks to conservativism, and a growing disaffection among white Republicans with Brownlow's administration steadily eroded Radical power. Although General Ulysses S. Grant carried the state in the 1868 presidential election, Governor Brownlow held a precarious grip on the state government.[42] Each step the governor took to protect black voters cost him white support. In the summer of 1868, the legislature had given Brownlow power to organize a militia and to declare martial law wherever he thought it necessary to quell Klan violence.[43] Removing limitations on Negro voting, officeholding, and jury service was one thing, but guaranteeing these rights through employment of the state militia and martial law was entirely different. Whites deserted the Radicals in droves. Growing opposition to the administration's economic policies, traditional sectional animosities in the state, incompetence and corruption within the Brownlow government, and widespread sympathy for disfranchised whites also played their roles in weakening Brownlow's power.[44]

In 1869, Radical control over Tennessee came to a swift and climactic end. Early in the year the state legislature elected Brownlow to the United States Senate, and the speaker of the state senate, DeWitt C. Senter, stepped up to the governor's office. Racked by factional rivalries, the Radicals failed to unite on a candidate in the 1869 gubernatorial election. Seeking to retain the office and fearing a loss of support among Radicals, Senter courted Conservatives by quietly and illegally opening the registration books to disfranchised ex-Confederates. Aided by these illegal ballots, he won the ensuing election by a landslide; Conservatives also captured a clear majority in the legislature.[45]

[42]Alexander, *Political Reconstruction*, 192–93; Taylor, *Negro in Tennessee*, 63.

[43]Taylor, *Negro in Tennessee*, 61; Patton, *Unionism and Reconstruction*, 190–94; Alexander, *Political Reconstruction*, 188.

[44]Alexander, "Political Reconstruction," 73–74.

[45]James A. Sharp, "The Downfall of the Radicals in Tennessee," ETHS *Publications*, No. 5 (1933), 105–24; Alexander, "Political Reconstruction," 75.

In his opening message to the new legislature, Senter, as expected, declared that it was time to repeal the laws disfranchising ex-Confederates. To the dismay of many of his recent Conservative allies, he also urged the legislature to ratify the Fifteenth Amendment in order that Negro suffrage might become "a fixed fact in Tennessee." The Conservative-dominated General Assembly, however, decisively rejected the proposed amendment, claiming it represented "class legislation of the most odious character" which would result in "ceaseless agitation" and a usurpation of power by the federal government.[46] Seizing the initiative, the legislature decided that the transition from Radical control demanded a complete revision of the state constitution, and a referendum calling for a January 1870 convention easily passed.

Before the convention met, however, the legislature repealed the Brownlow-sponsored Ku Klux Klan law, abolished the moribund state school system set up by the Radicals, and removed a statute prohibiting racial discrimination by railroads. With similar alacrity, the legislature moved to guarantee the economic dependence of blacks upon whites through the repeal of Radical protective legislation and the enactment of a crop-lien law.[47]

Faced by these somber events, Tennessee Radicals and blacks desperately appealed for federal intervention. Governor Senter hastily retreated from his alliance with Conservatives and requested federal troops. Black leaders also pressed for federal intervention, especially after Congress reinstituted military government in Georgia in 1869. While the all-white legislature was dismantling much of the Radical legislation, black leaders from across the state gathered in Nashville to participate in a convention set for February 21, 1869. Keenly sensitive to their vulnerable position, the delegates appealed to President Grant and the Joint Committee on Reconstruction to save black Tennesseans from the lawlessness that imperiled their property and their lives. The hostile state government offered no protection, they complained, against

---

[46]Taylor, *Negro in Tennessee*, 72–73.
[47]*Ibid.*, 73–74.

segregation on the railroads, the collapse of public schools, discrimination in state courts, and lynching.[48] The Grant administration, however, was determined to avoid intervention, and Tennesseans were left to resolve their racial problems in an atmosphere marked by tensions between white supremacy, black resistance, and the recurrent possibility of federal intervention.[49]

It was a foregone conclusion that the constitutional convention of 1870 would abolish the political restrictions against former Confederates, but opponents of Negro suffrage also viewed the convention as a welcome opportunity to eliminate black voters. In the 1869 elections for delegates to the convention, arguments against Negro suffrage covered a wide range of anti-Negro sentiments: since their enfranchisement in 1867, which some Conservatives insisted had been unconstitutional, the performance of black voters proved that they lacked sufficient intelligence, integrity, and virtue to vote responsibly; even worse, they tended to vote in a bloc; and, predictably, Negro suffrage would lead inevitably to social equality between the races, for, as whites would seek to secure favors from black officials, they eventually would be forced to engage in social intercourse with them.[50]

Other Conservatives, convinced that the Fifteenth Amendment would pass, viewed Negro suffrage as "a fixed, irrevocable fact" and counseled that raising obstructions would only risk driving all Negroes into the Republican party and, even worse, would court federal intervention.[51] Besides, blacks would vote with their former masters if the latter offered protection against lawlessness;

---

[48]*Ibid.*, 77–80.

[49]For a discussion of waning northern support for intervention in southern affairs, see J. G. Randall and David Donald, *The Civil War and Reconstruction* (2d ed., rev.; Lexington, Mass.: Heath, 1969), 678–80.

[50]Memphis *Appeal*, Aug. 10, 13, 25, 27, 30; Nov. 1869–Jan. 1870 (N.B. Nov. 22, 24–25, Dec. 3–4, 1869); Memphis *Avalanche*, Nov. 1869–Jan. 1870.

[51]Memphis *Avalanche*, Nov. 6, 1869; *Right to Vote*, p. 93. William Gillette cites selected southern newspapers to argue that the Fifteenth Amendment provoked little stir in the South, where blacks already voted. Insisting that Southerners believed the object of the amendment to be the enfranchisement of the Negro outside the South, Gillette concludes, "To most white southerners the Amendment appeared irrelevant." This interpretation does not hold up in Tennessee.

in any case, white economic control could be counted on to preserve white supremacy. Ironically, Conservatives in West Tennessee realized that black enfranchisement gave their section of the state greater representation in the legislature. Disfranchisement might not only be bad sectional politics but also be ruinous to white planters by provoking an exodus of black laborers.[52]

The constitutional convention of 1870 marked an important juncture in race relations in Tennessee. In mid-January the convention's suffrage committee presented its report: a majority recommended that the right to vote should not be withdrawn from Negroes, that the question should not be submitted to the electorate as an independent proposition, and that the payment of a poll tax should be made a prerequisite for voting. Despite a vocal minority's arguments for disfranchisement, the final draft of the suffrage article contained both impartial manhood voting and the poll tax.[53]

On March 26, 1870, Tennessee voters approved the new constitution by a substantial margin and launched the Conservatives, now calling themselves Democrats, into a decade-long run before the political winds of financial retrenchment, white supremacy, and "New South" progressivism.[54] Democratic dominance was firmly established in the elections of 1870; as long as Democrats

[52]Memphis *Avalanche*, Nov. 6, 21, 26, 28, Dec. 1, 3–4, 10, 16, 21, 1869.

[53]The suffrage article passed, 56–18. *Journal of the Proceedings of the Convention of Delegates Elected by the People of Tennessee, to Amend, Revise, or Form and Make a New Constitution for the State* (Nashville: Jones, Purvis, 1870), 92, 97–99, 177–81, 397–99. In his study of the poll tax in Tennessee, Frank B. Williams reached the conclusion, "It is difficult to connect the poll tax with Negro suffrage." He linked support for the tax with a desire to increase public school revenues and a general conviction among the majority of delegates that good citizens should pay taxes. "The Poll Tax as a Suffrage Requirement in the South, 1870–1901" (Ph.D. diss., Vanderbilt Univ., 1950), 76, 86. Another student, however, credited the minority who failed to block passage of the Negro suffrage measure with success in securing the poll-tax requirement. See Stephen B. Weeks, "The History of Negro Suffrage in the South," *Political Science Quarterly* 9 (Dec. 1894), 116.

[54]Alexander, *Political Reconstruction*, 233–38; Williams, "Poll Tax as a Suffrage Requirement in the South," 81; Robert E. Corlew, "The Negro in Tennessee, 1870–1900" (Ph.D. diss., Univ. of Alabama, 1954), 118–19.

maintained a reasonably united front, they could expect to retain the ascendancy.[55]

The Democratic party in Tennessee during the seventies was comprised of former Unionist Democrats, unrepentant rebels, and antebellum Whigs. Some Democrats wanted to build a new South based on industry and economic diversification; others viewed this goal as a threat to traditional values and customs; usually, however, these conflicts were submerged for the sake of maintaining a common front against radicalism and racial equality.[56] A few Negroes also supported the Democratic party. Some were coerced, but others cooperated with the Democrats in the interest of interracial harmony; still others preferred Democratic economic policies; and some argued that the black vote should be divided in order to use it as leverage for bargaining power.[57] Maintaining the Democratic coalition amid the sectional, economic, and racial troubles of the 1870s presented party leaders with a monumental challenge.

Perhaps the attitude of the Democratic party toward Negroes in the 1870s was best reflected in the actions of the state legislature. When it had abolished the nominal state school system in 1869, public education, especially for Negroes, had virtually ceased to exist.[58] On the other hand, the 1873 legislature, dominated by independent Democrats and cooperative Republicans, reestablished a state system of public schools which resulted in better

[55]Taylor, *Negro in Tennessee*, 244; Alexander, *Political Reconstruction*, 234.

[56]Philip M. Hamer, ed., *Tennessee: A History, 1673–1932* (4 vols.; New York: American Historical Society, 1933), II, 675; Daniel M. Robison, *Bob Taylor and the Agrarian Revolt in Tennessee* (Chapel Hill: Univ. of North Carolina Press, 1935), 134; Roger Louis Hart, "Bourbonism and Populism in Tennessee, 1875–1896" (Ph.D. diss., Princeton Univ., 1970), 8–12.

[57]August Meier, "The Negro and the Democratic Party, 1875–1915," *Phylon* 17 (2d Quarter, 1956), 173–91. For evidence of black identification with the Democratic party's position on economic issues, see the letter of Joseph E. Williams, leader of the Middle Tennessee Negro Conservatives in the late 1860s, and his speech at the 1867 state Conservative convention. Nashville *Republican Banner*, Apr. 6, 17, 1867.

[58]Ralph Samples, "The Development of Public Education in Tennessee during the Bourbon Era, 1870–1900" (Ph.D. diss., Univ. of Tennessee, 1965), 57, 61–62, 80; Taylor, *Negro in Tennessee*, 176–77, 182.

educational facilities for blacks as well as whites.[59] In other areas, however, Negroes did not fare so well under the Democratic legislatures. In 1875 a contract-labor law was passed which prohibited anyone from enticing a laborer to break a work contract, and another law of the same year subjected vagrants to a possible fine and imprisonment for as long as a year. While these laws ostensibly applied to both races, Negroes feared that they had been aimed specifically at black agricultural laborers.[60]

The Democrats also swiftly removed the Radical legislatures' legal barriers to segregation and reaffirmed existing legal bans against interracial marriages and racial mixing in the public schools. An 1868 civil rights law that prohibited racial discrimination on common carriers was repealed. Moreover, the Constitution of 1870 required segregation in the state's public schools and prohibited interracial marriages or cohabitation. Five years later, the state legislature retaliated against the passage of the federal Civil Rights bill by abolishing the common-law rule which permitted persons who were discriminated against in public accommodations to seek legal damages.[61]

The Republican party in Tennessee was hampered by many political encumbrances during the decade after the Democrats came to power. The smoldering resentments of ex-Confederates toward native Unionists had been enflamed by the disfranchisement measures of the Brownlow administration. Moreover, party leaders had committed the cardinal sin of calling for federal intervention against political opponents, and now their party suffered the consequences as northern Republicans lost interest in using federal power to maintain the Republican party in the South. In addition, the state party had bestowed political rights upon Negroes. Continuing national agitation of the race issue during the seventies, especially with regard to the federal Civil

---

[59] Robert H. White, *Development of the Tennessee State Educational Organization, 1796–1929* (Nashville: George Peabody Coll. for Teachers, 1929), 122–24; Taylor, *Negro in Tennessee*, 182–86; Samples, "Public Education in Tennessee," 87–101.
[60] Taylor, *Negro in Tennessee*, 137–38.
[61] *Ibid.*, 227, 230.

Rights Act of 1875, and frequent resort to "bloody-shirt" oratory by Republicans in the North and at home provided ample opportunity for Democrats to invoke their version of the bloody shirt to discredit the party as a threat to home rule and white supremacy.[62]

Although the vast majority of white Republicans opposed the advancement of blacks to political leadership, the Republicans' prospects depended upon their ability to steer a treacherous course that at once would retain the black vote and lure the former Whigs out of the Democratic camp. Repeated efforts to attract dissident Democrats met with little success.[63]

During the 1870s, although Negroes continued to appeal to Washington for protection against the assaults on their status in Tennessee, they turned more than ever toward state conventions to foster racial unity and to publicize their grievances. In 1871, and again in 1874, state Negro conventions complained of systematic discrimination against blacks by the state government, citing the courts and juries, the poll tax, segregation in public accommodations and schools, economic oppression, and unchecked Ku Klux Klan violence. Resolutions also condemned state and federal government for failure to enforce the 1866 Civil Rights Act and the Fourteenth and Fifteenth Amendments. The convention of 1874 petitioned Tennessee's congressmen to work for the passage of Senator Charles Sumner's civil rights bill and urged black voters to support only those candidates publicly favoring the bill and pledging not to discriminate racially in the appointment of jurors.[64]

Negroes gained few public offices in Tennessee during the 1860s and 1870s, exercised slight influence in Republican party

[62]*Ibid.*, 251–54. For the gubernatorial vote totals in the 1870s see Hamer, *Tennessee*, II, 679, 681–82, 684; and Taylor, *Negro in Tennessee*, 244.

[63]Queener, "A Decade of East Tennessee Republicanism, 1867–1876," ETHS *Publications*, No. 14 (1943) 59–85; and Verton M. Queener, "The Republican Party in East Tennessee, 1865–1900" (Ph.D. diss., Indiana Univ., 1940), 222; Hamer, *Tennessee*, II, 680, 689; Hart, "Bourbonism and Populism," 37.

[64]Tennessee *Tribune*, Mar. 6, 1871, quoted in Taylor, *Negro in Tennessee*, 227. See also *ibid.*, 101–2, 131, 227, 245; Nashville *Union and American*, Apr. 29–30, 1874.

councils, and received little patronage from either state or national party leaders. Only one black man, Sampson W. Keeble, served in the state legislature.[65] This bleak state of affairs has been attributed both to the absence of a large black population in the state and to the enmity with which most white Republicans viewed black officeholding.[66] The 322,331 Negroes of Tennessee in 1870 represented 25.6 percent of the total population. Understandably, the minority status of blacks sharply limited their political power, as did the racial antipathies of whites in the Republican party. Other reasons also help account for the political impotence of Negroes in Tennessee during the seventies. For example, even in the West Tennessee counties of Haywood, Fayette, Tipton, Madison, and Shelby, where Republican success was based largely on black votes, whites invariably harvested the fruits of political victory.

Lack of political expertise, money, and racial unity no doubt hampered black political aspirations. Moreover, the Republican party's general weakness in the state during the seventies provided Negroes with little opportunity for bargaining with Democrats or Independents. It also seems likely that blacks tended to defer to white leadership in the Republican party during the first decade of their enfranchisement. The economic dependency of blacks and the white willingness to resort to violence for political ends also curbed Negro political independence. Finally, the black churches and fraternal organizations of the 1870s did not provide the strong institutional bases for Negro politicians that they later would.[67]

[65]Keeble represented Davidson County in 1872. A former slave, he served only one term in the house. Monroe N. Work, "Some Negro Members of Reconstruction Conventions and Legislatures and of Congress," *Jour. Negro Hist.* 5 (Jan. 1920), 113; Daniel M. Robison, "Preliminary Sketches, Biographical Directory, Tennessee General Assembly" (Tennessee State Library and Archives, Nashville).

[66]Corlew, "Negro in Tennessee," 105, 146.

[67]This analysis is based on a critical reading of Taylor, *Negro in Tennessee*, 25–44, 244–65; Corlew, "Negro in Tennessee," 54–145; Queener, "Decade of East Tennessee Republicanism," 59–85; and Rayford W. Logan, *The Betrayal of the Negro: From Rutherford B. Hayes to Woodrow Wilson* (new enl. ed.; New York: Collier-Macmillan, 1965), 15–87, 105–21.

During the period from presidential reconstruction in Tennessee to the 1880s the struggle of blacks for political power had been largely thwarted. The efforts of Republicans to retain power during the late sixties brought an advancement in the civil and political rights of blacks but fell short of enabling them to achieve much representation in government. The weakness of the Republican party in the 1870s and the essential unity of Democrats further circumscribed black political influence until the eighties.

I

"Bourbons," Blacks, and "New South" Politics

From their enfranchisement in 1867 through the 1870s, black Tennesseans had little opportunity or incentive for seeking political gain by venturing outside Republican auspices. The Democratic factionalism that exploded in the 1880s created a new set of political options for black voters. The volatile issue that shattered the Democratic coalition of the 1870s and opened the door for a resurgence of Republican power was the state debt. Successive efforts to decide the amount of bonded indebtedness which should be paid produced such a fissure in the Democratic coalition that by 1880 Democrats could not agree on either a platform or a gubernatorial candidate. A state-credit faction advocated scaling down the debt only on terms acceptable to the bondholders, while a low-tax wing included those who favored outright repudiation or wanted a sharp reduction of the debt and submission to the voters of any agreement between the state and the bondholders. Each faction of the Democratic party ran a gubernatorial candidate in 1880, but most of the "Redeemers" who had "saved" the state from radicalism and had steered the party's course in the 1870s sided with the state-credit forces.[1]

This fierce internal battle among Democrats had an immediate impact on the way each faction perceived black voters. The much-publicized success of General William A. Mahone in Virgin-

[1]Hart, "Bourbonism and Populism," 8–36; Robert B. Jones, "The State Debt Controversy in Tennessee, 1865–1883" (Ph.D. diss., Vanderbilt Univ., 1972), 124–26, 259–73, 275; William A. Stanton, "The State Debt in Tennessee Politics" (M.A. thesis, Vanderbilt Univ., 1939), 69; Pulaski *Citizen*, Sept. 16, 1880. A full examination of the low-tax position may be found in the Nashville *Banner*, Aug. 10, 1880.

ia offered cause for alarm in the state-credit camp. In 1879 Mahone had bolted the Democratic party and won control of his state's government by entering into an open alliance with black voters on a debt-readjustment platform.[2] His success, threatening a major political realignment, heightened Democratic disunity in other southern states and posed a direct challenge to the economic and social policies of state-credit Democrats in Tennessee by accenting class and racial tensions.[3]

The Mahone-like fusionist movement, much feared by the state-credit Democrats, did not materialize in 1880; Negroes had little desire to desert the Republican party and forfeit what appeared to be certain victory. With Democrats racked by dissension, however, Republicans elected their gubernatorial candidate, Alvin Hawkins, and came close to winning a majority of the contested seats in the legislature.[4] Staunch state-credit Democrats joined Republicans in the ensuing legislature to fund the entire debt at face value. This action provoked a major realignment within the Democratic party. By supporting full payment of the debt, uncompromising state-credit Democrats had become isolated from the rank-and-file members of their party.[5] The low-taxers won a suit against the Republican administration's debt settlement in the state supreme court, and in the Democratic state convention of 1882 they won control of the party. When the convention adopted a low-tax platform, state-credit Democrats bolted and named their own gubernatorial candidate. Now low-taxers, although dominant within the party, faced a gubernatorial campaign in which success very likely depended upon their ability to offset the loss of state-credit votes.[6]

The nemesis of the state-credit purists and a remarkable ally of

[2]Wynes, *Race Relations in Virginia*, 17–19.

[3]For examples of the way in which state-credit Democrats used the case of Mahone to forestall a similar movement in Tennessee, see the Chattanooga *Times*, Feb. 12, Mar. 30, Nov. 25, 1880.

[4]White, *Messages*, VI, 639.

[5]Hart, "Bourbonism and Populism," 73–76; Hamer, *Tennessee*, II, 689–90; Jones, "State Debt Controversy," 287–97.

[6]Hamer, *Tennessee*, II, 689; John H. Savage to Howell E. Jackson, Nov. 24,

low-tax Democrats appeared in West Tennessee's Shelby County. Early in the spring of 1882 a large number of black voters in the county revolted against white Republican leadership and declared themselves in favor of a readjustment of the state debt along the lines advocated by the low-tax Democrats. These black low-tax Republicans were led by Edward Shaw, one of the most controversial black men in Tennessee during the 1880s.[7]

Apparently a man of considerable charisma among Memphis blacks, Shaw was a lawyer who had enjoyed minor patronage from the local Republican organization. In 1880 the local Democratic press had waged a vicious smear campaign against his unsuccessful candidacy for sheriff of Shelby County.[8] A prominent white Republican judge in Memphis, however, described Shaw as "a man of strong force of character, one of the most cogent speakers I have ever heard, and a clear thinker." Even Democratic Senator Isham G. Harris later praised him as "a very bright and able colored man."[9]

Available sources make it impossible to determine the primary motive behind Shaw's political activities in 1882. Since the inauguration of Republican Governor Hawkins in 1881, anger had been building among many black Republicans in West Tennessee's Tenth Congressional District. They resented Hawkins' unresponsiveness to black demands for patronage and educational improvements as well as his administration's state-debt measures. They also disapproved of the national Republican strategy for building a stronger party in the South by distributing patronage to white Independents and Democrats and playing down the race issue. They deeply resented the implication that black Republican votes were expendable, an idea they thought inherent in the presidential policy of using federal patronage to attract southern whites into the Republican camp. According to the black protes-

1881, Howell E. Jackson Papers (Manuscript Div., Tennessee State Library and Archives); Jones, "State Debt Controversy," 297–301, 310–15; Nashville *Banner*, June 22, 1882; Nashville *American*, July 12, 1882.

[7]Memphis *Avalanche*, Apr. 4, 1882.

[8]Memphis *Avalanche* and Memphis *Appeal*, July–Aug. 1880.

[9]Memphis *Avalanche*, July 5, 16, 1885.

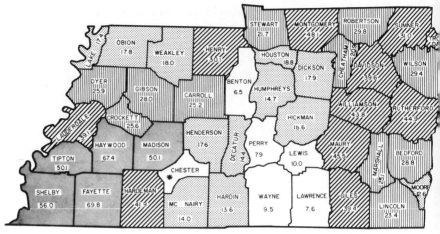

* Chester County, created in 1882, had 19.6% black
  population according to the census of 1890.

Map 1. PERCENTAGE OF BLACKS

tors, nine-tenths of the Republican voters in the Tenth District
were Negroes, yet patronage, the selection of party candidates,
and the party's policy lay in the hands of a small ring of white
federal officeholders. In the spring of 1881 the disenchanted black
Republicans of Shelby County held public meetings which resulted in resolutions calling for higher wages for Negro laborers, an
increase in state expenditures for Negro education, and greater
consideration of blacks in all local party matters. They also
denounced the administration's state-debt proposal on the
grounds that it would impose too great a tax burden and deprive
Negro schools of much-needed revenue. Though Negroes had
helped to elect a Republican governor and a Republican president, a Memphis black Republican pointed out, "both administrations turn around and give us the sack, and appoint only white
Republicans to office. If Republicans of the right color are not to

26

NORTHEAST NEBRASKA TECHNICAL
COMMUNITY COLLEGE - LIBRARY

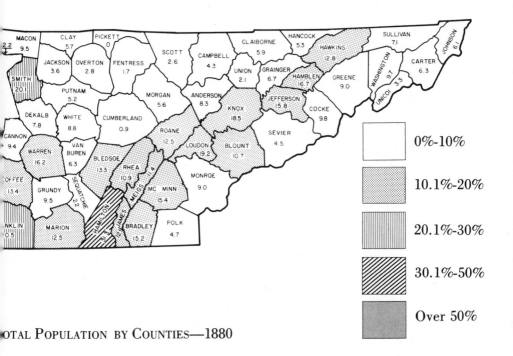

▢	0%-10%
▨	10.1%-20%
▥	20.1%-30%
▨	30.1%-50%
■	Over 50%

OTAL POPULATION BY COUNTIES—1880

be had democrats are appointed."[10]

To give substance to their bid for political power, the black insurgents began to organize local political clubs in each county of the Tenth District and in each ward of Memphis, which is situated in this district. Through these separate grass-roots organizations they hoped either to increase their influence within the Republican party or to be prepared for independent political action. In addition to serving as the political arm of the dissident black Republicans, each county organization was also to include an industrial association to encourage self-help and independence among black workers and was to strive for improvements in the black public schools. In their public rallies the insurgents urged Negroes to take full advantage of existing state educational facili-

[10]Memphis *Appeal*, Mar. 22, 1881; Memphis *Avalanche*, Apr. 15, 27, May 18, 1881.

ties and to insist upon full terms and competent teachers for their schools. To coordinate these political, economic, and educational objectives the Tenth District insurgents set up a central political club in Memphis, naming Benjamin K. Sampson president and Edward Shaw vice-president.[11]

The split in Republican ranks widened in 1881 as separate black Republican clubs became a reality and as insurgent blacks and regular Republicans became embroiled in the feud between President Garfield and Senator Roscoe Conkling of New York over patronage. When William R. Moore, congressman from the Tenth District and a major figure in the federal ring, joined Conkling in making war on the President, he was censured by the central organization of the black insurgents. Although little evidence exists by which to measure the amount of support Tenth District blacks gave the separate political clubs, the clubs did provide a forum for protests against the patronage and civil rights stance of the state and national Republican administrations; the central club also became a center of opposition to the state-debt settlement of Governor Hawkins' administration.[12]

When Shelby County Republicans gathered in the early spring of 1882 to nominate delegates to their state convention, the well-organized black insurgents seized the initiative. Under the leadership of Edward Shaw, they obtained approval of a set of resolutions favoring sharp readjustment of the state debt. Shaw vigorously defended readjustment, although he rejected the repudiationist label flung at him by the regular Republicans. The state-credit legislation passed by Hawkins' administration would not bestow any benefits upon blacks, he argued. Rather, it would benefit the rich at the expense of the poor. Under the high taxes necessitated by the debt settlement, Shaw asserted, the laboring man bore a disproportionate financial burden. "All over the city [Memphis], rental agents raised rents, thereby making the people pay the rich man's taxes." Responsibility for the debt did not rest on blacks, their leader declared, because most of them had been slaves when it was contracted. Shaw further stated that Governor

[11]Memphis *Avalanche*, May 18, 1881.   [12]*Ibid.*, June 5, Dec. 13, 1881.

Hawkins and the railroads had earned the special enmity of blacks—Hawkins, by signing "the infamous" Jim Crow law passed by the 1881 state legislature, and the railroads, by their persistent discrimination against Negro passengers. It was "time for the colored people . . . to protect themselves," Shaw concluded. Shaw alluded to the success blacks had enjoyed by joining the Mahone readjuster movement in Virginia and suggested that low-tax Democrats might be induced to cooperate with insurgent black Republicans in launching a similar movement in Tennessee.[13]

Not all black Republicans in Shelby County shared Shaw's sentiments. Apparently, those who had won patronage, been elected to office, or agreed with the Republican stance on the debt remained loyal. Led by Thomas F. Cassels and Carter Harris, they held another convention, condemned the low-tax views of the insurgents, and named an integrated delegation to the Republican state convention. Cassels, a black legislator from Shelby County, had voted for both debt-payment measures of the Hawkins administration and firmly advocated paying the bonded indebtedness on a basis satisfactory to the bondholders. Harris, a prominent black Memphis politician, was chairman of the Shelby County Republican Executive Committee.[14]

The breach in Republican ranks in Shelby County became irreparable when the state convention excluded the Shaw delegation and seated the state-credit men. In the August county elections, the insurgents, by combining forces with the Greenback party, drew enough black voters to enable the Democrats to overcome a previous Republican majority of 1,000 votes and elect the bulk of their ticket.[15]

After this show of force, and in preparation for the fall state elections, the insurgents held a meeting to nominate a ticket for the state legislature. By prearrangement they held their convention on the same day and in the same building as did the low-tax

[13]*Ibid.*, Apr. 4, 1882; Memphis *Appeal*, Apr. 4, 1882.

[14]Memphis *Appeal*, Apr. 4–5, 1882.

[15]Memphis *Avalanche*, Apr. 11, 28, May 30, June 7, 1882; Memphis *Appeal*, July 22, Aug. 1, 6, 1882.

Democrats of Shelby County. After consultations to iron out details, a delegation from each group announced that an alliance had been reached. By the terms of the agreement the insurgent blacks would support the readjuster-Democratic ticket for state office, including its candidate for governor, General William B. Bate. In return, two Negroes, Isaac F. Norris and William F. Price, were placed on a fusionist Shelby County legislative ticket. If elected, the two black representatives were pledged to vote for the reelection of Isham G. Harris to the United States Senate. Norris had served in the 1881 legislature, voting against the state-credit bills.[16]

Following announcement of the agreement, Edward Shaw, the principal architect of the fusion movement, addressed the low-tax Democrats. He surveyed the history of the insurgent movement in the Republican party, including a carefully selected list of black grievances which expediently focused on white Republican exploitation of the Negro vote and not black demands for offices. Shaw discredited the idea that blacks owed a debt to the Republican party. The Civil War had not been waged for Negro freedom, he stated, but for northern self-interest; Negro suffrage had been adopted to perpetuate the power of the Republican party. Shaw announced that he still viewed himself as a Republican on several issues but would not continue to be enslaved to the white bosses in that party. After outlining the views of his followers on the state debt, the redoubtable black leader prophesied that the readjuster-fusionists would carry Shelby County by a 2,000-vote majority. He joyously awaited the next Democratic administration, he said, for it would represent the "second emancipation" of his people.[17]

Shaw exhorted all black Republicans across the state to join the fusionist movement. The 80,000 Negro voters of Tennessee, he stated, had remained impotent under the tutelage of Republican bosses, and, while these conditions persisted, Negroes would be "politically disfranchised so far as holding any office." By asserting their political independence, blacks might accomplish more

[16]Memphis *Appeal*, July 20, Sept. 5, Oct. 5, 10, 1882; Memphis *Avalanche*, Sept. 10, Oct. 3, 8, 18, 1882.
[17]Memphis *Appeal*, Oct. 5, 1882.

than a low-tax solution to the state-debt question, he predicted. In two years, if they maintained their independence, they should be able to secure other goals; in any case, they would no longer be "political prostitutes" to white Republicans.[18]

In the words of Alfred A. Froman, one of the black insurgent leaders, the fusionist movement represented "an epoch in the life of the Negro in Tennessee." Many of the black fusionists probably joined Froman in interpreting the opportunity to participate in the councils of the Democratic party to be a milestone in their struggle for freedom. Froman said that he was honored to support Harris for reelection to the United States Senate, for he felt "bound to him by the warmest ties."[19] Indeed, the strength of the black vote in Shelby County gave the fusionist movement major political importance. Blacks constituted 56 percent of the total population of the county in the census of 1880, and the male voting-age population of the blacks outnumbered that of the whites by 467. With the state-credit Democrats and a normal Republican majority of at least 1,000 against them, the low-tax Democrats faced the alternative of embracing Shaw's followers or submitting to defeat. They chose fusion. At a biracial mass rally in Memphis, the white candidates on the fusion ticket publicly promised to work for the election of their black colleagues.[20]

Reverberations from the fusion movement in Shelby County reached throughout the state as state-credit men and Republicans alike feared that it might develop into a statewide political realignment similar to the readjustment movement in Virginia. The lack of low-tax newspapers outside Shelby County makes it difficult to determine whether fusionist alliances actually occurred in other parts of the state, although there is evidence that the movement spread to other West Tennessee counties in the Tenth District. In any case, state-credit newspapers in Knoxville, Nashville, and

[18]*Ibid.*

[19]*Ibid.*

[20]United States, Bureau of the Census, *Compendium of the Tenth Census of the United States, 1880*, Pt. I (Washington, D. C.: Government Printing Office, 1885), 371; Memphis *Avalanche*, July 24, 1880; Memphis *Appeal*, Oct. 10, 1882; Petition from D. T. Porter *et al.* to J. J. Vertrees, Nov. 18, 1882, Bate Papers (Governors' Papers, Tennessee State Library and Archives).

Chattanooga closely followed the events in Shelby County and warned of the dangers fusion posed. Influenced by a desire to attract capital for railroad and industrial expansion, by a fear of class conflict, by strong convictions about responsibility and personal honor, and by paternalistic racial attitudes, state-credit Democrats saw the fusion movement as a threat to their values and their power.[21] The Democratic fusionists were "political adventurers" engaged in a Mahone-type "nauseating political coalition" that threatened to disrupt the solid South, excite black demands for public office, and agitate an already incendiary element of "ignorant and malicious" Negroes who were "disruptionists, repudiators, and communists." Fusionists, in short, had sacrificed "principle, consistency, and decency" to ensure the reelection of Harris to the Senate and the election of Bate to the governorship.[22]

Edward Shaw and the two black candidates on the fusionist legislative ticket became the targets of special abuse from the state-credit press. A Montgomery County newspaper editor countered reports that Shaw was coming there to speak on behalf of the low-tax Democratic ticket by insisting that blacks and whites in his county were on "perfectly friendly terms." Local Negroes, he bluntly declared, did not want "these pleasant relations destroyed by incendiary speeches." The editor of the Nashville *Banner* acidly commented, "If Ed Shaw were an honest politician, representing an honest element, it would be of small consequence"; Shaw was, however, "a communist, a political adventurer of the worst character." It was not simply that the readjusters were willing to vote for two Negroes that rankled the *Banner* editor, but that they had allied with "the worst elements of the Republican party and had the audacity to embrace them as Democrats."

[21]Speech of W. J. Sykes delivered at Union City, Tenn., in defense of the state-credit position (Fall 1882), Scrapbook, Joseph H. Fussell Collection (Manuscript Div., Tennessee State Library and Archives); Clarksville *Weekly Chronicle*, Sept. 30, 1882; Hart, "Bourbonism and Populism," 87–92. For an analysis of the economic and social values that proponents of state credit identified with payment of the debt, see Jones, "State Debt Controversy," 125–67.

[22]Memphis *Avalanche*, Oct. 22, Nov. 4, 1882; Chattanooga *Times*, Oct. 7, 10, 16, 1882; Clarksville *Weekly Chronicle*, Oct. 14, 28, 1882.

Norris and Price, the two black legislative candidates on the fusionist ticket in Shelby County, were labeled "Shaw's tools," and castigated as "unprincipled Republican Negro characters" who were "too disreputable to do the dirty work of the Republican administration." Surely, a white Middle Tennessee editor cried, these associates of "an avowed communist, repudiator and general disruptionist" would be rejected by "every respectable, honest, fair-minded colored man in the state."[23]

Obviously, state-credit Democrats were only partially motivated by racial concerns; but, in one way or another, the race issue impinged upon every facet of the state-credit faction's blueprint for responsible government, personal honor, and economic progress. Fundamental to their perspective was a firm conviction that social order and harmony depended on all racial groups having a stake in society, either by owning property or by education. For political rights to be beneficial to society, they had to be earned, rather than received gratis, by the groups seeking them.[24]

Their paternalistic racial policy represented an amalgam of concern for status, a sense of responsibility for the direction of blacks, economic self-interest, and convictions that presumed Negro inferiority but saw race relations as amenable to change.[25]

[23]Clarksville *Semi-Weekly Tobacco Leaf Chronicle*, Oct. 24, 1882; Nashville *Banner*, Oct. 7, 1882; Chattanooga *Times*, Oct. 7, 1882; Clarksville *Weekly Chronicle*, Oct. 14, 21, 1882.

[24]Hart, "Bourbonism and Populism," 87–92. Hart assigns major significance to concern over status as the motivating force behind the state-credit bolt. See also Chattanooga *Times*, Oct. 7, 1882.

[25]George M. Fredrickson offers a sophisticated analysis of the attitudes associated with the paternalistic racial policy of New South theorists in the 1880s. Fredrickson argues that this "optimistic neopaternalist school" came under attack from two sides during the 1880s. At one extreme were the "die hard racists," while at the other end of the spectrum were white proponents of a policy of "genuine public equality." *The Black Image in the White Mind: The Debate on Afro-American Character and Destiny, 1817–1914* (New York: Harper, 1971), 198–227. It seems highly plausible, however, that in Tennessee the greatest threat to the paternalistic position of the state-credit advocates came from low-tax fusionists who were neither "die hard racists" nor proponents of "genuine public equality." Instead, they represented political pragmatists who displayed a willingness to engage in biracial politics.

For other examples of advocates of a paternalistic racial policy in Tennessee, see the *Christian Advocate*, Oct. 20, 1883; Apr. 9, 1890; Memphis *Avalanche*,

To the extent that a clear set of interracial guidelines emerged from these views, they were forcefully articulated by Colonel John E. MacGowan, Democratic editor of the Chattanooga *Times*. A native of Ohio, MacGowan had served as an officer in the First United States Colored Artillery during the Civil War. Mustered out in Chattanooga at the close of the war, he practiced law there until 1872, when he became editor of the *Times*.[26]

Editorially in the early 1880s MacGowan pondered the "wholesale, indiscriminate and sudden enfranchisement of the liberated blacks," but he believed "the legal status of the Negro as a citizen" to be "fixed and irrevocable"; therefore, disfranchisement was impossible—and unwise even if possible. The best assurance for continuing the progress that blacks had made under "the parental discipline of slavery" lay in education and the extension of a paternalistic white tutelage designed to replace slavery. Through education the evils of impartial manhood suffrage eventually would be remedied, for as black voters gained education and acquired property they would divide over economic issues and end bloc voting. "The government owes it to its own safety," Mac-Gowan insisted, "to provide for the proper training and advancement of all its citizens." MacGowan's adherence to a paternalistic racial policy was also reinforced by his conviction that black leaders like ex-Senator Blanche K. Bruce and Frederick Douglass were "indebted to slavery for the foundation of that discipline which has enabled them to pull to the front."[27]

With words clearly intended for Democratic fusionists, however, MacGowan condemned the "flippant folly" of those who treated "the destiny of six million citizens of the black race as so much capital, so many pawns on the political chessboard." Mac-Gowan scorned a racial policy based on "a whimsical, hysterical, sentimentalism . . . that can see nothing but what is lovely and of

---

Nov. 20, 1880; the policy is analyzed in Guion Griffis Johnson, "Southern Paternalism toward Negroes after Emancipation," *Jour. Southern Hist.* 23 (Nov. 1957), 483–509.

[26]Charles D. McGuffey, ed., *Standard History of Chattanooga, Tennessee* (Knoxville: Crew & Dorey, 1911), 145–46; Chattanooga *Times*, May 6, 1886.

[27]Chattanooga *Times*, May 22, 1881; Mar. 13, 1882.

good report in the portion of mankind which is bound in black, while it is ready enough to see all manner of wickedness in every member of the white race which fails to fall in with its maudlin philosophy." MacGowan shared with most white Tennesseans a belief that if Negroes immediately entered into full participation in politics, southern society would undergo radical alterations. The proper criteria for participation in self-government, therefore, were "competency and honesty." In MacGowan's estimation, blacks fell short on three counts: they were ignorant; they were subject to prejudice "as just having emerged from a servile condition"; and they were vulnerable to "the vile uses political adventurers constantly seek to make of them, taking advantage of their ignorance and credulity." For proof of the last he cited the "open alliance" between "the worst Negro element in the State" and "the machine which runs by the power of hope in the possession of office and spoil, and has been labeled by Isham G. Harris 'Democracy.' "[28]

In response to the state-credit attack, and to counteract general skepticism among blacks about the efficacy of an alliance with Democrats, readjuster spokesmen waged a campaign focused on the economic interdependency of both races, abstract commitments to Negro education, and auspicious statements about how fusion would lead to racial harmony.

The pro-fusionist Memphis *Appeal* proclaimed the advent of "a new era." The *Appeal* was edited by John McLeod Keating and Matthew C. Galloway, both of whom were antebellum Democrats, former Confederate colonels, and enthusiastic supporters of Harris. Keating and Galloway hailed "the break in the solid colored vote in the South" and prophesied that it would "liberalize the Southern whites and bring the two races, whose interests are identical, to a better and more harmonious understanding." The time had arrived for a new politics devoid of racial hostilities. For these reasons, the *Appeal* declared, whites and blacks of Shelby County had "in good faith united" to elect men who were "in sympathy with the popular masses." Fusionists would be unde-

[28]*Ibid.*, Oct. 10, 1882.

terred, therefore, by those "busily engaged in trying to breed jealousies" between the two races. "For years," the *Appeal* reflected, "the color line" had worked "to the great detriment of the material interests of both races." Overlooking the expediency of fusion, the *Appeal* concluded that "statesmanship" had required "an obliteration of the color line," because "no people can prosper without first becoming homogeneous."[29]

The low-tax Democrats struck deftly to coax Shelby County's black voters away from their traditional Republican ties. They condemned the firing of blacks with fusionist sympathies from federal jobs, gave repeated assurances that the two blacks on the fusionist legislative ticket would receive the full support of whites, and romantically praised the Negro's "fidelity during the civil war." Southern whites, proclaimed the editors of the Memphis *Appeal*, "are the best friends—the only true friends—of the colored people."[30]

Josiah Patterson, ex-Confederate officer, close friend of Senator Harris, and a candidate for the legislature on the fusionist ticket, offered a far more tangible pledge to the biracial audiences he addressed during the campaign. He promised, if elected, to "make it one of the chief objects of my labors to so shape legislation as to secure for them [Negroes] and for all the people of Tennessee the most effectual means of educating their children." Patterson identified Negro education as "the most important question of the day" and insisted that it was "paramount to the public debt or any other issue." In joint speaking engagements with Edward Shaw and the two black legislative candidates, Patterson proclaimed that he wanted "to show the black man that he stood equally with the white man." He condemned Republican efforts to intimidate black fusionists, endorsed a mechanics' lien law, urged whites to vote for the blacks on the fusionist ticket, and

[29]Keating, who had been a quiet opponent of slavery and a reluctant secessionist, supported education and full civil rights for Negroes, championed women's rights, and displayed a favorable attitude toward labor unions. William S. Speer, comp. and ed., *Sketches of Prominent Tennesseans* (Nashville: Albert B. Tavel, 1888), 346–50, 378–86; Memphis *Appeal*, Aug. 8, Oct. 22, Nov. 3, 1882.

[30]Memphis *Appeal*, Aug. 10, Oct. 22, Nov. 2–4, 1882.

defended the interracial political alliance as something which "should have been done years ago." Edward Shaw, in return, praised Patterson's views on education, rejoiced over the abolition of the color line in politics, and predicted that 2,500 blacks would vote the fusionist ticket in Shelby County.[31]

Democratic fusionists attempted to reduce the outcry against their breach of the color line by claiming that those Negroes who had joined the fusionist ranks had purged themselves of Republican vices and were largely without any "personal political ambitions." Norris and Price, the two black candidates on the fusionist legislative ticket, therefore, were "men of fine practical sense and good judgment" who understood "the wants of the 35,000 colored people in Shelby County" and, at the same time, entertained "sympathies and sentiments in perfect accord with the whites." Although blacks had previously erred by placing themselves in the hands of "irresponsible adventurers," they now had "learned wisdom by experience" and "cut loose from the rule of the carpetbagger." It was "the duty of the whites to hold their hands and show that they meet them half way in the effort to exterminate race prejudices." The mutual interests of blacks and whites could be served only by "mutual kindness and confidence," reasoned the Memphis *Appeal*. To Josiah Patterson, it seemed obvious that blacks had begun "to see at last that the Democratic party is the party of the people, the party of the constitution, and the especial guardian of the rights and liberties of the citizen." Patterson thought that black voters, ennobled by association with men like himself, might "become the instrument in the hands of the Almighty" for restoring the Democratic party to power.[32]

Despite the campaign rhetoric, the election results revealed that, for many white Democrats, breaking the political color line did not include voting for black candidates. William B. Bate, the low-tax candidate, won the governor's race, defeating Republican Alvin Hawkins, 118,821—90,660. The 4,599 votes of the state-credit candidate indicated that most Democrats ignored or dis-

[31]*Ibid.*, Oct. 22, 31, Nov. 2, 1882; Speer, *Prominent Tennesseans*, 266–68.
[32]Memphis *Appeal*, Oct. 18, 22, Nov. 3, 1882.

counted the acrimonious charges leveled at the low-taxers and supported Bate. The fusionist movement apparently allowed the Democrats to carry the election in Shelby County. The Republican gubernatorial vote in Shelby County fell from 7,758 in 1880 (a presidential election year) to 5,421 in 1882, while the combined vote of the low-tax and state-credit Democrats fell from 6,915 in 1880 to 5,781 in 1882. Thus the Republican vote declined by 2,337, while the Democrats lost only 1,134. Since the state-credit candidate received only 257 votes in Shelby County in 1882, it appears that approximately 1,000 blacks may have voted for the low-tax Democrats. About 5,000 blacks, on the other hand, remained loyal to the Republicans. After the election, Memphis newspapers estimated the black low-tax vote in the county at 1,500. Black support in Shelby County also probably enabled the Democrats to win the Tenth District congressional seat. Casey Young, the Democratic candidate, defeated his Republican opponent by a 22-vote margin. Ironically, Norris and Price, the two black candidates for the legislature on the fusionist ticket, were defeated, running from 700 to 1,000 votes behind their victorious white allies. Nevertheless, their substantial vote seems to indicate that they received either sizable white Democratic support or a large vote from black Republicans. Leon Howard, one of the two blacks on the Republican legislative ticket, won his race.[33]

White leaders in the fusionist movement in Shelby County lamented the fate of the two black candidates on the low-tax ticket. "Universal regret was expressed by the Democrats at the defeat of Messrs. Norris and Price," declared the Memphis *Appeal*, which blamed their fate upon "a few malignants" in the Democratic party who did not wish to see it "allied with the colored people." The editor of the Memphis *Avalanche* predicted that the scratching of Price and Norris by the readjusters would aid the Republicans in the long run by proving to the blacks that there was nothing to be gained by an alliance with Democrats.[34]

Nevertheless, the victorious white Democrats of Shelby County

[33]*Ibid.*, Nov. 10, 1882.
[34]*Ibid.*; Memphis *Avalanche*, Nov. 9, 1882.

hoped to salvage what remained of the postelection fusionist sentiment among blacks by pushing Shaw, Norris, and Price for minor appointments in the new state administration. William W. McDowell, an ex-Confederate officer and a Memphis judge, congratulated his friend, Governor-elect Bate, upon his victory and pointed out that black support had been crucial in Shelby County: "The truth of the matter is that the negroes saved Casey Young and the white members of the legislative ticket and increased your vote more than 1,000 votes and they are now being taunted for their trust in Democratic promises." McDowell urged Bate to appoint Shaw or Norris to the lucrative office of Memphis coal oil inspector, a position already held by a black man appointed by Governor Hawkins. Although some white men wanted the position, McDowell advised Bate that "they should not stand in the way of a political necessity like this."[35] With assurances of support from white leaders in the Shelby County Democratic party, Memphis low-tax Negroes also met to petition Bate's appointment of Shaw as inspector.[36]

Shortly thereafter, the successful white candidates on the fusionist ticket sent a similar petition to the chairman of the state Democratic executive committee. They candidly disclosed the reasons for the fusionist movement in Shelby County: "With at least one thousand majority against us, added to the disaffection from our own ranks, the alternative was forced on the Shelby Democracy to make the alliance or submit to defeat." Shaw had done yeoman work in stemming white Republican efforts to win the black vote for Hawkins. "Since the election," the petitioners continued, "these allies of ours have been taunted and ridiculed as the dupes of Democracy." Something would have to be done "to show them that we are not unmindful of their services." Appointing Shaw coal oil inspector would not antagonize whites and, more importantly, would "permanently secure Shelby County and this congressional District for years to come," they declared. Further-

[35]W. H. Rhea to William B. Bate, Jan. 18, 1883; William W. McDowell to William B. Bate, Nov. 9, 1882, Bate Papers.
[36]G. W. Gordon et al. to William B. Bate, Nov. 9, 1882, ibid; Memphis Appeal, Nov. 11, 1882.

more, if the black fusionists in Shelby were rewarded, the movement was certain to spread, notably to Montgomery, Obion, and Fayette counties. Otherwise, "they will conclude there is no such thing as political recognition at our hands, and return to the Republican party." The question had to be viewed purely from the standpoint of what was best for the Democratic party.[37]

On into the spring of 1883, Bate hedged over appointing Shaw to the Memphis coal oil inspectorship. By April the governor seemed to be on the verge of appointing a personal friend, W. H. Rhea, who had held the position during earlier Democratic administrations. The Democratic executive committee of Shelby County anticipated Bate's action in a set of resolutions crediting the victory of the regular Democrats in the Tenth Congressional District to their black allies. They reiterated their reasons for demanding Shaw's appointment, and protested the anticipated nomination of a man who had not even been in accord with the low-taxers. They reminded Bate of his political commitments to the black low-taxers when, while campaigning in Memphis, he had "assured these men (calling heaven to witness) that if they stood by the democracy in this contest he would stand by them." Bate's refusal to honor his commitment, they stated, would be "unwise, hurtful, pernicious and ruinous to the best interests of the party." Nevertheless, in May Bate passed over Shaw and appointed Rhea to the position.[38]

Whatever their expectations, Shelby County Negroes received few tangible benefits from the fusionist movement in 1882. Not only were the two blacks on the legislative ticket defeated, but Edward Shaw failed to receive any appointment to office by the Bate administration. In a sad epitaph to the fusionist movement, the Memphis *Appeal* defended Bate's appointment of Rhea by fatalistically proclaiming that the governor "could not do otherwise."[39] Perhaps Governor Bate had concluded that his substantial margin of victory in 1882 justified his writing off the black vote in Shelby County rather than risking the loss of white support by

[37]D. T. Porter *et al.* to J. J. Vertrees, Nov. 18, 1882, Bate Papers.
[38]Memphis *Avalanche*, May 8, 1883.
[39]Memphis *Appeal*, May 8, 1883.

extending patronage to blacks. In any case, the meager benefits of the fusionist movement for blacks indicates the limited power they wielded in Tennessee politics even in areas like Shelby County, where the black population was heaviest and most vocal. The refusal of the Democratic administration to encourage fusion with tangible rewards also reveals that most white Democrats felt constrained from using patronage to build an interracial alliance. The failure of the movement to produce significant results for blacks did not augur well for their future in Tennessee politics.

Nevertheless, the fusionist movement in Shelby County was more than a brief political union of blacks and whites outside the Republican party. The cooperation of blacks and whites in a political alliance may have eased racial tension in Shelby County, although bloody-shirt and racist attacks by state-credit editors probably agitated racial hostilities elsewhere in the state. Limited though their power might be, as long as blacks held the vote, they at least stood as bargainers in the political arena rather than as specters exhumed to discourage political deviation among whites. The promising rhetoric of the low-taxers in the 1882 campaign may have been shallow and opportunistic, but their racial views, however narrow, offered blacks a far more attractive political environment than the one that would confront them a few years later.

Although blacks would be wary in the future of placing much stock in white political alliances outside the Republican party, for a brief spell, real political competition had made the black vote an important ingredient in Shelby County and had presented an opportunity for blacks to exercise limited power. Though unsuccessful immediately, it stimulated blacks throughout Tennessee to renewed political activity. At least this was the warning of the editor of the Chattanooga *Times*, who blamed the Shelby County fusionists for stirring up racial tensions in Chattanooga: "Radicalism is something new in Chattanooga. We have been the most conservative and prudent of communities. Never have we experienced, until within the past few weeks, anything like a collision of races. The policy of the city has been to build schoolhouses for the colored people; to treat them with consideration and kindness; to forbear with their weaknesses and follies as if they were children of the town."[40]

The victorious low-tax wing of the Democratic party, under the leadership of Governor Bate and a cooperative legislature, quickly settled the state-debt issue. Most of the debt was scaled down fifty cents on the dollar and funded with new bonds bearing 3 percent interest.[41] Harris, the indomitable symbol of the old Democracy in Tennessee, was reelected to the United States Senate. Resolution of the debt issue did not end strife within the Democratic party but simply diverted it to other issues—principally, railroad regulation, tariffs, and federal aid to education. While the factions within the Democratic party shifted somewhat from issue to issue and no continuous and permanent alignment existed, the Bate-Harris forces generally attacked consolidation of economic and governmental power and opposed special-interests legislation; consequently, they favored state regulation of railroads and opposed a protective tariff and federal aid for education. They met opposition from the more business-minded members of the party, often former Whigs, who talked of building a "New South" based on industry and agricultural diversification. The Bate-Harris forces were derisively labeled "Bourbons" by political enemies who charged that, like the French ruling family of that name, they had learned nothing from past experiences. Confronted by powerful foes within the party and a viable Republican opposition, the Bourbons struggled to broaden their base of support in order to maintain power and to steer the party in the direction they thought it ought to go.

Intraparty strife between the New South and Bourbon factions in the state Democratic party was heightened by deteriorating agricultural conditions and by moderate industrial growth. Amid the New South industrial propaganda of the 1880s, Tennessee farmers were working harder and producing larger and larger crops but receiving less money.[42] Agrarian unrest resulted in the

[40]Chattanooga *Times*, Nov. 16, 1882.
[41]Hart, "Bourbonism and Populism," 102; Hamer, *Tennessee*, II, 690–92.
[42]United States, Bureau of the Census, *Compendium of the Eleventh Census, 1890*, Pt. II, Miscellaneous Statistics (Washington, D. C.: Government Printing

entrance of farmers into Tennessee politics with such increasing force that by the end of the decade they would win temporary control of the Democratic party. Through the mid-eighties, therefore, Bourbon and New South factions fought for dominance within the party, and each keenly understood the influence that the black vote could have in determining the outcome of their struggle. With the state-credit bolters back in the Democratic party, Bate won reelection in the gubernatorial contest of 1884, but by a majority of only 7,000 votes. The administration's efforts to attract black votes, especially in West Tennessee, met slight success,[43] but the Bourbon wing of the party soon found an issue that offered promise of winning greater black support.

Early in 1883 the Bourbons, led by Governor Bate, had created a state railroad commission in an attempt to end unjust discrimination in transportation rates. Republicans and New South Democrats, wanting to encourage railroad expansion, weakened and, in the 1885 legislature, killed the commission as an effective agency. Elements in the Bourbon camp, however, continued to press for some form of regulation. In March 1885, John J. Vertrees, a close associate of Governor Bate, assumed control of the most prestigious Democratic newspaper in Tennessee, the Nashville American. Upon launching a campaign to stir up flagging public support for railroad regulation, Vertrees sought to attract Negro voters to the Democratic party, claiming that a regulatory commission would enforce the state law requiring railroads to furnish separate facilities for blacks equal to those enjoyed by whites. Under existing practices the railroads operating in the state largely ignored the 1881 separate-car law and either confined black passengers to a mixed smoking car, whether or not they paid first-class fare, or, in some cases, allowed them to sit wherever they wished.[44]

The issue of railroad regulation became ensnarled in racism as

---

Office, 1891), 671, 686–87; State of Tennessee, *Biennial Report of the Bureau of Agriculture, Statistics and Immigration, 1889–90* (Nashville: Albert B. Tavel, 1891), 49–52.

[43]Memphis *Appeal*, Sept. 17, Oct. 26, Nov. 1, 5, 1884.

[44]White, *Messages*, VII, 58–59, 73; Nashville *American*, Aug. 28, 1885.

Vertrees began to attack the unjust policies of the railroads. Here was an opportunity to befriend blacks, and, at the same time, to complement the Bourbons' drive for an effective railroad commission. To secure equal accommodations on the state's railroads, blacks were encouraged to help the Bourbons create an effective regulatory commission—one that would enforce the 1881 law requiring equal but separate first-class facilities.

To entice blacks into the Bourbon camp without repelling whites, the Nashville *American* traveled much the same ground covered by the low-tax Democrats in 1882. Vertrees revived the well-worn argument that the masses of both races in the South had identical interests and promised blacks patronage and a share of party nominations as they joined the Democratic camp. "Let the colored people feel that, in so far as they become Democrats," he wrote, "they are entitled to have their interests considered in the party, and to have a share in the shaping of its policy. Let them feel that they are thoroughly at home in the Democratic party." He urged Democrats not to "make the mistake their opponents have made on this question" and at least to "meet the colored people half way, as they come within the organization, and to accord to them a share of its responsibilities and emoluments." The Bourbon editor waged a relentless campaign to educate white Democrats to the political and moral advantages of abolishing the color line in politics. Not only would such a course greatly reduce corruption among white politicians and strengthen the Democratic party by adding black votes but also would solidify party unity by eliminating "any inducement for the formation of 'Independent' log-rolling combinations with the Republicans."[45]

The editorial pages of the *American* also bristled with indignation at the unjust treatment of Negroes by the state's railroads. The *American* stressed the injustice of assigning blacks to second-class facilities even when they paid first-class fares and pointed to a railroad commission as the remedy. On the other hand, in an effort to escape the stigma associated with courting blacks, the

[45]Nashville *American*, Apr. 6, May 17, 31, July 7, 25, Aug. 2, 4, 16, 1885.

Bourbon journal appealed to white racial sensibilities by condemning the railroads for allowing the races to intermingle illegally on trains.[46]

The *American* faced mounting criticism from within the party. New South editors angrily charged that the Bourbons were attempting to replace old Whigs in the party—men who opposed regulation of railroads, reduction of the tariff, and fusion with Negroes—with blacks who would support the machine. In short, the Bourbons were proselytizing among black Republicans "by pretense of advocacy of rights upon public conveyances" in order "to replace losses the machine has incurred and is daily incurring among white democrats." The New South press also attacked the Nashville *American* on the grounds that, as spokesman for the Bate administration, it was exciting racial tensions and promising Negroes social equality. Referring to "the nigger flop" of the *American*, the editor of the Pulaski *Citizen* complained that the Nashville newspaper was trying to force Negro social equality and was calling on blacks "to help the 'democrats' (God save the mark!) establish a railroad commission that will give them equal access to the sleeper and the ladies car." Courting Negro votes was fraught with grave dangers, warned the *Citizen*, for the *American* "even sent a man around interviewing prominent negroes, calling them Mr. this and Esq. that." It was "this hobnobbing with negroes, inciting them to renewed demands" that misrepresented the Democratic party. White people would not permit social equality, he asserted, and black people did not expect it; continued debate of the matter would only "lead to anarchy and bloodshed." The Bourbon machine had chosen its new course not out of "a love of the negro," concluded the editor of the *Citizen*, "nor for justices sake," but "to gain recruits to itself from ignorant and daring negroes to help it and its men seize and hold the offices in Tennessee." A Henderson County editor, quoted in the *Avalanche*, vowed that if the Bourbons' racial policies prevailed, white men "who don't want their wives and daughters to mix up in the same car, board at the same hotel and

[46]*Ibid.*, July 30, Aug. 11, 19, 21, 25, 28, 1885.

tend the same theater with the negro, will desert that party."[47]

Although the bulk of the editorial opposition to the Bourbon campaign for black support centered on political and racial fears, business-minded Democrats of the New South persuasion also feared that enforcement of the Jim Crow law would discourage railroad expansion by saddling the companies with the extra expense of maintaining separate first-class facilities. The New South press, therefore, obliquely defended the prevailing railroad policy of unofficially ignoring the law and assigning most blacks to the smoking cars. The Memphis *Avalanche*, for example, warned that any tampering with existing practices either would lead to social equality or would drive railroads out of the state. New South Democrats apparently reasoned that if the separate-facilities issue were pushed, railroads in the state quietly would allow blacks access to all cars rather than assume the extra financial burden of providing separate first-class facilities; if the law were enforced, the economic burden would curb railroad expansion in the state. Agitation of the issue, therefore, promised to result either in social equality born of economic expediency or in separate facilities and economic stagnation.[48]

In response to these attacks, Vertrees, editor of the Nashville *American*, defended the political wisdom of an alliance with Negroes and assured critics that he was interested only in securing justice and ending racial intermingling on the railroads, not in introducing social equality. "According the Negro the simple rights involved in his citizenship," he argued, "in no way involves the social question. That is a question already settled by inexorable natural law." The persistent editor called upon southern Democrats to insure the Negro his rights, not only to disarm

[47]Memphis *Avalanche*, July 23, Aug. 8, 11, 1885; Chattanooga *Times*, July 23, 1885; Pulaski *Citizen*, July 30, Aug. 6, Sept. 10, 1885.

[48]Nashville *American*, Aug. 17, 18, 1885; Memphis *Avalanche*, Aug. 8, 11, 1885. In a 1974 article, a student of the 1898 Jim Crow law in South Carolina argues that a principal reason for the late passage of railroad segregation laws in that state was the opposition of business-minded Democrats who "feared that separate coach laws might harm the railroad industry." See Linda M. Matthews, "Keeping Down Jim Crow: The Railroads and the Separate Coach Bills in South Carolina," *South Atlantic Quarterly* 73 (Winter 1974), 117–29.

northern critics and "inspire the negro himself with confidence" but also "to assume an impregnable moral position."[49]

The Nashville editor saw the malign influence of the Louisville and Nashville Railroad behind his New South critics. They were stirring up the racial issue to divert attention from the need for a railroad commission, he said. The greatest threat to railroad expansion in the state was not a regulatory commission, Vertrees charged, but the monopolistic practices of the Louisville and Nashville empire which used its power to eliminate rival lines in Tennessee. A writer to the *American* stated this issue candidly when he argued that "to overcome the influence of the Louisville and Nashville corporation in Tennessee politics the party must stand together and the colored vote must be divided." Another writer to the same paper saw the cry of social equality raised by the *American's* critics as a scheme "by unscrupulously designing men" to "excuse the railroads from the extra expense of providing and running separate cars."[50]

Whatever Vertrees' motives, there were clear limits to his concern for the rights of Negroes. The more he came under fire from the New South press, the more forthrightly he stressed that separate facilities were necessary to protect whites from offensive Negroes and played down earlier concern that refined Negroes should be protected from the coarse behavior of lower-class blacks and whites.[51]

Blacks responded to this call for a new departure in politics through a series of interviews conducted by the *American*. Their attitudes ranged from hearty approval to cautious skepticism. The interviews with prominent black Nashvillians reveal the difficulties the Bourbons confronted in courting black support and attest to the political sophistication and integrationist goals of Nashville's black elite in the mid-eighties. James C. Napier, a member of the Nashville city council and an avid Republican, viewed the extensive discussion of the race question as a healthy development but firmly declared: "I am opposed to the *American's* idea of

[49]Nashville *American*, Aug. 2, 19, 1885.
[50]*Ibid.*, July 7, Aug. 18, 23, 1885.
[51]*Ibid.*, July 30, Aug. 21, 1885.

separate institutions such as railway coaches set apart for the two races." Joseph H. Dismukes, a prominent lawyer and active local Republican organizer, also regretted that the *American* could not "go a little further with us in the matter of railroad accommodations, instead of insisting upon separate cars, though each may be equally comfortable." On this question, Dismukes said, he was "uncompromising." George W. Bryant, a minister already in the Democratic camp, applauded the efforts of the *American* to attract more members of his race into the party and observed that "intelligent" Negroes increasingly were affiliating with the Democratic party. Attorney William Henderson Young, however, cautiously advised Negroes to stay out of the intraparty dispute because "any interference by the colored people will frighten off the party making the overtures." Young did venture the opinion that political demagogues had divided black and white Southerners and that there was a growing political independence among blacks, although black fear "of insincerity on the part of Democrats" acted as a constraining influence. "The negro is going to stand by the party that demonstrates to him that he shall be supported in his political and civil rights," Young asserted. Like Young, a number of the blacks interviewed wanted a more tangible manifestation of the Bourbons' commitment to a biracial political alliance than mere editorial blandishments. One respondent urged the Bourbons to incorporate the *American's* pledges to protect Negro rights into the Democratic party's platform before asking for the black vote. The blacks interviewed by the *American* uniformly agreed that they did not want social equality and that they had not interpreted the newspaper's editorials to favor it. A crisp, if not final, word on this subject was Dismukes' perhaps tongue in cheek observation: "I don't believe the colored people want social equality with any one outside their own race. As our intelligence increases we grow less inclined for social intercourse with the whites."[52]

The Bourbon campaign for black support also included promises of patronage. When news spread in the summer of 1885 that

[52]*Ibid.*, July 25, Aug. 17, 20, 1885.

Edward Shaw again was being considered for an appointment at the hands of the Bourbons, the New South press exploded. Shaw had campaigned enthusiastically for Governor Bate and the national Democratic ticket in the election of 1884.[53] His position as the central figure over whom the two Democratic factions waged their internecine war on the race question was assured when Senator Harris, in conjunction with other Bourbon leaders in Tennessee, recommended that he be appointed head of the federal customs office at Memphis. For two weeks in July 1885, the editorial pages of the Memphis *Avalanche* bristled with personal invective aimed at Shaw. This "bitterest of radicals" was condemned for his role in reconstruction politics in Memphis, accused of delivering "communistic speeches" which advocated violence, and labeled "a mean and despicable individual." The Chattanooga *Times* branded him a "criminal politician who had travelled marvelously close to the dizzy edge of felony for years," and saw the black leader as "wholly dishonest, treacherous, thoroughly bad, morally rotten and corrupt." The following of this "ignorant and dishonest scoundrel," according to the *Times*, was "solely of the criminal and rowdy class" and came "from the slums and the workhouse."[54]

The New South press condemned the proposed appointment of Shaw as an "infamous scheme" undertaken by Senator Harris and his "machine Democrats" to control the Democratic party by using Negro votes and warned that it would cause the downfall of all who took part in it. The Chattanooga *Times* warned, "No, gentlemen of the machine, you can't retrieve the losses your agrarianism and dishonesty have caused the party by conscripting from the negro slums." The Bourbon politicians who supposed that this was the way to divide the black vote and to augment their diminishing strength were wrong, argued the Memphis *Avalanche*, and they would find that they "have mistaken the wishes of the public." The Bourbons and their organ, the Nashville *American*, represented "a dead and rotten corpse," the *Avalanche*

---

[53]*Ibid.*, Oct. 18, 1884; Memphis *Appeal*, Oct. 28, 1884.
[54]Memphis *Avalanche*, July 1–10 (N.B. July 5), 1885; Chattanooga *Times*, July 7, 1885.

declared, predicting that "a time of reckoning" would come, "and when it does woe be unto those who have tried to make of the democratic party the unworthy instrument of their personal advancement." For recommending the Shaw appointment, Senator Harris came under heavy fire in the Democratic press. The *Avalanche* quoted the Jackson *Whig* warning Harris that, if he should secure the appointment of Shaw, "the righteous indignation of Tennesseans" would "follow him to his grave." The Lawrence County *Democrat*, also quoted in the *Avalanche*, suggested that Harris should hide his head in shame "for the complimentary language he has already used in speaking of this brutal deformity of the human race [Edward Shaw]."[55] New South leaders undoubtedly hoped to exploit the race issue in order to stir up opposition to the Bourbons and, ultimately, to remove Harris from the United States Senate.

In the face of this torrent of abuse, Bourbon leaders defended Shaw's character and once again advanced their reasons for trying to recruit blacks into the Democratic party. Since the Memphis customs office was already headed by a black Republican, the *American's* Vertrees saw no harm in a patronage policy which would attract black votes to the Democratic party. Josiah Patterson, Bourbon leader from Memphis and a close friend of Senator Harris, described Shaw as the man "who best represented the colored democratic element" in Tennessee. Praising Shaw's intelligence, courage, and independence, Patterson stated that he believed the South's best interests lay in promoting racial unity by encouraging black Democrats.[56]

Writing to the Memphis *Avalanche*, Shaw defended his past activities as a leader of his people and challenged his traducers to produce evidence that "I ever said anything about burning southern homes" or "spoke disrespectfully of the white women of the south." Such charges were "circulated through motives desperate, diabolical and insane and to gratify a hellish malignity," he replied. The Nashville *American* interviewed Republican Thomas

[55]Chattanooga *Times*, July 12, 1885; see also July 7, 18, 1885; Memphis *Avalanche*, July 5, 7, 10–12, Sept. 4, 1885.
[56]Nashville *American*, July 7, 1885; Memphis *Avalanche*, July 8, 1885.

A. Sykes, a former member of the Tennessee legislature from Davidson County, who considered the disposition manifested by the Democratic party to elevate black men "full of promise" for his race. Sykes predicted that Shaw's appointment "would be hailed with joy" by blacks and "would cost the republican party many thousands of votes." At a nonpartisan meeting in Memphis black citizens denounced the *Avalanche's* editorial war on Shaw as "a mad conspiracy . . . calculated to prejudice the unthinking, arouse the passions of the ignorant, and injure the man only to defeat him." The "unscrupulous vilifications" circulated against Shaw were patently absurd, they declared, for "it is known to every intelligent mind that no colored man could have uttered those charges and lived in this community."[57]

In August, the Memphis papers carried stories of a grand jury indictment brought against Shaw for perjury in a civil case, but he was soon exonerated before the criminal court. The Nashville *American* viewed the episode as harassment by Shaw's opponents. Protesting that he favored the appointment of qualified blacks to office, Senator Harris nevertheless refused to stand by Shaw and in early October announced that a white man would fill the position for which Shaw had been proposed.[58]

With the Democratic party sharply divided over the state debt, railroad regulation, and the tariff, Bourbon efforts to establish a biracial base of support were of major political importance and attracted national attention. However unsuccessful, the support for Shaw's appointment seemed to presage to some national observers "great changes in the division of voters in the South."[59] Perhaps the Bourbons wished to offset losses from dissidents within the party, as the New South press claimed, or perhaps they sincerely believed that the political interests of both races were similar and that abolition of the color line in Tennessee politics would ease racial tension. Indeed, it is likely that both motives

[57]Memphis *Avalanche*, July 12, 14, 1885; Nashville *American*, July 15, 1885.
[58]Memphis *Avalanche*, Aug. 5, Sept. 8, Oct. 13, 1885; Memphis *Appeal*, Aug. 5, 1885.
[59]E. P. Clark, "The Negro in Southern Politics," *Nation* 41 (July 23, 1885), 67.

were influential. In any case, as the focus in Tennessee politics shifted from largely internal matters, such as the debt and railroad regulation, to national issues, such as federal aid to education and national protection of voting rights, Bourbon attitudes toward Negro voters would undergo a monumental change.

The question of federal aid to education provided New South leaders in the party with an opportunity to combine self-interest with political expediency and to court black support themselves. In 1883 Republican Senator Henry W. Blair of New Hampshire stimulated national discussion of the issue when he proposed a bill that would have provided for a ten-year period of annual federal appropriations—beginning at $15,000,000 and diminishing by $1,000,000 each year—to be distributed to the states on the basis of their illiteracy rates. The money was to be proportioned between both races in each state; otherwise, the bill avoided any interference with state control of the funds.[60] During the Tennessee gubernatorial campaign of 1886, the issue gained statewide importance when the Democrats turned to Robert L. Taylor as a candidate who might conciliate the two rival factions within the party, but, when both New South and Bourbon leaders sought to identify "Bob" with their respective camps, the Blair Education bill became the crucial test of the candidate's ideological persuasion.

Rallying to the support of the Blair bill, New South editors asserted that federal aid for Negro education would benefit blacks and whites alike. It would help counteract the sudden enfranchisement of a large mass of "ignorant" voters, make black labor more reliable and capable of intelligently utilizing the implements of an industrial society, and instill in Negroes an appreciation for the responsibilities of propertyholding. Southern whites, reasoned the editor of the Memphis *Avalanche*, would benefit if their black

---

[60]Woodward, *Origins of the New South, 1877–1913* (Baton Rouge: Louisiana State Univ. Press, 1951), 63; Otto H. Olsen, ed., *The Negro Question: From Slavery to Caste, 1863–1910. Major Issues in American History* (New York: Pitman, 1971), 173–74; Knoxville *Chronicle*, Mar. 6, 1883; Daniel W. Crofts, "The Black Response to the Blair Education Bill," *Jour. Southern Hist.* 37 (Feb. 1971), 41–65.

neighbors "should receive the education that makes him [sic] more capable as laborers, more trustworthy in business, quiet and peaceable neighbors, and good citizens." The editor of the Chattanooga *Times* concluded that the "negro is here as a citizen and to stay. To keep him in barbaric ignorance is to perpetuate forever a menace to social order and the industrial progress of the section."[61]

An early advocate of the Blair bill in Tennessee was Senator Howell E. Jackson, whose alignment with the New South forces pitted him against his colleague in the Senate, Bourbon leader Harris. Elected to the Senate in 1881 by a combination of Republican and state-credit Democrats in the legislature, Jackson voted for the Blair bill in 1884 and again in 1886, and spoke often in its behalf. Addressing the Tennessee State Teachers' Association in August 1885, Jackson defended the constitutionality of the Blair bill, warned of the dangers of an illiterate voting population, pointed out the financial inability of Tennessee to provide the kind of education its citizens needed, and proclaimed the growth of a skilled labor class as an immediate consequence of improvements in the state's educational program. The editor of the Memphis *Avalanche* applauded Jackson's speech. Black labor would be improved by education, argued the editor, for Negroes were "especially capable of profiting by technical education." More significantly, perhaps, federal aid would enable Negroes to advance by education rather than by political agitation.[62]

The Bourbon wing of the Democratic party was not united in its opposition to the Blair bill. Colonel Keating, one of the editors of the Bourbon-oriented Memphis *Appeal*, was a long-standing advocate of Negro education, but Senator Harris, a steadfast opponent of the Blair bill, probably more accurately expressed the views of the Bourbon Democrats in Tennessee. He branded the bill a subterfuge to allow the Republicans to maintain a high protective tariff by draining the United States treasury of its surplus revenue, claimed that each state should assume responsibility for education

[61]Memphis, *Avalanche*, June 2, Oct. 18, 1883; Aug. 5, 1885; Mar. 25, 1886; Nov. 7, 1886; Chattanooga *Times*, Mar. 28, 1886.
[62]Memphis *Appeal*, and Memphis *Avalanche*, Sept. 11, 1885.

without interference from the national government, and maintained that federal handouts violated state rights and individualism.[63]

Throughout his 1886 gubernatorial campaign, Taylor sat on the fence between Bourbon and New South Democrats, issuing vague statements favoring federal aid to education through public-land sales, while opposing use of the existing treasury surplus for anything other than payment on the public debt. Taylor, however, had endorsed the Blair bill in a private letter to Senator Jackson, and after his election the new governor quickly fell out with the Bourbon element by forthrightly advocating the principles of the Blair bill and by favoring the New South wing with patronage.[64] While Bourbon leaders charged that Taylor and his "mugwump" allies had sold out to the New South wing of the party, Taylor's position was hailed by New South enthusiasts: "Tennessee in the front rank of the 'New South' must be kept abreast of these advancing times, and her people look to you to see that she is not suffered to lag and be smothered in the atmosphere of fifty years ago," a Memphis lawyer wrote Taylor. "Your stand for education," he continued, "demonstrates the accuracy of your comprehension of the needs, the happiness and the general welfare of your people." Another writer, the head of an industrial plant in Cleveland, Tennessee, urged Taylor to stand firm in insisting that the federal government help pay for the damages wrought by the Civil War: "They (I mean the Radical party) destroyed our property[,] burned our building and fencing, freed our negroes and left us not content with the irreparable damages done—but with the burden to carry of educating the negroes—now if we can get them to help *I say do it.*"[65]

[63]John M. Keating, "Twenty Years of Negro Education," *Popular Science Monthly* 27 (Nov. 1885), 24–37; Dan M. Robison, "Governor Robert L. Taylor and the Blair Educational Bill in Tennessee," *Tennessee Historical Magazine*, 2d ser., 1 (Oct. 1931), 32–35.

[64]Robison, "Taylor and the Blair Educational Bill," 40–45; Robert L. Taylor to Howell E. Jackson, Oct. 1, 1885, Harding-Jackson Papers (Manuscript Div., Tennessee State Library and Archives).

[65]Taylor also appointed an outspoken advocate of the Blair bill to be state superintendent of public schools. Nashville *American*, Feb. 13, 1887; Knoxville

Through their defense of the Blair bill, New South exponents in Tennessee further advanced their paternalistic racial policy. Based on a recognition of the interdependent needs of southern blacks and whites, the New South idea of racial progress, like that of the Bourbons, presupposed inherent Negro inferiority, white supremacy, and a belief that southern economic prosperity depended upon interracial cooperation. Although bitterly hostile to the Bourbons' courting of black voters, New South leaders were more solicitous when they saw a chance to win black support themselves. In his 1886 campaign for Congress, for example, James Phelan, owner of the Memphis *Avalanche* and a vigorous New South ideologue, explained what the New South racial formula meant to Democrats of his persuasion:

It means a hearty sympathy with all people of all classes. It means . . . to accept in good part and in good faith the citizenship of the negro race. They are our fellow-Tennesseans. Their rights are as sacred as ours. Socially God has placed a wide and running river between us. This river of race no one of liberal mind can desire to see bridged over. But they are our fellow-citizens, and on opposite sides of this river they are, or ought to be, moving with us toward the common goal of a higher order of civilization. In civil life they are as much entitled to receive the full worth of their money as we and they can demand as a right all the privileges that flow from a free ballot and a fair count. The New South, in full sympathy with the lower plane upon which they stand, accepts them with hearty acquiescence and turns cheerfully and earnestly toward the solution of the problem that involves their moral, intellectual and industrial development.[66]

Those who championed federal aid to education in Tennessee sought to convince Negroes that the path of progress lay in vocational education rather than politics, while, at the same time, they held out to conservative whites the vision of a disciplined and

Tribune, Feb. 26, Mar. 10, 19, 27, 1887; M. B. Trezevant to Robert L. Taylor, Feb. 25, 1887; Joseph H. Hardwick to R. L. Taylor, Feb. 22, 1887, Taylor Papers (Governors' Papers, Tennessee State Library and Archives).

[66]*The New South*, (Memphis: S. C. Toof, 1886); copy of speech delivered at Covington, Tenn., Oct. 2, 1886.

docile black work force speeding the economic metamorphosis of the South. Nevertheless, like the dream of a reinvigorated South pulsating with the energy unleashed by industrialization, the hope of federal aid for education would have to await fulfillment until a later era. The Blair bill suffered its final defeat in the Senate in 1890, and white Southerners became increasingly suspicious of federal interference. As Republicans threatened to institute federal supervision of southern elections through passage of the Lodge election bill, the moderating and nationalizing influence of the New South rhetoric gave way to bitter racial recriminations, the bloody shirt, and heightened sectional animosities.[67]

The great majority of Tennessee Negroes remained Republicans, but some joined the ranks of the Democracy and actively worked to recruit other black voters for the party. Although they generally have been lumped together as "accommodationists," black men joined the Democratic party in the 1880s for a variety of reasons. Some of them continued to support the Democrats on the same grounds as they did in the 1870s: economic coercion and physical intimidation by whites, hope that cooperation with whites would lead to interracial harmony, belief that a divided black vote would allow Negroes to exercise greater bargaining power, and preference for Democratic economic policies.[68] Many of those Negroes who considered Democratic economic policies more suitable to their needs undoubtedly agreed with Charles H. J. Taylor, a Negro lawyer and newspaper editor who served as minister to Liberia under President Cleveland. Highly regarded by the Democratic press in Tennessee as a "sensible" Negro, Taylor advised members of his race that they were natural Democrats: they favored low taxes, preferred a low tariff, and were opposed to legislation favorable to business.[69] Other blacks joined the Democrats after becoming disenchanted by the white

[67]Allen J. Going, "The South and the Blair Education Bill," *Mississippi Valley Historical Review* 44 (Sept. 1957), 275; Logan, *Betrayal of the Negro,* 70–74.

[68]Memphis *Avalanche,* July 27, Oct. 6, 1880; Nashville *American,* Aug. 17, 24, 1880; Oct. 28, 1888; Memphis *Appeal,* Aug. 5, Oct. 6–7, 1880; Nov. 3, 1888.

[69]Charles Henry James Taylor, *Whites and Blacks; or, The Question Settled* (Atlanta: J. P. Harrison, 1889), 43; Memphis *Avalanche,* Oct. 3, 1888.

Republicans' failure to share offices as a reward for black votes, and an increasing number turned to the Democratic party in an effort to secure their civil rights.[70] With dwindling confidence that the Republican party would use its national power to protect black rights, they either organized independent groups which fused with local Democrats or moved boldly into the Democratic party.[71]

The most prominent black convert to the Democratic party in Tennessee was Edward Shaw. While campaigning for the party in 1884, Shaw exemplified the guarded militancy of those blacks who turned to the Democratic party for patronage, for the chance to run for office, and for recognition of their civil rights. He counseled blacks that for their own benefit they should vote for the party in power in the state. Speaking in Nashville to a large racially-mixed crowd, he urged black voters to emulate him, to "shake off the yoke of Republicanism and stand shoulder to shoulder with their best friends, the Democrats of the country." Shaw argued that he had served the Republican party earnestly and faithfully for years without receiving any office. "You were made voters by these white Republicans," he told the members of his race, "in order that you might vote for white Republicans and not for your-selves."[72]

Several other Tennessee Negro political leaders joined Shaw in supporting the Democratic party. Henry C. Smith of Chattanooga, appointed to a federal clerkship under President Cleveland, campaigned for the Democratic party throughout the 1880s. A graduate of Roger Williams University in Nashville, Smith praised the efforts of Tennessee Democrats on behalf of Negro education, defended the Democratic position on the tariff, and lauded President Cleveland's appointment policies regarding Negroes. At the same time he assailed white Republicans for refusing to support

[70]Memphis *Appeal*, Oct. 6, Dec. 29, 1880; Nov. 3, 1883; Nashville *American*, Oct. 28, 1888; Washington *Bee*, Nov. 20, 1886.

[71]August Meier, *Negro Thought in America, 1880–1915* (Ann Arbor: Univ. of Michigan Press, 1963), 26–41. For a similar trend in North Carolina, see Logan, *Negro in North Carolina*, 21–23.

[72]Memphis *Appeal*, Oct. 28, 1884; Nashville *American*, Oct. 18, 1884.

black candidates, for being interested only in the Negro's vote, and for practicing discriminatory policies in the North.[73]

Perhaps Alfred A. Froman best represented those black Democrats who combined a desire for interracial harmony with a keen disenchantment with Republicanism. Froman was a Memphis lawyer who had participated in the fusionist movement of 1882 and 1884 and had run unsuccessfully for the state legislature on the Democratic ticket. Also in 1884 he had toured the country campaigning for Cleveland. An ex-slave who had escaped from bondage before the Civil War and had lived in the North, Froman was praised by white Democrats for his conciliatory efforts "to harmonize discordant elements" and "to bring about a better feeling between the white and colored people." Although denouncing Froman's policies, Harry C. Smith, the Negro editor and owner of the Cleveland (Ohio) *Gazette*, thought that Froman had assumed his position "without fear or favor." Acknowledging Froman's consistency, Smith described him as an able man who saw his mission to be that of harmonizing the races. Froman wrote Governor Bate after the latter's successful reelection in 1884, applauding the Democratic party's efforts for Negro education in Tennessee and subtly reminding the governor of his promise to create the position of state assistant superintendent of education to be filled by a Negro who would supervise the black public schools. Froman later applied for the position and was heartily endorsed by West Tennessee Democratic leaders, including the Bourbon editors of the Memphis *Appeal*, but the position he sought never materialized.[74]

Like Shaw, Froman defended his Democratic allegiance on the basis that the Republican party had long since turned its back on the Negro, leaving black Southerners with the only realistic alternative of "making terms for ourselves." Writing to the editor of the *Gazette*, he argued that the Democratic victory of 1884 would "create a better and more friendly feeling between the

[73]Washington *Bee*, Nov. 20, 1886; Nashville *American*, Oct. 28, 1888.
[74]Memphis *Appeal*, Jan. 15, Oct. 10, 1884; Cleveland (Ohio) *Gazette*, Dec. 13, 1884; Alfred A. Froman to William B. Bate, Dec. 31, 1884; A. J. Vaughn *et al.* to William B. Bate, Feb. 1885, Bate Papers.

former master and slave." For "so long as the southern white man has been feeling himself ostracised by the General Government," Froman reasoned, "the colored man would remain an eyesore, engendering bitterness and causing much unavoidable persecution and abuse to the untutored Negro who could never find any redress from the Republican administration." The South was Democratic, and since the great majority of black people lived in the South, Froman regarded it as "nonsense that they being poor, dependent, uneducated, should be trained to disregard their interest, and to wield their votes against the very men from who [sic] they get employment, only for the sake of being called a Republican." The greatest needs of black Southerners, he declared, were bread, protection, and education. Pointing out that these could be obtained only from the local government and not from Washington, Froman concluded that Negroes should adhere to "home influences," utilizing them for the good of the race. Their loyalty to the Republican party had reaped only "blood, slaughter and death." Now, he argued, it was time for peace, time to "let the South have its turn."[75]

Although most blacks remained loyal to the Republican party, Negro support for the Democrats gradually increased during the 1880s in every section of the state. Tennessee blacks organized local Democratic clubs to support the party's national candidates in 1880, 1884, and 1888. Discontent with Republican racial policies, desire for racial harmony, preference for Democratic economic policies, concern over local protection for civil rights, as well as white intimidation, apparently produced a larger black vote for the Democratic ticket in 1886 than ever before. The increased Democratic majorities in Nashville and the Democratic victories in Memphis and in West Tennessee's Tipton and Madison counties were credited in part, at least, to a growing black Democratic vote in each area.[76]

[75]Cleveland (Ohio) *Gazette*, Jan. 3, 1885.

[76]Memphis *Appeal*, Aug. 6, 1880; Memphis *Avalanche*, Aug. 6, Nov. 3, 1886; Nashville *American*, Aug. 4, 1886; New York *Freeman*, Aug. 21, 1886; Knoxville *Journal*, Jan. 16, 1886; J. A. Trousdale to William B. Bate, Nov. 17, 1884, Bate Papers; Memphis *Avalanche*, Aug. 6, Nov. 3, 1886.

Negroes who voted the Democratic ticket risked denunciation, social ostracism, and even occasional physical violence from black Republicans. Although some of the charges of black political intolerance represented Democratic campaign propaganda, extreme partisanship was not an exclusive preserve of whites. A black schoolteacher, witness in the contested Fayette County election of 1883, testified that local black Republicans were "extremely hostile" toward Negroes who voted Democratic, adding that the latter were "socially ostracised and often threatened with violence and death." In the state elections of 1884 a group of black Republicans in Chattanooga assaulted a member of their race who voted the straight Democratic ticket. A year later, the editor of the Chattanooga *Times* said that this antagonism was "more pronounced than ever before." Although overt intimidation of black Democrats by members of their own race had apparently declined by 1886, incidents continued to occur at the polls throughout the 1880s. Harassment, ostracism, and violence only gradually gave way to an apparent reluctant toleration of black Democrats by black Republicans.[77]

By 1888 growing white Democratic hostility toward black voting and officeholding, continued pressure from black Republicans, and the possibility of federal intervention to protect black voting made Negro loyalty to the Democratic party tenuous at best. The great majority of Tennessee Negroes steadfastly remained Republicans. Those Negroes who had joined the Democratic party out of optimistic hopes for racial harmony or expectations for office received few offices and by the end of the 1880s faced a resurgence of racial animosities. For a brief period in the eighties, though, Democratic factionalism had augured well for blacks in Tennessee politics. Ironically, the way by which each faction had attempted to marshal black support for its policies only created

[77]Petitions, Memorials, Reports, 43d General Assembly, 1883, Secretary of State Papers (Archives Div., Tennessee State Library and Archives); Chattanooga *Times*, Nov. 5, 1884; Oct. 16, 1885; Memphis *Appeal*, Aug. 18, 1886; Chattanooga *Times*, Oct. 19, Nov. 7, 1888; affidavits, W. W. Wilson to Robert L. Taylor, Nov. 19, 1888, and M. M. Henderson to Robert L. Taylor, Nov. 3, 1888, Taylor Papers.

greater ill will among whites toward blacks and provided part of the rationale, at the end of the decade, for legislative attacks on black voting. The similarities of the racial formulas advanced by the warring factions of the Democratic party in Tennessee outweighed their differences, but, for a time, the political contours in the state led Bourbon politicians—presumably the fossilized creatures who forgot nothing and learned nothing—to forge pragmatic political alliances with Negroes. If nothing else, this created a racial atmosphere that was more open and flexible than the one that would exist a few years later.

II

Black Militancy and the Republican Party

Throughout the 1880s Negroes played a vital role in determining the strength of the Republican party in Tennessee. According to the census of 1880, the total voting population of the state was 330,305, of which nearly one-fourth was black.[1] The vast majority of the state's approximately 80,000 black voters in 1880 were Republicans, and most would remain so, although as the decade advanced there was a perceptible shift of blacks toward the Democratic ranks. Dominated usually by East Tennessee mountain whites, the Republican party also attracted white support from the hilly sections and the cities of Middle and West Tennessee. An active core of whites generally controlled party operations even in West Tennessee, where blacks comprised the great majority of Republican voters. Republicans usually fared well in Montgomery, Williamson, and Davidson counties of Middle Tennessee because of the existence of large black populations in Clarksville, Franklin, and Nashville—the respective county seats. Three of the five consistently Republican counties in West Tennessee—Carroll, Henderson, and Hardin—were part of a hilly strip with only small black populations, but the other two—Fayette and Haywood—both contained large black majorities in 1880. The black majorities in Tipton and Madison counties carried them for the Republicans through the middle of the eighties, and the growing black population in Memphis insured a strong Republican party in Shelby County until the end of the decade.[2]

[1]*Compendium of the Tenth Census*, 596; Memphis *Appeal*, Sept. 12, 1882; Chattanooga *Times*, Oct. 23, 1888.

[2]The crucial role of East Tennessee in the state Republican party is discussed

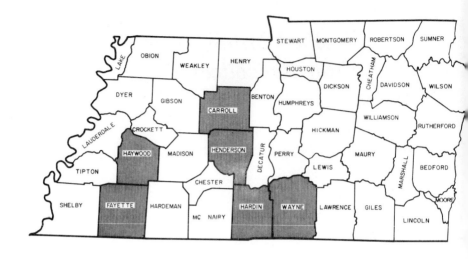

Map. 2. COUNTIES (SHADED) WITH REPUBLICAN MAJORITIES IN OVER

Overall, the Republican party remained competitive in Tennessee until the latter part of the eighties. Of the state's ten congressional districts, the Republicans controlled the First and Second in East Tennessee throughout the 1880s. They were able to elect

in Verton M. Queener, "The East Tennessee Republicans in State and Nation, 1870–1900," *Tennessee Historical Quarterly* 2 (June 1943), 100 (hereinafter cited as *Tenn. Hist. Quar.*).

County-by-county voting statistics for gubernatorial and presidential elections during the eighties are found in the following sources: for 1880, *Cumberland Almanac for the Year 1881* (Nashville: American Pub., 1881), 22, 24; for 1882, White, *Messages*, VII, 18–21; for 1884, *Cumberland Almanac for the Year 1885* (Nashville: American Pub., 1885), 18, 20; for 1886, Chattanooga *Times*, Dec. 3, 1886; for 1888 and 1890, Charles A. Miller, comp., *The Official and Political Manual of the State of Tennessee* (Nashville: Marshall & Bruce, 1890), 257–59, 278–80 (hereinafter cited as *Official Manual*). For the percentage of Negroes in the total population of each county in 1880, see United States, Bureau of the Census, *Negro Population, 1790–1915* (Washington, D. C.: Government Printing Office, 1918), 787–88.

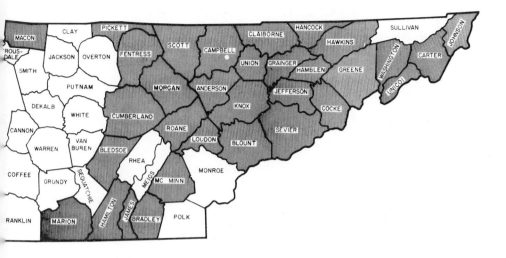

their candidate in the Third, which encompassed Chattanooga, in 1888, and won in the Tenth in 1880 and 1884. Republican strength in the Tenth District, which lay in West Tennessee, was dependent on the district's large black population. Republican power in the state legislature during the 1880s fluctuated from 20 to 40 percent of the seats in the senate and from 20 to 50 percent of the seats in the house of representatives. Moreover, according to one estimate, the Republicans tallied from 28 to 49 percent of all votes cast in state elections from 1870 to 1900.[3]

Negroes participated in Republican party politics at all levels of state and local government in the eighties. Although none succeeded in representing Tennessee in either the United States Senate or the House of Representatives, several sought such posts. In the state legislature, where not a single Negro had served

[3]Queener, "East Tennessee Republicans," 99–128.

REPUBLICAN-DEMOCRATIC RATIO IN THE TENNESSEE
GENERAL ASSEMBLY, 1881–1891

Legislature	Democrats	Senate Republicans	Republican percentage	Democrats	House Republicans	Republican percentage
1881	15	10	40	37	37	50
1883	27	6	18	75	24	24
1885	19	14	42	63	36	36
1887	21	12	36	62	37	37
1889	24	9	27	70	29	29
1891	25	8	24	79	20	20

during Radical reconstruction and only one during the 1870s, twelve were elected during the 1880s. They would be the last Negroes to be seated in the Tennessee legislature until the 1960s. A peak of black political activity occurred on the local level in the eighties also, as Negroes filled a variety of elective and appointive offices in both county and city governments.

Through the mid-eighties Tennessee Republicans exuded confidence in the prospects for their party's ascendancy. Following increases in the Republican vote in the election of 1884, the state Republican executive committee predicted that Tennessee would be "the first state to secede from the solid south." From 1876 to 1884 the Democratic margin of victory in presidential elections in the state steadily declined from 43,600 to 9,180, and from 1882 to 1884 the Democratic majority in the governor's race dramatically fell from approximately 27,000 to about 7,000.[4] Democratic intraparty strife, continued black voting, and rising interest in Republican economic policies among industrialists and businessmen all increased the competitive position of the Republican party until the mid-eighties and enabled it, at times, to challenge Democratic control. In light of this trend, the editor of the Knoxville *Chronicle* responded to overtures Democrats were making to Negro voters with charges that they were "endeavoring to mislead the colored voters in order to save themselves and their party from an ignominious defeat." Because of their anxiety, the *Chronicle* continued, "the democratic leaders are proposing to swap off the Old Whig in an even trade for the Negroes."[5]

[4]Knoxville *Chronicle*, Dec. 21, 1884; Chattanooga *Times*, Dec. 3–4, 1884.
[5]Knoxville *Chronicle*, Aug. 10, 1885.

Indeed, the chief hope Republicans had of building a majority in Tennessee lay in proselytizing among the antebellum Whigs and in retaining the vast majority of black voters. The editor of the *Chronicle* reasoned that the Whigs and Negroes clearly belonged in the Republican party: Negroes, because of "principle, intuition, and education," and Whigs, because, even though they had "acted with the democrats through sentimental prejudices," they should follow their "better judgement" and act on the basis of their beliefs "in the principles and policies of the republican party." Twenty years had intervened since the war; consequently, "these old Whigs ought to come into and vote with the republican party because they believe it right."[6] Thus Republicans hoped to keep the black vote, take in the Whigs, and win control in Tennessee.

White Republican leaders in Tennessee, as in other southern states, found the alliance with Negroes a lamentable necessity. The paradoxical relationship between southern white Republicans and Negroes is highlighted by a recent claim that whites in the southern mountain regions voted Republican more because they did not have to contend with a large black population than because of any economic differences they may have had with low-country Democrats. Most white Republicans adamantly opposed black candidates for public office, only reluctantly distributed patronage to Negroes, and sought to restrict their participation in party affairs to voting for white candidates.[7] Even when blacks received an occasional nomination, white Republicans usually either voted for the Democratic candidate or stayed at home. District Judge David M. Key, the postmaster general in President Rutherford B. Hayes' Cabinet and a self-styled Independent Democrat, depicted the attitude of most white Republicans as he described the dismal prospects of black Republican candidates in his native East Tennessee—a plight he blamed on "pride and prejudice of race. If one's affections and sympathies

---

[6]*Ibid.*, July 20, 1884; see also Aug. 10, 1885.

[7]Gordon B. McKinney, "Mountain Republicanism, 1876–1900" (Ph.D. diss., Northwestern Univ., 1971), 35–39, 58, 161–63; Chattanooga *Times*, Oct. 15, 1884; Sept. 11, 1885; Aug. 10, 12, 1890.

are such that he takes sides with the colored race against his own, he becomes no favorite with his own race, but is relegated to the companionship of the other." Key claimed that the white Republicans in his section of the state would rather vote for a former Confederate than a black.[8]

Finding themselves bound politically to Negroes, however, white Republicans aroused themselves periodically in defense of the right of blacks to vote, to earn a living, and to acquire an education. For the most part, white Republicans struck a paternalistic pose toward blacks, but, ironically, argued for a governmental policy of laissez-faire on the race question. Thus, they championed black rights but opposed federal interference. The Knoxville *Journal* voiced the sentiments of many Republicans when it observed that the special legislation and educational opportunities given to Negroes during reconstruction had been "laudable and noble," but "a serious mistake." It had "led to the pushing forward of colored men, for no other reason than that they were colored, faster than they were able to go, and to places in which they could not sustain themselves." The Republican editor suggested that the best racial policy would be to "stop talking about the negro, let him alone, throw no obstructions in his way, treat him fairly, give him a chance and let him work out his own salvation." By the end of the decade, the Republican editor had concluded that it was time for the Negro to "paddle his own canoe." He believed that all blacks would benefit from a "root hog or die" philosophy. Although the editor acknowledged that some whites would like to deny blacks a place as well as a right "to root" by assuming that "all the good ground for rooting . . . is reserved for the white pigs," he opposed any "special radical legislation" to guarantee Negroes equal opportunities.[9] This not only represented the prevailing liberal viewpoint in the late nineteenth century, it also gave southern Republicans the best hope of gaining votes from the former Whigs.

Throughout the eighties, tension mounted within Republican

[8]Nashville *Banner*, Dec. 2, 1889.
[9]Knoxville *Journal*, Feb. 15, 1888; May 3, Aug. 26, Sept. 16, 1889; Jan. 23, Aug. 6, 1890; Knoxville *Chronicle*, c Aug. 20, 1884 (date illegible).

ranks as blacks and whites clashed, sometimes among themselves, but more often interracially, over the proper course their party ought to take. The more volatile issues were nominations, patronage, and the party's stance on civil rights. As the presidential election fever swept Tennessee early in 1880, for example, Republicans divided into two camps: the first, comprised of rural whites and most of the black voters, backed former President Grant for an unprecedented third term; the second, which included federal officeholders and businessmen, supported John Sherman, President Hayes' secretary of the treasury. Disillusioned with the southern policy of Hayes, blacks supported Grant on the assumption that he was the candidate most likely to use federal power for the protection of their civil rights and to give them a proportionate share of federal patronage.[10]

Disagreement over the presidential nomination revealed the cross-purposes which national Republican policy and local black interests often assumed and the way in which blacks entered into the political calculations of white factions in the party. In January, Joseph R. Dillin, an influential Middle Tennessee white Republican who would soon serve as chairman of his party's state convention, advised his close political confidant, Second District Congressman Leonidas C. Houk, that the state's Negroes "unanimously supported Grant." Although Houk favored John Sherman, Dillin warned the East Tennessee party leader that Grant was "the only living Republican" who could carry Tennessee. In reply, Houk noted that the Hayes administration's appointments and southern policies had caused a rapid decline in his own enthusiasm for Sherman, whose presidential candidacy was supported by Hayes. Houk agreed with Dillin's estimate of Grant's popularity in the South, saying, "I have one of the largest, if not the very largest correspondence of any member of either House of Congress, from the South, and from this, I am fully convinced that Grant can poll

[10]Nashville *American*, May 2, 1880; Stanley P. Hirshson, *Farewell to the Bloody Shirt: Northern Republicans and the Southern Negro, 1877–1893* (Bloomington: Indiana Univ. Press, 1962), 59–62; H. Wayne Morgan, *From Hayes to McKinley: National Party Politics, 1877–1896* (Syracuse: Syracuse Univ. Press, 1969), 62.

more votes in the Southern States than any other man living."[11]

As Houk moved into the Grant camp, Dillin warned him that fully "two-thirds of the Federal office holders in Middle and West Tennessee are democrats"; in Rutherford, his home county, Dillin added, the federal officeholders opposed Grant and were "at work to organize against him in the face of such large numbers who are for him."[12]

Vigorous contests erupted at the county Republican meetings to select delegates to the party's state presidential nominating convention. Battling white supporters of James G. Blaine and John Sherman in an effort to name delegates pledged to Grant, Negroes faced a variety of tactics designed to minimize their influence in the party. Local whites usually appointed white majorities on the nominating committees, insisted that all delegates agree to support the nominations of the convention, and, more deviously, often held their conventions during workdays, when blacks had difficulty attending. Blacks protested white bulldozing and warned that, since they constituted the majority of the state's Republican voters, they would not be ruled by the white minority.[13]

A few weeks before the state convention, Dillin advised Houk that the Grant forces would have to select the temporary chairman of the convention in order to triumph. "He must be a man of nerve and distinction," Dillin admonished. "He will probably shape the committee on credentials, also the committee on permanent organization. If we get a stout hearted chairman who is not dispeptic [sic] or annoyed with a tender conscience we will have things right."[14] When the Republicans gathered at Nashville in

[11]Joseph R. Dillin to Leonidas C. Houk, Jan. 22, 1880; L. C. Houk to J. R. Dillin, Feb. 5, 1880, Houk Papers (Lawson-McGhee Library, Knoxville). For a biography of Houk, see Amos Lee Gentry, "The Public Career of Leonidas Campbell Houk" (M.A. thesis, Univ. of Tennessee, 1939). The best analysis of Houk's political machine and of his functions as Republican party boss in Tennessee is found in McKinney, "Mountain Republicanism," 99–106.

[12]Joseph R. Dillin to Leonidas C. Houk, Mar. 2, 1880; Lee Nance to L. C. Houk, May 28, 1880; G. S. Garrett to L. C. Houk, May 30, 1880, Houk Papers; Memphis *Avalanche*, June 5, 1880; see also the Nashville *American*, Mar. 11, 1880.

[13]Nashville *American*, May 1, 1880; Chattanooga *Times*, May 1, 1880.

[14]Joseph R. Dillin to Leonidas C. Houk, Apr. 16, 1880, Houk Papers.

May, a staunch Grant supporter was selected to fulfill this role. He was William H. Young, a black lawyer from Davidson County. In nominating Young, Houk asserted that Republicans should "be the last to pander to a discrimination on account of race or color or previous condition of servitude." On the contrary, Republicans should stand "willing to recognize their [Negroes'] equality in the politics of this county, and in the deliberations of the Republican party." In a similar vein, Colonel James Scudder, a white delegate from Bedford County, assured his white colleagues that Negroes were "Republican to the core" and, acknowledging the strength of blacks in Middle Tennessee party affairs, proclaimed, "We are all ready to stand upon equal rights. The Republican party recognizes no distinction of color or race. . . ." As temporary chairman, Young not only helped carry the day for Grant but also success-fully opposed efforts by some blacks to fix a quota giving them one-third of the delegates to the national convention at Chi-cago.[15]

Despite the lofty sentiments expressed at the state presidential nominating convention, the anti-Grant delegates had fiercely resented the political influence wielded by the Negroes. Accord-ing to the Nashville *American*, a Blaine delegate had said that "anti-third termers [anti-Grant men] had the brains opposed to the muscle and nothing but the weight of muscle and numbers gave the best opinion a back seat and success to the third-term advocates." It was only a matter of time until the "brains" of the party would regain control, concluded the *American*, and the "negro element, failing to obtain that control it seeks," likely would divide its vote.[16]

Whatever unity Grant's candidacy had brought among Tennes-see's black Republicans quickly disintegrated in the contests over nominations for state office. In both Davidson and Shelby counties blacks fought over the number of places they should have on the legislative tickets. Although in the majority, black delegates to the Davidson County nominating convention split when William H.

[15]Nashville *American*, May 6, 1880.
[16]*Ibid.*, May 9, 1880. See Clarence Albert Bacote, "The Negro in Georgia Politics, 1880–1908" (Ph.D. diss., Univ. of Chicago, 1955), 75.

Young spoke against the inclusion of two blacks on the ticket. Young specifically opposed the candidacy of John H. Burrus, chairman of the county convention, Nashville lawyer, graduate of Fisk University, and recent delegate to the national Republican convention. Young charged that Burrus, by insisting upon black nominees for two legislative slots from Davidson County, was furthering his own selfish interests at the expense of the overall ticket. The ticket eventually selected excluded Burrus and contained only one black candidate, Thomas A. Sykes, a federal revenue collector who had served in the North Carolina legislature before coming to Tennessee. Sykes had also been a delegate to the recent national Republican convention.[17]

A similar fight occurred in Shelby County when a group of blacks led by Edward Shaw bolted the county nominating convention and challenged the predominantly white federal ring that had controlled local party affairs there. The nominating convention had placed two blacks in the six-man slate for the house of representatives and had nominated William R. Moore for Congress. Now the Shaw faction demanded, without success, that two additional black men of their choice be placed on the legislative ticket. They also claimed that their candidate for the congressional nomination, Thomas H. Hamilton, had been cheated out of the nomination at the convention. As in Davidson County, blacks divided. Aligned with the whites were Carter Harris, the chairman of the county Republican executive committee; Fred Hunt, a veteran Memphis political organizer and county official; William H. Porter and Robert H. Hurley, skillful orators and ministers in the black community; and the two black legislative candidates, Isaac F. Norris and Thomas F. Cassels. Cassels, a lawyer who had attended Oberlin College, had held several political appointments in Memphis, serving as assistant attorney general of the city in 1878.[18] In the ensuing campaign Shaw declared that black voters had been duped long enough and that the time had arrived when

[17]Work, "Some Negro Members of Reconstruction Conventions," 114; *Proceedings of the Republican National Convention, 1880* (Chicago: Jeffery Printing & Pub. House, 1881), 28; Nashville *American*, Sept. 19, 1880.

[18]Memphis *Avalanche*, Sept. 22, 24, Oct. 6, 1880; Memphis *Appeal*, Sept. 14,

they should "unite on the color line" even if it resulted in defeat. Despite his defiant statements, Shaw mysteriously reached an accord with the federal ring before election day, deserted the Hamilton camp, and belatedly endorsed William R. Moore for Congress.[19]

Interracial discord within the Republican party in 1880 was probably moderated by the likelihood that Democratic division over the state debt would allow Republicans to win the gubernatorial contest and, perhaps, a majority in the legislature. Three months before their gubernatorial nominating convention, Joseph Dillin assured Congressman Houk that the party was "in better organization and condition in every way than it has been in ten years," and Middle Tennessee Republicans, he insisted, were united behind a state-credit position on the debt issue. In their convention the Republicans adopted a platform renouncing any alteration of the debt not volunteered by the creditors, vaguely reaffirmed the state party's commitment to national Republican principles, and named Judge Alvin Hawkins, a lawyer from Carroll County, as the party's gubernatorial candidate.[20]

Hawkins conducted his campaign for the governorship with skill and confidence. He appealed to former Whigs and traditional Republicans by stressing his party's tariff policy and emphasizing the necessity of maintaining the state's credit. Meantime, he solicited black support as he cited the Republican party's past stands on civil rights, denounced the state's work-contract law that made persons who broke a work contract to improve their position liable for damages, and condemned the leasing of convict labor.[21]

In order to parry independent tendencies and to thwart a black

Oct. 5, 1880; Charles S. Brown to Donald M. Love, May 6, 1961 (Alumni File, Oberlin College Archives, Oberlin, Ohio).

[19]Memphis *Appeal*, Sept. 29, 1880; Memphis *Avalanche*, Sept. 19, 22, 24, Oct. 9, 16, 1880.

[20]Joseph R. Dillin to Leonidas C. Houk, Jan. 27, 1880; L. C. Houk to J. R. Dillin, Feb. 5, 1880, Houk Papers; Nashville *American*, May 7, 1880; White, *Messages*, VI, 627–29.

[21]Memphis *Avalanche*, Aug. 20, 1880; Knoxville *Chronicle*, Nov. 7, 1880. For an analysis of the state-debt controversy's influence on the election of 1880 see

exodus to the low-tax Democrats on the state-debt issue, Republicans alternated in the campaign of 1880 between civil rights rhetoric and paternalistic lectures to Negroes on the duties of citizenship. Republican leaders tediously reminded black voters that the state debt had largely been created during the long travail of Civil War and reconstruction. "There never was a debt more sacred," William R. Moore told a black audience in the Tenth District. "It is a part of the sacred price paid for the purchase of freedom."[22] The Republican editor of the Knoxville *Chronicle* also viewed the debt as "only a part of the immense price paid for the freedom of the colored people of the state." In light of this fact, he predicted, Tennessee's black citizens would rally to support the state's credit: "They will not be so ungrateful as to disown the sacred obligations which stand today as evidence of a part of the cost of their freedom."[23] Before a largely black audience in West Tennessee, Alvin Hawkins also reasoned that Negroes, like other responsible citizens, had a duty to help meet the state's obligations.[24] Furthermore, John Mercer Langston, the United States minister to Haiti, who campaigned in Tennessee for Hawkins and the Republicans, told a large Negro audience in Nashville that, as free men, they were "equal partners in the government with the white man" and were obligated to help pay the state debt.[25]

Dissension in the Shelby County Republican party in 1880 apparently had little to do with the state debt, for there were noticeable differences within each faction over the proper solution. Isaac F. Norris and Thomas Cassels, for example, the two black candidates for the state legislature on the regular Republican ticket in Shelby County, held slightly different views on the question of the debt. Cassels condemned repudiation and un-

Robert B. Jones, "Tennessee Gubernatorial Elections, II, 1880—The Collapse of the Democratic Party," *Tenn. Hist. Quar.* 33 (Spring 1974), 49–61.

[22]Memphis *Avalanche*, Oct. 6, 1880.

[23]Sept. 8, 1880.

[24]Memphis *Avalanche*, Aug. 20, 1880.

[25]Langston had supported Hayes' southern policy. See Vincent P. De Santis, *Republicans Face the Southern Question–The New Departure Years, 1877–1897* (Baltimore: Johns Hopkins Univ. Press, 1959), 129–30; Knoxville *Chronicle*, Sept. 30, 1880.

equivocally favored payment of "the honest debt"—a position which apparently left room for possible readjustment. Norris frankly desired a compromise settlement between the bondholders and the taxpayers, after which he thought "the people should then come forward and pay it honestly." Another black leader in the regular Republican camp took a different view of the matter: as far as the railroads were concerned, argued the Reverend William H. Porter, he "would not vote to pay a dollar; for when colored people ride on the cars they are charged as much fare as Gen. Grant or President Davis, but put in dirty smoking cars with horse thieves and murderers."[26]

With the Democrats divided, the Republicans won the gubernatorial contest, sharply increased their power in the state legislature, and elected three congressmen, including William R. Moore of the Tenth District. The vast majority of Negro voters apparently supported Alvin Hawkins, for he polled 102,969 votes compared to the state-credit candidate's 79,191 and the low-tax candidate's 57,424. In the state legislature Democrats saw their majority in the senate reduced from 22 to 15 and a house majority of 39 completely wiped out. Democrats and Republicans evenly divided 74 seats in the house, leaving the one Greenbacker elected the power to wield a potentially tie-breaking vote. Moreover, four Negroes, including Norris and Cassels, would sit in the new legislature, the only blacks to do so since 1872, when Sampson W. Keeble had become the first Negro to serve in the Tennessee General Assembly. In the presidential contest the Democrats carried Tennessee by approximately 23,000 votes, although James A. Garfield, the Republican presidential candidate, outpolled Hawkins by almost 8,000 votes.[27]

With a Republican in the governor's chair, a strong minority in the General Assembly, and a Republican administration in Wash-

[26]Memphis *Appeal*, Oct. 5, 1880; Memphis *Avalanche*, Oct. 6, 1880.
[27]Nashville *American*, Mar. 30, 1880; Nashville *Banner*, Nov. 3, 1880; Memphis *Avalanche*, Nov. 6, 1880; Memphis *Appeal*, Nov. 3, 5, 7, 1880; for tabulation of the vote in the gubernatorial election see White, *Messages*, VI, 639; for the state vote in the presidential election see *Cumberland Almanac, 1881*, 22–24, and Memphis *Appeal*, Nov. 5, 1880.

ington, the prospects for Negroes in Tennessee seemed brighter than at any time since the victory of the white Conservatives in 1870. Many blacks looked to the new state administration to inaugurate civil rights and educational reforms and to distribute political offices fairly. White Republicans in the 1881 legislature did, in fact, support the unsuccessful efforts blacks made to repeal the 1875 state law allowing racial discrimination in public facilities, although they later voted almost unanimously for the 1881 Jim Crow law requiring separate but equal accommodations for Negroes in first-class railroad cars. On the other hand, white Republican legislators helped secure an appropriation for the education of Negro teachers and solidly backed the adoption of stiffer penalties against law officers who were negligent in protecting a prisoner in their custody against mob violence, but they backed away from black efforts to repeal the state law banning interracial marriages.[28]

Dissatisfaction with these meager gains and opposition to the administration's state-debt measures provoked a revolt among blacks in the Tenth District which resulted in their fusion with low-tax Democrats in the gubernatorial campaign of 1882. When the low-tax Democrats swept into power in the aftermath of the 1882 state elections, however, it proved to be a Pyrrhic victory for their black allies.[29]

Disillusioned as they were with local Republican policies, black Tennesseans still looked for federal intervention in their behalf as long as Republicans held power in Washington. In 1883, however, the Supreme Court dashed their hopes by ruling that Congress could only prohibit racial discrimination by the state, not by privately controlled agencies. The federal Civil Rights Act of 1875, therefore, was unconstitutional.[30] This development kindled a

[28]The response of white Republicans in the 1881 General Assembly to legislation dealing with black civil rights and education is discussed in Ch. III.

[29]See Ch. I.

[30]One of the five cases included in the 1883 decision had been filed in Tennessee; it involved a suit brought by a black couple against the Memphis & Charleston Railroad Co. for refusing them access to the train's first-class car. Robinson and Wife v. Memphis & C. R. Co. 109 *U.S. Reports* (1883), 3–4; Memphis *Appeal*, Oct. 16, 1883; Memphis *Avalanche*, Nov. 4, 1883.

NORTHEAST NEBRASKA TECHNICAL
COMMUNITY COLLEGE - LIBRARY

spirited debate among black leaders regarding the wisdom of their continued loyalty to the Republican party. A year later, for example, when over 300 black leaders from seventeen counties met in Nashville to discuss the plight of blacks, heated opposition arose to resolutions praising the Republican party. Ostensibly nonpartisan, the convention had been called, in the tradition of similar Negro conventions held over the past two decades, to consider topics ranging across a broad spectrum of social, political, and economic concerns. James C. Napier, the keynote speaker, stressed the importance of the approaching national and local elections and counseled his audience to proceed "with united purpose and concert of action" in order to secure all the "privileges and blessings of American citizenship." Napier contended that this goal could best be attained if Negroes remained in the Republican party.[31]

Samuel A. McElwee, a Republican legislator from Haywood County, set off a volatile debate by igniting resentments which apparently still smoldered in his listeners' minds because of the Civil Rights decision. Employing a militant rhetoric, McElwee received rousing applause when he proclaimed that the rights of blacks had to be respected and that blacks would "declare eternal war" until they secured them. When McElwee attempted to forge black political unity behind the Republican party, however, the cheering stopped. Thomas F. Cassels, who served as chairman of the 1884 convention, declared that the recent Supreme Court decision had "given rise to serious questions concerning the legal status of Negroes" and concluded that many of Tennessee's laws violated the constitutional rights of the state's black citizens. Therefore, he maintained, it was all the more important that blacks should deliberate carefully on the best means of securing their rights. Edward Shaw, although labeling McElwee's address a good Republican stump speech, declared that it was out of place and opposed a resolution which called for its endorsement as the sentiments of the black assembly. He then proceeded to attack the

[31]Nashville *American*, Feb. 29, Mar. 1, 1884; New York *Globe*, Jan. 5, Mar. 15, 1884.

Republican party for refusing either to share important offices, or, in those places where Republicans controlled the public schools, to give blacks a voice in their operation. However divided they were on the advisability of blacks voting solidly Republican, the delegates did unite on a resolution denouncing "those white republicans who attempted to control the colored vote without giving the colored race a fair division of the offices." Other resolutions condemned the Supreme Court's civil rights decision and declared that black voters should not support any candidate "who would not pledge himself to use his influence for the repeal of all laws making invidious distinctions and discriminations on account of color." Black disillusionment at the convention stopped short of an open split with the Republican party, but a clear warning of future independence had been issued. In fact, to further the interests of blacks, the convention called for the creation of local political clubs throughout the state.[32] "Our experience with political parties has taught us a lesson," one delegate ominously wrote, "and we see that if we want anything done we must do it ourselves."[33]

The Nashville convention mirrored a growing uncertainty among black leaders about the way their interests could best be served. It was a question not merely of party affiliation but, more fundamentally, of the accountability and tactics of black politicians themselves. Some blacks of an accommodationist persuasion continued to argue that a politics of deference to white leadership would be their most realistic and, eventually, most rewarding course. Whether these pragmatists spoke out of altruistic convictions or had in mind only their own aggrandizement, an increasing number of blacks rejected the political strategy of accommodation on the grounds that it had redounded only to the benefit of whites. Wanting black politicians to be more accountable to their constituents, they recommended that black voters select their own leaders and reject those chosen for them by white political manipulators. Faced with rising concern over accounta-

[32]Nashville *American*, Mar. 1, 1884; New York *Globe*, Mar. 15, 1884.
[33]Nashville *American*, Mar. 8, 1884.

bility, many Negroes who had been prominent in politics were forced to fight for greater power within the Republican party in order to make it more responsive to blacks, regardless of how their action might affect the party at the polls.

In preparation for the Republican party's state convention and the subsequent elections of 1884, blacks asserted their voice in local party deliberations but divided over the political wisdom of selecting black-dominated tickets. Davidson County Negroes, under the leadership of James C. Napier, outmaneuvered what one of them labeled the local "clique of old bosses and wire pullers" and selected a slate of delegates of their choice to the Republican state convention. "Our zeal was burning," one of these later wrote; "we felt the justness and righteousness of the cause some of us had advocated and supported all our lives, and even with our life-blood." Unwilling "to retire to the shades of Democracy, as some had done," he continued, the black delegates decided "to take matters into our own hands, find new and more worthy leaders, and place them at the head of our columns."[34] Negro domination of the local convention in Middle Tennessee's Giles County prompted the prophetic response from white Republicans there that they did not intend for the "damned nigger to rule."[35] In the Knox County Republican convention, the rejection of two blacks who sought to run for the state legislature provoked a vow from their supporters not to vote for any of the convention's candidates.[36] In Hamilton County, however, blacks succeeded in naming a Chattanooga Negro, William C. Hodge, as a candidate for the state legislature. Although Hodge admitted that his candidacy might weaken the Republican ticket among white voters, he stated that, since there were 1,400 black voters in the county and only 400 white voters, the time had come for whites to be "educated up" to accept black candidates. In order to demonstrate the influence of the black vote and to avert an exodus of white Republicans to the Democrats in November, Chattanoo-

[34]Undated letter to the Nashville *American*, c Apr. 1884, James C. Napier Papers (Fisk University Library).
[35]Pulaski *Citizen*, Apr. 10, 1884.
[36]Knoxville *Chronicle*, Aug. 16, 18, 1884.

ga Negroes threatened to boycott white Republican candidates in the upcoming city elections. On the eve of the city election they circulated a pamphlet warning white Republicans that every one of them who held office in the city and county did so by virtue of Negro votes, yet, now that a Negro had been nominated for the legislature, the white leaders of the party "turn up their noses and roll their eyes in holy horror, and say well! well! we can't stand the 'nigger' out of his place."[37] Whether aided by these tactics or not, Hodge won election to the state legislature in November and became the first Negro to represent Hamilton County in the Tennessee General Assembly.[38]

Although blacks probably had greater political leverage in Shelby County than elsewhere in the state in 1884, they could not agree at the local Republican convention whether to push for a predominantly black slate of candidates for the state legislature or to allow whites to dominate the ticket. Greene E. Evans, a mulatto businessman aligned with the white federal ring, declared that it would be foolish to ignore the existence of prejudice. If more blacks than whites were on the ticket it would be defeated, he predicted. Evans favored naming only two blacks on the six-man slate. Indeed, he argued, "if the Republican party can be successful with one colored man on it, why, let us have but one." When the final ticket listed only two Negroes, one of whom was Evans himself, the more militant blacks met and declared themselves Independent Republicans not bound to the regular ticket.[39]

Republican strategy in the gubernatorial campaign of 1884 further strained the party loyalty of many blacks. White leaders, under Congressman Leonidas C. Houk's direction, minimized black participation in the state convention and adroitly blunted black protests, while pressing the party's claims upon black voters for past services rendered and urging party unity. The platform focused on economic issues, calling for a protective tariff, opposing a state railroad commission, and condemning Democratic repudiation of the state debt. Planks endorsing national aid for

[37]Chattanooga *Times*, Oct. 12–13, 1884.
[38]*Ibid.*, Oct. 15, Nov. 6, 1884.
[39]Memphis *Appeal*, Oct. 12, 15, 18, 1884.

education and denouncing the convict-lease system gave blacks some cause for enthusiasm. In the end, however, only six of the twenty-four delegates to the party's national convention were black; they also failed to block the nomination of an ex-Confederate soldier, Judge Frank T. Reid, for governor.[40]

The relegation of blacks to a minor role in the convention infuriated the editor of the *Knights of Wise Men*, a journal published by a Nashville Negro fraternal organization. The editor, himself a delegate to the convention, blamed black leaders for quietly taking a back seat in the convention in order to make the party more attractive to whites. He charged that James C. Napier, Thomas F. Cassels, Samuel A. McElwee, and Carter Harris were especially culpable. "The white bosses showed by almost every word, look, and act that the ordinary Negro delegate was a stench. Ignored in the temporary and permanent organization and not recognized on committees, the Negro's voice was hushed on the floor of the convention by the plain evasive and biased rulings of his 'monarchy' Houk." In fact, the editor complained, "These leading Negroes who are honored and looked up to by their race were not known on the floor of the Republican assembly, and knew not, nor cared, what transpired." He called upon blacks to spurn "the gross and cowardly insults heaped upon them by the so-called Republican convention," which in truth was but "a set of 'machine' Negro hating white Republicans, alias 'sheep in wolf's clothing'."[41] When the Democratic press in Nashville gave this editorial wide circulation, the publishers of the *Knights of Wise Men* disclaimed responsibility for the editorial, apologized, and in the next issue of their journal endorsed the Republican ticket.[42] As the Republican gubernatorial campaign got underway, however, there would be a noticeable lack of black enthusiasm for Reid and the Republican campaign strategy.

Reid based his campaign on appeals to former Whigs in the state, urging them to realign themselves with "their true inter-

[40]Knoxville *Chronicle*, Apr. 20, 1884; Nashville *American*, Apr. 18, 1884; unidentified newspaper clipping dated Apr. 17, 1884, Napier Papers.
[41]Knoxville *Chronicle*, May 3, 1884; Nashville *American*, Apr. 29, 1884.
[42]Nashville *American*, May 3, 1884.

ests." The firing upon Fort Sumter had not "converted them to the doctrines of state sovereignty," he argued. "The passion and bitterness" of the reconstruction era and race prejudice, however, had "forced them in their action to antagonize their own principles." These "Republicans at heart" had the power to decide whether the state "shall longer be tied to the corpse of a dead tradition, or whether she will come out of the moonlit graveyard of the past and battle in the living present for the rich prizes the future has in store," Reid dramatically declared. While Republicans, in the tradition of the former Whigs, represented "great national interests," the Democrats were "anticentralization." Thus, Republicans favored national aid to education, but Democrats opposed it; on the other hand, Republicans opposed the economic policies of the Tennessee Democrats—the convict-lease system, the repudiation of part of the state debt, the railroad commission, and the increase in taxes under the incumbent administration.[43] Republican strategy shrewdly focused on economic issues to win the former Whig vote and played down racial issues by consigning them to the politics of the past.

Many blacks resented Republican proselytizing among antebellum Whigs, but others remained uncritical party boosters. A black correspondent to the Knoxville *Chronicle*, for example, viewed Reid as the candidate who could best unify the Republican party and lead it to victory. Illustrating the deep rifts among blacks over political strategy, the writer contended that Negroes who constantly criticized the Republican party were "enemies of their race" with "no influence whatever," who maliciously misrepresented the state's Republican leaders and craved "notoriety at the expense of truth and common justice." This ardent Republican partisan also decried those white renegades who, "through the medium of the democratic press," were "continually hurling their billings gate [*sic*]" at the leaders of the Republican party.[44]

The cool reception that Reid received in traditionally enthusiastic black Republican areas indicated continued black resentment

---

[43]Memphis *Avalanche*, June 21, 1884; Knoxville *Chronicle*, Sept. 1, 1884.
[44]May 3, 1884.

toward the party's campaign. One Democratic editor cryptically explained the sparse Negro attendance at a Reid rally in Brownsville: "This Whig talk was new to the Haywood County Negro voter, and he could not relish it." The editor quoted a local observer who crudely, but perhaps accurately, had suggested that "there was too much Whig in the speech for the nigger, and too much nigger for the Whig." As the campaign progressed and the lack of Negro enthusiasm became obvious, the Republican gubernatorial candidate began to court black support. At a large rally in Memphis, for example, he devoted a major part of his speech to crediting the Republican party with a "divine mission" to establish equality for all.[45]

The Republican bid for white support in 1884 probably cost the party as many votes as it won. In the rural counties of West Tennessee, where Negroes constituted a majority of the Republican voters, Blaine, the Republican presidential candidate, outpolled Reid. Judge Reid lost the gubernatorial election by approximately 7,000 votes, yet he did attract white support away from the Democrats. In the urban counties of Shelby, Davidson, Hamilton, and Knox, for example, Reid fared significantly better than Blaine, who lost the state by slightly over 9,000 votes.[46]

Following the gubernatorial election of 1884, blacks increased their efforts to attain a greater share of power within the Republican party, threatened to divide their votes between the two major parties, and generally displayed a growing political independence. Rising black political aspirations collided with the Republican strategy of broadening the white base of the party by avoiding the civil rights issue and by confining blacks to a minor role in the party's affairs. There were other reasons for the trend toward black independence in Tennessee politics in the mid-eighties: the growing political independence among northern Negroes, the unexpected appointment of a few black leaders to office by President Cleveland, a reexamination of Republican claims to be the exclusive guardian of Negro rights, the conviction of some

[45]Memphis *Appeal*, July 26, Oct. 5, 1884.
[46]*Cumberland Almanac, 1885*, 18–20.

blacks that the whites who controlled both parties shared similar racial views, and a growing disposition to reject the image of political enslavement to the Republican party.[47]

By the mid-eighties an increasing number of national Negro leaders began urging blacks to stop voting *en masse* for the Republicans—to divide their votes. Bloc voting, they argued, had presented an unfavorable image of black voters as mindless political slaves who followed the dictates of their self-styled benefactors among the white Republicans. Formerly stalwart Republican W. Calvin Chase had clear advice for his fellow black voters in 1885: "The only thing to be done to liberate the colored man from political slavery is to make a division and go where his interest is better subserved."[48]

Advocates of a divided black vote also began advancing the theory that blacks would be fully assimilated into American life only when they began to vote as individuals rather than as a group. This was a broader version of the popular idea that southern blacks could insure racial harmony by voting with their white neighbors. In 1886 John Mercer Langston, a nationally prominent black politician whose only daughter was married to James C. Napier, advised blacks in a Nashville address that once they divided their vote, the color line would cease to exist. By joining the white people of the South, the Negro could "blunt the edge of their past enmities towards him" and through political action secure not only economic, social, and educational advantages but also "peace through reconcilement." Langston commended the black voter for a greater disposition to vote "according to his business interests, his personal inclinations and his convictions with regard to the advancement of that section of the country in which he resides."[49]

[47]For a general account of the trend of northern Negroes toward independent politics and sporadic black support for the Democratic party, see Meier, *Negro Thought in America*, 28–30. The erratic political course of one prominent northern Negro and his favorable response to President Cleveland is discussed in Emma Lou Thornbrough, *T. Thomas Fortune: Militant Journalist* (Chicago: Univ. of Chicago Press, 1972), 58–63, 86–91.

[48]Editor Chase's editorial, Washington *Bee*, May 9, 1885.

[49]Chattanooga *Times*, Jan. 4, 1886; Memphis *Avalanche*, Jan. 2, 1886.

Despite Langston's visionary expectations, blacks were beginning to embrace a "hard politics of using black votes as bait to gain
concrete political rewards and to reject the "soft" politics of
rhetoric and lofty pronouncements about the idealistic principles
of the Republican party. In his Nashville speech, for example,
Langston also declared that he saw no existing differences between the two parties "on the questions of freedom and enfranchisement."[50] In 1885, a similarly straightforward statement
came from a black political leader in Nashville who informed a
reporter from the Democratic *American*, "If the Democratic party
prove a better friend to the Negro than the Republican party, the
vote of the Negro will certainly divide and go with you, increasing
as the friendly relation increases." An even blunter declaration of
these views came from a black voter who frankly wrote the editor
of the *American*, "I offer my vote to the highest bidder, not for
money, but the greatest measure of justice."[51] A few years later,
Charles S. Wallace, a black journalist who published the Chattanooga *Tribune*, converted sentiment into political strategy in
analyzing a congressional race in his district for a reporter from the
Chattanooga *Times*. "We [blacks] don't want to forget that they
are both white men," he said of the candidates, "and different
party views will not push them far enough apart to allow us, as a
race voting solid, to walk in between them." The "best lick"
blacks could strike, he advised, would be to divide their votes and
ignore the fulminations of the "few big mouth, ignorant Negroes
who, afraid they will be returned to slavery" go "up and down the
streets crying [against] democratic Negroes."[52]

The impact these views had upon the way blacks actually voted
cannot be fully determined, but in the elections of 1885 and 1886 it
became abundantly clear that black support for the Republican
party waned, in some cases drastically. "Negroes were never so
much displeased with the Republicans," declared a black political

[50]Memphis *Avalanche*, Jan. 2, 1886.
[51]Aug. 17, 20, 1885.
[52]Chattanooga *Times*, Sept. 2, 1888; McGuffey, *Standard History of Chattanooga*, 255.

leader in Chattanooga during a municipal campaign there in 1885. This dissatisfaction stemmed from a variety of local black grievances: a few months earlier, a black prisoner in the custody of the Republican sheriff had been lynched; white Republicans had recently abandoned a black candidate in a magistrate's race; and, despite Negro efforts to have two blacks placed on the Republican municipal ticket, an exclusively white slate had been chosen. Unhappy blacks further complained that white Republicans would not confer with them in party caucuses and that Republican newspapers refused to print their criticisms of the party.[53]

Indicative of the new style of black politics in Tennessee, the Chattanooga dissidents organized separately, censured local white Republican leaders, and selected two blacks to run for aldermen in the upcoming city election. One-half the delegates at the regular party convention had been black, the insurgents pointed out, but their leaders had betrayed them, deferring to the white bosses either to keep, or to obtain, city jobs under the incumbent Republican administration. These white-appointed Negro leaders, one of the insurgents declared, were under a form of slavery worse than any they had ever before experienced. He exhorted blacks to rise up and assert their manhood rather than to submit to the "kicks and cuffs" of their white overseers. Another outspoken leader of the insurgents, Styles L. Hutchins, added that any Negro who supported the regular ticket would be "a fool" deserving "the contempt of every honorable man." In an outburst of anger that doubtless reflected the frustration of other black political leaders, Hutchins denounced those blacks who would continue to be blinded by white leaders. "Are you dogs and slaves to act like that?" he asked. White Republicans had won black support by giving a few leaders powerless petty offices which had no connections with the public schools, the water supply, the tax rates, or the conditions of streets in black neighborhoods, Hutchins declared. Even if the Independent ticket failed, Hutchins reasoned, it would "make the white Republicans think and do our race more justice."[54]

[53]Chattanooga *Times*, Aug. 18, Sept. 12, 14, 16–17, 22, 26, 1885.
[54]*Ibid.*, Sept. 27, 1885.

Although the Chattanooga insurgents claimed to represent at least 1,000 voters, in the municipal election only 250 to 300 blacks actually joined the rebellion against the victorious white Republican ticket.[55] The revolt gathered momentum in 1886. In February about 40 leaders in the movement met, reiterated their grievances against the white Republicans, and formed an independent black political organization. By May approximately 150 men were participating in a central club composed of representatives from each ward and district in Chattanooga. Threatening all-out war, the Independents succeeded in pressuring the regular Republicans into nominating a Negro for the office of circuit court clerk in the August county elections. The insurgents swung their vote to the Democratic candidates for sheriff and county judge, however, enabling them to win, while the remainder of the offices went to Republicans. The number of black Independents can probably be gauged by the 600 to 1,000 votes by which the Republican candidates for sheriff and county judge fell behind the rest of their ticket. Although the black candidate for circuit court clerk, John J. Irvine, won, he ran about 400 to 500 votes behind the Republican ticket, probably reflecting his loss of white support. A former slave, Irvine had moved to Chattanooga after the war, had become a skilled machinist, and had won election as a constable in 1882. Because he was an active member of the Knights of Labor, disgruntled whites attributed his election in 1886 to the biracial support he received from that union.[56]

Black militancy within the Republican party took a similar course in Shelby and Davidson counties in 1886. Prior to the local elections in Shelby County, Negroes protested the token representation usually given their race on the Republican ticket, demanded three positions on it, and urged the 8,000 black voters in the county to "get out from under the party lash" and assert their independence instead of being "driven about like cattle by the 100 men who claimed to be the leaders." The ubiquitous rebel Edward Shaw advocated the nomination of Negroes for every office in the

[55]*Ibid.*, Oct. 14, 1885.
[56]*Ibid.*, Feb. 4, 6, May 1, 5, 8, June 23, July 23, Aug. 6–8, 1886; May 11–12, 1890.

county and called upon black voters "to throw off the yoke of allegiance to white men." In the county Republican convention, however, only two Negroes were included on the eleven-man ticket: Isaac F. Norris for county court clerk and Louis H. Fields for county registrar. This slender concession did not satisfy some black leaders, who urged Negroes to bolt the party. A Negro-owned and-edited Memphis newspaper, the *Watchman*, exulted in the determination of black voters to reject white Republican leadership and encouraged those Negroes who had begun to realize their political value.[57] Enough blacks cast Democratic ballots in the ensuing county election to help substantially in defeating the Republicans.[58] Similarly, in Davidson County, one exasperated black politician vowed "to show these would-be leaders, at the August elections, that their nominations amount to nothing without our support and worse than nothing with our combined strength, our united power hurled like a sweeping tornado against them."[59] In the election, Democrats, aided by Negro votes, polled one of the highest majorities recorded in Nashville since the Civil War. One traditionally Republican district in the county, almost totally inhabited by Negroes, went Democratic for only the second time since the Civil War.[60]

These examples of black militancy within Republican ranks represented a statewide trend in 1886. The black Democratic vote in the November elections, although not as great as that cast in the local elections of the preceding August, apparently contributed to the landslide victory of Democratic gubernatorial candidate Robert L. Taylor. While the statewide Republican vote in 1886 fell about 16,000 short of that cast in the previous governor's race, the Democratic vote was only 6,000 less. Aside from the expected falloff in state voting during a nonpresidential election, the sharp Republican decline, coupled with election-day observations, lent support to the view that many blacks either voted Democratic or

[57]Memphis *Avalanche*, June 24, July 4, 6, 1886; Washington *Bee*, July 3, 1886.
[58]New York *Times*, Aug. 24, 1886.
[59]Chattanooga *Times*, June 27, 1886.
[60]Nashville *American*, June 22–23, Aug. 7, 1886.

did not go to the polls. The reduction in the Republican vote was especially pronounced in Hamilton, Davidson, and Shelby counties—all areas in which Negro dissatisfaction with Republican policies had been conspicuous.[61]

Black political insurgency in Tennessee gained nationwide attention. To a New York *Times* correspondent, the elections of 1886 in Tennessee offered proof that the Negro vote was losing its solidarity.[62] Chase, editor of the Washington *Bee*, pointed to the Tennessee elections as evidence that Republicans would have to be more responsive to black interests.[63] Evaluating the elections in his native East Tennessee, William H. Franklin, a black minister who served as a correspondent for T. Thomas Fortune's politically independent New York *Freeman*, lamented the refusal of white Republicans in Knox County to support black candidates. "Such foolish and unreasonable prejudice must be laid aside if the party [Republican] is to be respected and the colored vote retained," he warned. "No colored man worthy of the name of a freeman and a citizen can ally himself with a party of men or give them his support who fail to recognize his worth and manhood."[64] Two years later, Franklin again wrote Fortune's New York paper. Whatever else might be made of the growing political militancy among blacks, Franklin now was certain that "the Negro will never be as subservient again as he has been." Black political ambition, however, was beginning to stand in the way of racial harmony. "Some Negroes will not know their places," Franklin curtly stated. "They seem to think they have a right in the first rank, at the head if they can get there. This unrighteous and unnatural thought and aspiration in the Negro is making trouble all along the line."[65]

In the face of rising Negro insurgency white Republican leaders assumed conflicting strategies. Some, alienated by the upsurge in

[61]County-by-county votes in the state elections of 1884 and 1886 are found in *Cumberland Almanac, 1885*, 18–20, and in White, *Messages*, VII, 232–34; Nashville *American*, Nov. 3, 1886; Clarksville *Semi-Weekly Tobacco Leaf Chronicle*, Nov. 5, 1886.

[62]Aug. 24, 1886.   [63]Aug. 21, 1886.

[64]New York *Freeman*, Aug. 21, 1886.   [65]New York *Age*, Aug. 18, 1888.

black demands, adopted a lily-white policy and sought to eliminate all black participation in party councils. Others, hoping to recover wayward black voters and prevent a major defection, reaffirmed the party's commitment to civil rights. The renewed Republican commitment to civil rights was reflected in the local, state, and national party deliberations of 1888. In the spring, Shelby County party leaders endorsed an outspoken civil rights advocate and former congressman from the Tenth District, William R. Moore, for vice-president of the United States. The Shelby County Republicans also adopted resolutions protesting the convict-lease system, favoring the Blair Education bill, demanding "a fair ballot and an honest count," and urging that two black delegates be sent to the national convention—one to represent the Tenth District and the other, the state at large.[66] This conciliatory tone was sustained at the state convention in Nashville, where blacks constituted about one-third of the delegates. Roderick R. Butler, First District congressman and longtime East Tennessee party leader, urged the convention not to repudiate blacks or act in such a way as to alienate them from the party. Judge A. M. Hughes, prominent Middle Tennessean and chairman of the state Republican executive committee, also counseled white delegates to give blacks a voice in party deliberations. Hughes subsequently seconded the nomination of Samuel A. McElwee as a delegate-at-large to the national convention. To the delight of black Republicans, McElwee was elected unanimously, and four other blacks were included in the Tennessee delegation.[67] McElwee assumed leadership of the delegation at the national convention, representing Tennessee on the important credentials committee and nominating William R. Moore for vice-president. In this nominating speech McElwee cited the obstacles that blacks had confronted in remaining loyal to the party and predicted that Moore's nomination would revive southern Republicans and insure the party's victory in Tennessee.[68] The Republican platform called for the enactment of "effective legislation to secure the integrity and

[66]Memphis *Appeal*, May 15, 1888.
[67]Nashville *American*, May 17, 1888; Chattanooga *Times*, May 17, 1888.
[68]Moore withdrew from the race for the vice-presidential nomination. *Proceed-*

purity of elections," and the party's presidential nominee, Benjamin Harrison, paid increasing attention to civil rights during the campaign.[69]

Following the Republican national convention, William R. Moore led Tennessee in reclaiming the party's avowed civil rights tradition. Although the tariff was "of the most vital interest," he stated that it was "nothing compared with the unspeakably higher question" of "a lawful ballot and an honest count." Later in the year, Moore responded to attacks launched by the Memphis press against Senator John Sherman for "waving the bloody shirt" on the Negro question. Moore joined Sherman in urging the Republicans to take steps to provide federal protection for the black vote in the South. The state party's platform in 1888 paid homage to the national party's commitments to a free ballot and a fair count and condemned Democrats for suppressing the ballot. Although black delegates at the state convention had wielded little influence, in the ensuing gubernatorial campaign the party's nominee, Samuel Hawkins of Carroll County, endorsed the Blair Education bill, condemned the convict-lease system, and demanded protection of the ballot. Republican leaders in the state also launched repeated attacks against Democratic racial policies in an apparent effort to draw a clear distinction between the two parties on civil rights questions.[70]

The revival of Republican interest in Negroes provoked an enthusiastic response among black politicians in Tennessee. Black Republicans held a rally in Nashville to endorse the national

ings of the Ninth Republican National Convention, 1888 (Chicago: Blakely Printing, 1888), 236; Nashville American, June 29, 1888.

[69]Kirk H. Porter and Donald B. Johnson, eds., National Party Platforms, 1840–1956 (Urbana: Univ. of Illinois Press, 1956), 80; Logan, Betrayal of the Negro, 62–63; De Santis, Republicans Face the Southern Question, 193–97; H. Wayne Morgan, From Hayes to McKinley, 310. Whereas De Santis, Logan, and Morgan see a clear-cut national Republican commitment to Negro rights in the campaign of 1888, Hirshson considers the platform vague on civil rights and emphasizes the efforts of Republican strategists to play down the Negro question during the campaign. See Farewell to the Bloody Shirt, 143–66.

[70]Memphis Appeal, Aug. 29, Oct. 11, 1888; Memphis Avalanche, Mar. 25, 1887; Sept. 10, 1888; Nashville American, June 22, July 19, 1888; Chattanooga Times, Oct. 20, 1888; Knoxville Journal, Sept. 29, Nov. 2, 1888.

ticket, and a succession of speakers heartily approved the party's defense of Negro voting rights. William H. Young was one of several who saw the Republican party as "the only refuge" from mob law and ballot box stuffing in the South. He also defended the Republican tariff policy as being beneficial to black laborers. Stalwart party worker, Joseph H. Dismukes, joined him in denouncing mob law in the South, complaining that no black man could be tried in the Nashville courthouse "except before a white jury who would rather see the Negro dead than alive." Such conditions would have to be corrected at the ballot box, he predicted, or Negroes would "remain in perpetual slavery."[71]

The sincerity of the renewed Republican avowals of friendship would soon be tested, however. In Middle Tennessee's Sixth District, Negroes wrested control of the congressional nominating convention from whites and put up William H. Young for Congress. Young had been prominent in Republican circles since the late 1870s and had been a prime mover in the municipal reform campaign in Nashville in 1883. In 1888 he received the congressional nomination amid a scene described with typical overstatement by the Democratic Nashville *American* as "the most violent race upheaval that has occurred in Tennessee since the Negro was set free." Forty-eight of the sixty-three delegates to the convention were avid black Young supporters; most were from Davidson County. When blacks took charge of the convention, the majority of the white delegates walked out. According to a hostile Nashville newspaper, the black delegates had made "a direct and distinct appeal for the negro to array himself . . . without fear, as negroes, [*sic*] against the white race." The same source noted the "bold and uncompromising" manner in which blacks expressed their bitterness over the long years of service they had given the Republican party without reward. A young Negro schoolteacher in Nashville, C. N. Clark, drew the special wrath of the local press for allegedly stirring up animosities against whites. Although the older generation might submit to being ignored, Clark told the delegates, "the young black men of today are not going to stand

[71]Nashville *American*, June 28, 1888.

this kind of thing any longer." The time had come for the black man to say what he thought: "We no longer ask for recognition, we demand it and we are going to have it. We are not afraid of any man, white, black, yellow, or blue, nor do we fear to go into every corner of every county of this district and say these things."[72]

The militancy of blacks in the Sixth District and the nomination of a Negro for Congress ended interracial cooperation in the Republican party there. One observer, noting that most whites intended to bolt the party, summarized their attitude by quoting a white Republican who had responded to his queries by saying, "Let the negroes go to the democratic party or to hell as they please." The independent Nashville *Banner* wryly predicted that, despite Young's excellent Republican record, he would be "knifed," for "white republicans have no particular predilection for the negro" except for his vote. Indeed, a manifesto shortly appeared in the Nashville press in which white Republicans proposed to form a separate political organization. "We are throwing off an incubus; we are in earnest," their proclamation bluntly declared. One unidentified leader in the lily-white movement delivered the presumed *coup de grace* to the black-white Republican alliance: "We are done with the mercenary, shiftless Negro. The Republican party has had to bear the odium of having him inside the ranks as a claimant for favors"; now white Republicans have "thoroughly tired of this class and will have no more of them as our party allies."[73]

Thus Young's nomination drew racial lines taut in Davidson County and provoked a movement among white Republicans to dissociate themselves from blacks. At the county convention to select candidates for the state legislature, James C. Napier denounced the lily-whites and demanded two places for blacks on the six-man slate. A nominating committee dominated by whites conceded blacks only one of the nominations. While angry blacks, led by Napier, spurned the compromise and announced their

[72]*Ibid.*, July 20, 1888.
[73]Chattanooga *Times*, July 20, 1888; Nashville *American*, July 20, Aug. 5, 1888; Nashville *Banner*, July 20, 1888.

determination to defeat the ticket, several of the white nominees threatened to withdraw because the slate contained a Negro. Fearing that the existence of a Prohibition candidate in the congressional race might attract enough votes away from the Democratic candidate to elect Young, the Nashville *American* raised the racial standard throughout the campaign. The *American* repeatedly charged Young with "maliciously sowing seeds of race prejudice," depicted him as an "inflammatory" speaker and a "revolutionary," and urged whites to unite behind the party of "Old Hickory and James K. Polk." When Young was arrested during the campaign for allegedly carrying a pistol, the *American* headlined the story and then tersely reported his acquittal.[74]

In no other Tennessee election of the 1880s were the political problems confronting Negroes so apparent. A candid report by the editor of the Nashville *Banner* analyzed the forces behind the lily-white movement. According to the *Banner*, white conservatives had gained control of the Republican party and were intent upon drawing a rigid color line even if their actions resulted in Negroes decamping to the Democrats. In fact, it declared, the leaders of the movement believed that, by ridding themselves of blacks, white Republicans would make large gains among Democratic voters.[75]

It is difficult to assess the geographical extent of the lily-white movement in Tennessee in the late eighties, although it definitely was not confined to Nashville. Apparently many white party leaders resisted the movement; one of these, T. C. Muse, chairman of the Republican party in Madison County, fought the emergence of white Republican clubs by forming integrated organizations in each district of his county.[76] The correspondence of black Republican leaders in the state to Leonidas C. Houk indicates that the East Tennessee congressman attempted to maintain a biracial coalition throughout the decade.[77] Some evi-

[74]Nashville *American*, July 20, 21, 26, Aug. 5, Sept. 27, Oct. 5, Nov. 6, 1888; Nashville *Banner*, Sept. 27, 1888.

[75]Sept. 27, 1888.

[76]T. C. Muse to Leonidas C. Houk, Jan. 15, 1890, Houk Papers.

[77]Black Voters of Lincoln County to Leonidas C. Houk, May 5, 1889; Black

dence indicates that the movement represented more of a grass-roots hostility among whites in the Republican party than any definite decision by party leaders to write off the black vote. A white Nashville Republican office seeker proudly informed Congressman Houk that he had been "one of the prime movers" in organizing a "strickly [sic] white" Republican club in Nashville in order to put down the "white and negro leaders that have been selling out our party."[78] In the Third District, white Republicans barred blacks from participating in party rallies and parades, providing the Democratic Chattanooga Times with further ammunition with which to chide black voters for slavishly accepting the "air of proprietorship republican bosses assume when colored votes are under consideration."[79]

Despite the lily-white movement, the vast majority of Negroes remained Republicans. In the November election, however, William H. Young polled a competitive vote only in the two counties—Davidson and Montgomery—which had the highest black populations in the Sixth District. He won every predominantly black ward and district in Nashville and Davidson County but lost the election, 12,677–18,956.[80]

Reports from West Tennessee indicated that Democratic victories there were enhanced in part by black apathy and in part by Democratic intimidation of black voters. Events in Haywood County in 1888 doubtless revealed part of the reason for the sharp decline in Republican votes and the corresponding Democratic victories in West Tennessee. Whites had "redeemed" Haywood County from Republican rule in the previous August elections. Negroes constituted over 60 percent of the county's population, and throughout the 1880s more than half of the male population of voting age was black. Haywood and adjoining Fayette County had

Republican Leaders in Nashville to L. C. Houk, Feb. 18, 1889; James C. Napier to L. C. Houk, Feb. 26, 28, Dec. 16, 1889; Jan. 4, Apr. 18, Sept. 25, 1890; W. A. Crosthwait to L. C. Houk, Mar. 13, 1889, *ibid.*

[78]J. W. Langford to Leonidas C. Houk, Apr. 18, 1889, *ibid.*

[79]Oct. 29, 1888.

[80]Nashville *American*, Nov. 7, 1888; Nashville *Banner*, Nov. 6, 1888; Miller, *Official Manual*, 261.

been Republican since the Civil War. Both had sent Negro representatives to the state legislature; Haywood had been represented since 1883 by Samuel A. McElwee. Prior to the August elections in Haywood County whites had drawn up a "citizens' ticket," which, according to an approving newspaper account, "worked with a vengeance" to redeem the county from Republican rule. The white citizens' organization had formed an armed patrol to insure the "safety of the ballot box" on election day. As rumors spread that blacks were "laying in a supply of ammunition" to protect themselves, attention across the state focused on Brownsville, the county seat. A Democratic Memphis newspaper reported that heavily armed whites were flocking to Brownsville from West and Middle Tennessee communities. On the day of the election the white citizens' organization, with its armed assistance, enabled the Democrats to carry Haywood County for the first time in over twenty years. Additional whites arrived in Brownsville on the night of the election "armed with shotguns, Winchesters, carbines—to squelch any inclinations among the defeated Republicans to rise."[81]

McElwee, who was a candidate for reelection to the state legislature in November, traveled through the county on election day to bolster the courage of black voters, but an armed band of whites forced him to stop, and those Negroes who voted had to do so in the face of armed whites stationed at the polls. It was not surprising that even the predominantly black precincts in Haywood County went Democratic; in the subsequent November election, the county reports laconically stated that those Negroes who voted were "mainly voting the Democratic ticket." McElwee received only 723 votes in a county with a Negro voting-age population of almost 3,000. Shortly after the election, McElwee left Brownsville and moved to Nashville, apparently because of white threats against him.[82]

[81]Nashville *American*, Aug. 3, 1888; Memphis *Appeal*, Aug. 3, 1888.

[82]Nashville *American*, Aug. 3, 1888; Nashville *Banner*, Nov. 6, 1888; *Eleventh Census, 1890*, Pt. I, Population, 782; see also Miller, *Official Manual*, 261; Edward B. Stahlman to Leonidas C. Houk, Feb. 26, 1889; J. C. Graham to L. C. Houk, Feb. 11, 1889, Houk Papers.

In Shelby County in 1888, newspaper reports simply declared that Negro voters had not taken their usual interest in voting; the county moved firmly into the Democratic column after going Republican in 1880 and 1884. The total Republican vote in the five counties of West Tennessee that had black majorities had fallen from 17,885 in 1880 to 13,615 in 1888; the Democratic vote had risen from 15,081 to 23,477 in the same years. On the other hand, the four predominantly white counties of West Tennessee that consistently voted Republican from 1880 to 1888 saw the Republican vote increase from 5,804 in 1880 to 7,012 in 1888. In the statewide election of 1888 the Democrats carried the gubernatorial race, 156,799–139,014 for the Republicans and only 6,893 for the Prohibitionist candidate. Cleveland carried Tennessee over Harrison in the presidential election, 158,799–138,933.[83]

During the heat of the 1888 campaign, the Nashville *Banner* had outlined some unpleasant truths for blacks in Tennessee politics: both political parties wanted the Negroes' votes, but neither wanted to divide the rewards of office with them. While white Republicans gladly would swap the Negro vote for one-half of the state's white vote, Democrats only sought enough black votes "to keep the republicans out of office," and preferred that the mass of black voters remain Republican because such a situation allowed Democrats to exploit the race issue. The editor of the *Banner* concluded that it would not be in the self-interest of Negroes to form a separate party, for he did not think they would be able to maintain a compact political organization. In light of their bleak prospects in politics, Negroes should "realize that the moral and intellectual progress of their race is far more desirable than representation in official life, purchased by servile adherence to any party."[84]

The editor of a Negro Republican newspaper, the *Tennessee*

[83]Miller, *Official Manual*, 259. Following is the 1880 Republican gubernatorial vote in each of the five counties as compared to that in 1888: Haywood, 3,520-1,223; Madison, 2,078-1,475; Shelby, 7,758-8,382; Tipton, 1,584-1,485; Fayette, 2,945-1,050. For the 1880 vote, see the Nashville *American*, Nov. 6, 1882; for that of 1888, see Miller, *Official Manual*, 258–59.

[84]Sept. 27, 1888.

Star, reached a similarly dreary verdict. "Things are looking very poorly for God's despised poor in these parts," he wrote. "Every time when the Negro sticks his head up for office he is slaughtered by those with whom he affiliates, and for whom he always works and votes." Citing the results of the local August elections of 1888, the Nashville journalist lamented the fate of black Republican candidates in Knox, Hamilton, and Davidson counties who had been defeated while whites on the same ticket had won. Indeed, in Davidson County, there had been "bad blood" since the nomination of William H. Young for Congress, and "white Republicans swear they will not vote for the 'nigger'." To the black editor it seemed that white Republicans in Tennessee did not want the state to be carried for the party but intended to control the organization in order to distribute patronage and campaign funds as they pleased. "Ham is permitted to whoop 'em up and vote. That's all."[85]

As the editor of the *Tennessee Star* indicated, the determination of some white Republican leaders to control patronage and party funds doubtless fed the lily-white movement. Many white leaders also adhered to the simple political logic that black participation in party councils would cost more votes than it would win and that blacks had no real alternative but to vote Republican anyway. The intensity of the state lily-white movement in the 1880s came from at least two other sources, however, for whites had controlled the party throughout the early eighties without cutting loose from black support. The dynamic ingredients in converting white supremacist sentiment in the Republican party into a drive to rid the party of blacks came, it seems, from the efforts of white Republicans to broaden the appeal of the party by focusing on economic issues, on the one hand, and the rising political expectations of blacks within the party, on the other. Whites could be won over to Republicanism only if the party blacks remained passive and submitted to white direction. As blacks began to demand power within the party, they threatened not only the power of

[85]Quoted in Nashville *American*, Aug. 13, 1888 and Cleveland (Ohio) *Gazette*, Aug. 25, 1888.

traditional leaders but also the strategy of those whites who wanted to shape the party in the interests of conservative businessmen. In short, the Republican party in Tennessee in the late 1880s was torn by a conflict between a growing number of blacks who were determined to make the party the vehicle of black political equality and freedom, and the majority of white party leaders who were equally determined to draw industrial-minded Democrats into their camp. Ironically, before the decade ended both sides had lost.

III

Black Legislators of the 1880s

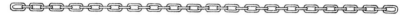

In the white press, black voters were generally stereotyped as an uneducated, irresponsible, and irrational horde, easy prey for demagogues and corrupt politicians. The twelve Negroes elected to serve in the Tennessee legislature in the 1880s, however, were men of ability, experience, and influence in the communities in which they lived. Four of them were lawyers, six had experience as businessmen, four had taught school, one was a minister; at least half of them had university educations. Seven of the twelve had had previous experience in public service on the federal, state, or local level, ranging from minor positions in the customs service and Treasury Department to city councilman and city jailer. Most of them actively participated in the work of the house of representatives, introducing legislation, taking part in debates, and sharing in the duties of the respective committees to which they were assigned. Collectively, their legislative record stands as a significant protest against many facets of the emerging system of racial discrimination in the state.

Although the influence of the twelve Negroes in the General Assembly was not strong, the legislation they sponsored, the votes they cast, and the arguments they presented all highlighted distinct issues. The black legislators challenged racial segregation in public transportation, fought for a fairer distribution of public educational funds, and attempted to halt economic proscription, lynching, and mob violence directed against members of their race. In fighting for these goals, they reflected the political and economic interests of the large black populations in the counties they represented: nine of them came from the five West Tennessee counties in which blacks outnumbered whites; one represented Davidson County, where Negroes composed almost 40 percent of the total population; the other two came from Hamilton County, which had a black population of better than 30 percent during the 1880s. All the black representatives of the 1880s were Republicans, representing areas where the majority of Republican voters were black and where many white Republicans inevitably refused to vote for black candidates on the party ticket; consequently, their major electoral support had come from members of their own race.

One of the primary concerns of Tennessee's black legislators during the eighties was the practice of racial discrimination in the use of public facilities, especially the railroads. To counteract the federal Civil Rights Act of 1875, the Tennessee legislature that same year had abolished the common-law right of "any person excluded from any hotel or public means of transportation, or place of amusement" to institute legal action. Although there is no evidence that this common-law right had been explicitly recognized in the past, the Tennessee legislature had acted to prevent a rash of suits under the federal Civil Rights Act. The Tennessee law permitted proprietors of public facilities to control the admission or exclusion of persons from their establishments on a basis "as perfect and complete as that of any private person over his private house, carriage, or private theater, or places of amusement for his family."[1] Under the provisions of the 1875 state law railroad companies had adopted the policy of charging Negroes first-class fare, then assigning them to second-class accommodations in the smoking cars. On some railroad lines the smoking cars were actually baggage cars; on others they were simply second-class cars in which drinking and the smoking and chewing of tobacco were allowed. In any case, passengers were not segregated in these cars. Blacks complained that they reeked of tobacco and that they were patronized by unsavory whites whose cursing and disrespectful behavior made them totally unsatisfactory to respectable Negroes, especially women. Also, because they were

---

[1]*Acts of the General Assembly of the State of Tennessee,* 1875, pp. 216–17 (hereinafter cited as *Acts*).

charged first-class fare, Negroes argued that they should have access to first-class accommodations on a nondiscriminatory basis.[2]

The four Negroes serving in the General Assembly in 1881 waged a vigorous battle to abolish racial discrimination in the use of public facilities. Thomas A. Sykes, a representative from Davidson County, initiated the effort by introducing a measure to repeal the act of 1875, and thereby gain the right of access to public accommodations. Sykes, who had served in the North Carolina legislature before moving to Tennessee, had also received minor federal patronage, serving successively as an internal revenue gauger and as an employee of the customs house in Nashville before his election to the state legislature. A white newspaper in Nashville described him as a man of "excellent character," a "fluent speaker, and gentlemanly in his bearing."[3] With the aid of his black colleagues and with substantial support from white Republicans, Sykes piloted his controversial bill through to a third reading, at which point it was vigorously debated. Although Republicans held half of the seats in the house and had controlled its organization, the black legislators could not muster enough support to pass Sykes' bill. It was narrowly defeated, 31–29. With twenty-six of the thirty-one opposition votes coming from Democrats, the five Republican opponents in the house more than assured its defeat. Later in the session, the house reconsidered the measure, but it failed again by only a few votes, receiving a simple, but not a constitutional, majority.[4]

Following the bill's second defeat, the four Negro legislators submitted a formal protest against the action of the house. They called the act of 1875 "a palpable violation of the spirit, genius and letter of our system of free government"—a law which "wickedly, cruelly and inhumanly" denied access to the state courts to those whose rights were violated, thereby forcing them into lengthy and

[2]Stanley J. Folmsbee, "The Origins of the First 'Jim Crow' Law," *Jour. Southern Hist.* 15 (May 1949), 235–47.
[3]Nashville *Banner*, Nov. 3, 1880.
[4]*Journal of the House of Representatives of the State of Tennessee* (Nashville: Tavel and Howell, 1881), 89, 420, 837 (hereinafter cited as *House Journal*).

expensive trials in the federal courts. Under the provisions of the act of 1875, the protestors declared, 400,000 citizens of Tennessee were "entitled to no rights that railroads, hotels, and theaters are bound to respect."[5]

Although their protest went unanswered, blacks in the legislature would make two other efforts during the eighties to repeal the 1875 law permitting racial discrimination. Leon Howard, a representative from Shelby County in the 1883 legislature, and William C. Hodge, representing Hamilton County in 1885, both introduced measures calling for its repeal. Howard's proposal was laid on the table and never came up for a vote, while Hodge's failed, 21–49. Thirteen of the fourteen legislators voting for Hodge's bill whose party affiliation could be identified were Republicans.[6]

Unable to abolish the law that permitted racial discrimination to go unchallenged in Tennessee's courts, the black legislators sought other relief. In 1881, Representative Isaac F. Norris introduced a bill to prohibit racial discrimination on railroads in Tennessee, but it never came up for a vote. Meanwhile, a compromise measure which had passed the senate, 18–1, stipulated that all railroads should provide "separate but equal" facilities for Negroes. This bill required railroad companies either to provide separate first-class cars or to partition off part of a first-class car "which all colored passengers who pay first-class passenger rates or fare, may have the privilege to enter and occupy." Such cars or portions of a car set aside for Negroes were to be equal in all physical respects to those used by whites. The measure passed the house April 7, 1881, 50–2. Significantly, two black representatives, Isaac F. Norris and Thomas A. Sykes, cast the only negative votes; of the other two Negro legislators, John W. Boyd was absent and Thomas F. Cassels abstained.[7]

From all indications Tennessee's black legislators did not favor the separate but equal principle, for later in the same session,

---

[5]*Ibid.*, 840–41.

[6]*House Journal*, 1883, pp. 429, 458; 1885, p. 486.

[7]*House Journal*, 1881, pp. 830, 868, 987, 993; *Acts*, 1881, pp. 211–12; see also *Senate Journal of the General Assembly of the State of Tennessee* (Nashville: Tavel and Howell, 1881), 575, 625 (hereinafter cited as *Senate Journal*).

during a heated debate on a bill to create a railroad commission, Representative Cassels offered an amendment to invest the proposed commission with the responsibility of prohibiting racial discrimination on all railroads in Tennessee. Cassels' amendment was defeated by only two votes.[8] The close vote probably represented an effort by opponents of railroad regulation to destroy the commission by saddling it with the burden of enforcing racial equality.

Further evidence of black dissatisfaction with the separate but equal law of 1881 surfaced in the 1882 extra session of the legislature when Representative Norris succeeded in stiffening the fine for violation of the law.[9] Apparently, Norris feared that the original penalty of only $100 for violators who were successfully prosecuted would not deter railroad companies from continuing to assign Negro passengers to the smoking cars. Through the imposition of a higher penalty railroad companies might be forced either to incur the heavy cost of maintaining separate first-class facilities or to abandon racial discrimination completely.

Black representatives made their opposition to the separate but equal law of 1881 even clearer in the succeeding two legislatures. In 1883, for example, John W. Boyd, a holdover from the previous legislature, sponsored a bill which would have prohibited racial discrimination of any sort on railroads in the state, but it was amended to allow a continuation of the separate but equal provisions of the existing law. In this meaningless form it passed the house by a large vote, with Boyd voting against it, two other Negro legislators abstaining, and only one, David F. Rivers of Fayette County, voting for it. Since it did not alter existing legislation, it never came to a vote in the senate. One of the Negro abstainers, Leon Howard, had made his opposition to the separate but equal principle clear earlier in the same legislative session by attempting to repeal the 1875 law permitting racial discrimination. Defeated in that endeavor, he sought to repeal only the provision of the 1875 law that pertained to railroads, but this bill, too, was decisively

[8]*House Journal*, 1881, pp. 777, 781.
[9]*House Journal*, 1882, 3d Ex. Sess., 17, 37, 90–92, 129, 134; *Senate Journal*, 1882, 3d Ex. Sess., 94–95; *Acts*, 1882, 3d Ex. Sess., 12.

beaten. After failing in both these efforts, Howard apparently acquiesced to the separate but equal bill by abstaining on the final vote. In 1885, Representative Greene E. Evans from Shelby County launched a bill to repeal Tennessee's 1881 Jim Crow statute. Evans, a graduate of Fisk University and a former school-teacher, was at the time of his election a successful Memphis businessman. His repeal bill, however, like the earlier antidis-crimination measures, met swift defeat.[10]

Although the Negroes in the legislature were not united in their voting on the bills pertaining to segregation, their persistent efforts to repeal the 1875 statute and the 1881 separate but equal law indicate that there was substantial black opposition to the emerg-ing pattern of Jim Crow in public accommodations. Since the Tennessee legislative journals do not record the debates on bills under consideration, it is impossible to assess the attitudes of whites as they voted down black efforts to abolish segregation measures. The close vote in 1881 on Representative Sykes' effort to repeal the Tennessee statute permitting discrimination in public facilities and the twenty votes that Representative Hodge's repeal measure of 1885 received in the house indicate that white attitudes toward segregation legislation remained somewhat fluid in the early 1880s. Even the overwhelming white support for the separate but equal measure of 1881 does not indicate unanimity among whites on segregation, for the 1881 law did not require complete separation of the races on the railroads; it only called upon railroads to provide first-class facilities for blacks.

Tennessee's 1881 law might best be explained as an effort by the legislature to sanction racial discrimination on the state's railroads on a more systematic basis than before. Earlier racial discrimination on the railroads, although pervasive, was unsys-tematic and subject only to the whims of each company. Under the

[10]*House Journal*, 1883, pp. 458, 514, 759, 812; 1885, pp. 359, 372. House Bill 447, 44th General Assembly, 1885, Secretary of State Papers. For a brief biographical sketch of Greene E. Evans see Mrs. L. D. Whitson, *Personal Sketches of Members of the Forty-fourth General Assembly of Tennessee* (Nashville: Southern Methodist Pub. House, 1885), 91–92; Memphis *Appeal*, Nov. 13, 1884.

terms of the 1881 law, a more uniform policy could be adopted. It was, as Stanley J. Folmsbee has maintained, an attempt "to clarify a rather confused legal situation."[11] In actuality, the law made little difference in the quality of accommodations provided for Negro passengers. Most of the railroad companies in the state either ignored it, continuing to assign all blacks to the smoking car, or simply partitioned off a part of the smoking car and labeled it the first-class section for Negroes. In any case, it was hardly the "concession to Negroes" that Folmsbee supposed it to be; rather, the law represented an important transitional step from the 1875 Tennessee statute which allowed proprietors to discriminate in their public businesses as they saw fit to the uniform segregation codes adopted by Tennessee and other southern states between 1890 and 1910.[12] The 1881 law simply provided legal guidelines for racially discriminatory practices during a period of transition from laissez-faire to full statutory regulation of segregation.

Tennessee's black representatives of the eighties also called upon the legislature to improve the quality of Negro education. They fought for state aid for a black normal school, federal aid for public education, greater control by blacks over their public schools, compulsory attendance, and a more equal distribution of state, federal, and philanthropic funds for education. Despite their vigorous opposition to segregation in public accommodations, Tennessee's black legislators, surprisingly, did not challenge racial segregation in public education; perhaps they assumed that integration of the public schools was an unrealistic goal. In any case, they simply sought more racially equal facilities and funds.

[11]Folmsbee has argued that Tennessee's 1881 law was not the prototype of the Jim Crow statutes passed throughout the South at the turn of the century. Folmsbee cited white Republican support for the 1881 law and what he judged to be the acceptance of the bill by the Negro legislators as proof that the law was a "concession" to Negroes, and therefore not of the same intent as later Jim Crow legislation in the South.

[12]In 1891 the Tennessee legislature passed a more comprehensive law requiring railroads to provide separate but equal accommodations for all Negro and Caucasian passengers, with the exception of black nurses who were allowed to accompany their white employers in the white cars. See *Acts*, 1891, pp. 135–36.

In 1881, for example, when Thomas A. Sykes secured the adoption of a bill that required officials to admit Negro students into the school for the blind at Nashville and the school for the deaf and dumb at Knoxville, it specifically stipulated that they were to be assigned to separate facilities. All four Negro legislators voted for the measure.[13]

Blacks also encouraged the Tennessee legislature to support federal aid for education and to divide any funds so attained equitably between the races. In the extra session of 1881, Thomas F. Cassels, a member of the house Committee on Education and Common Schools, offered an amendment to a joint resolution requesting Tennessee's congressmen to vote for federal aid to common schools. Cassels' amendment stated that any money obtained from the federal government should be distributed on a basis of "equal justice to all claims of citizens." Although the resolution passed, 48–18, Cassels' "equal justice" amendment was tabled. In 1885, Representative Samuel A. McElwee of Haywood County sponsored a resolution urging Tennessee's congressional delegation to support the Blair Education bill, but consideration of it was postponed indefinitely, 51–42.[14]

While they fought for federal aid, Negro legislators also campaigned for an increase in the state allocations for the education of their race. In 1881, Isaac F. Norris presented a petition from a group of black educators who represented the Negro State Teachers' Institute, a self-improvement group organized by black public school teachers in the state. Foremost among the needs they cited was state aid for the education of prospective Negro teachers. This resolution pointed out that, although the state helped finance the normal school at Nashville and four other public universities in Tennessee, "the colored youth of the state are not allowed to attend any of them, and the state makes no provision whatever for the higher education or normal training of her colored children." The Negro educators further noted that, although the state received approximately $13,000 from the Peabody Education Fund

[13]*House Journal*, 1881, pp. 345–46, 958.
[14]*House Journal*, 1882, 2d Ex. Sess., 95, 100; 1885, p. 122.

for the benefit of the state normal school, graded schools, and teacher institutes, less than $500 of that money went for Negro education. Apparently most of the money Negroes received went for teachers' institutes held throughout the state. The educators also complained that the money Tennessee received from the Land-Grant College Act of 1862 went entirely to the University of Tennessee, a school which barred Negro students. "It is not to be supposed Congress intended that gift to be for the exclusive use of either the white people or the colored people but for the whole people of Tennessee," they declared.[15]

Friends of Negro education had struggled in vain since the late 1860s to get the state to assume part of the responsibility for training black teachers.[16] Finally, in 1881, the legislature responded by allocating the sum of $2,500 for this purpose. In contrast, the state normal college at Nashville received an annual appropriation of $10,000 from the state, plus an equal amount from the Peabody Education Fund. The money for the education of Negro teachers was allotted in the form of tuition scholarships to be awarded competitively to two students from each senatorial district. Since black students were not admitted to the state normal school, they could attend any "good colored normal school" of their choice. This measure passed the house unanimously, 60–0. Despite its segregation provisions and its inequitable allocation of funds for black teacher education, all the black representatives voted for it. No doubt it was better than nothing. The obstacles confronted by blacks in fighting for better public education were starkly outlined later in the same session when they had to battle an effort to cut off the appropriation after one year; with prodding from Governor Hawkins, however, the General Assembly allocated continuing, albeit meager, funds.[17]

In the succeeding legislature, Samuel A. McElwee endeavored

[15]Petition in Favor of the Higher Education of the Colored Children in Tennessee, 42nd General Assembly, 1st Session, 1881. Memorials, Petitions, Reports, Miscellaneous Papers, Secretary of State Papers; *House Journal*, 1881, p. 768.

[16]Taylor, *Negro in Tennessee*, 188–89, 200–21.

[17]*Acts*, 1881, pp. 209–11; White, *Messages*, VI, 687–88; *House Journal*, 1881, 1st Ex. Sess., 44–45, 66, 70; *Senate Journal*, 1881, 1st Ex. Sess., 52, 53, 58–59.

to increase the appropriation for the education of Negro teachers. During his three terms from 1883 through 1887, McElwee emerged as one of the more active members of the legislature. Apparently as a gesture of interracial goodwill and to solidify the loyalty of blacks to the party, the Republican lawmakers nominated McElwee speaker of the house in 1885. Since Democrats decisively outnumbered Republicans in the house, there was no chance of his actually being elected, although he received almost full support from the Republican representatives.[18]

McElwee, born a slave in Madison County in 1858, exerted efforts to obtain an education which foreshadowed his later drive and initiative as a legislator. At the age of sixteen, after attending school sporadically and farming with his father, he began teaching in Haywood County. A year later, he entered Oberlin College, paying his expenses by working at menial jobs. After a year at Oberlin, he accepted a teaching job in Mississippi, but when his school closed after only a few months, he returned to Tennessee. Although soon teaching again, McElwee trudged ten miles two nights a week to recite Latin, German, and algebra to a white tutor who was a student at Vanderbilt University. Fortunately, the tutor informed officials at Fisk University of McElwee's industriousness, and in the fall of 1878 he enrolled there, graduating with an excellent record in 1883. McElwee represented Haywood County in the legislature during his last year at Fisk. While serving his second term in 1885, he worked on a law degree at Central Tennessee College in Nashville. The Democratic Nashville *American* described him as "a magnetic speaker, forcible debator and indefatigable worker" who had earned the "high regard" of his colleagues in the legislature because of his "ability, integrity and loyalty to his constituency." According to the *American*, McElwee's popularity among blacks was "unbounded."[19] Portraits show that the young legislator was a man of dignified bearing, with

---

[18]*House Journal*, 1885, pp. 7–8.

[19]For an autobiographical sketch of McElwee, see the New York *Globe*, Feb. 2, 1884; see also the Nashville *American*, June 9, 1888, for an assessment of his influence and character; see also letter from Madison County Republicans to Leonidas C. Houk, Feb. 22, 1889, Houk Papers.

fashionable long sideburns, who dressed in the most refined style of the eighties.

In his first legislative session, McElwee sponsored a bill to increase the appropriation for the education of Negro teachers from $2,500 to $5,000.[20] In a speech quoted in full in the Nashville *American* and favorably commented upon in the New York *Globe*, the young black legislator marshaled a formidable battery of reasons why the Democratic-controlled legislature should substantially increase the appropriation for Negro teacher education. According to McElwee's statistics, Negro education had been given only $300 of the $390,000, plus interest, Tennessee had received under the Land-Grant College Act of 1862. The state university, largely financed by the federal land grants, excluded blacks, thereby depriving them of most of the benefits of that act.

McElwee combined a romantic image of Negro faithfulness and industriousness, a shrewd appeal to political self-interest, and a call for justice in urging the legislature to provide greater aid for Negro education. Tennessee's black citizens, he said, had earned the right to an adequate education by their long years of "patient, unrequited toil and industry," and by their faithfulness during the war. Speaking in a more practical vein, he pointed out that Democrats now had an opportunity to draw Negroes from the Republican party, for if his bill passed, it would have to have Democratic support. Many blacks had joined forces with the Democrats in 1882, he remarked, in response to pledges that the Bate forces had made to improve Negro education. The Democratic party's record on Negro education, however, did not justify black support, he warned, and in the future black voters would search the record to determine what political course to pursue. Leaving the plane of politics, McElwee broadened his appeal and, in the best fashion of the New South enthusiasts, argued that there was no more momentous question before the South than that of education. If Tennessee should take an advanced stand on this

[20]*House Journal*, 1883, pp. 397–98; Memphis *Appeal*, Feb. 16, 1883; House Bill 12 and House Bill 235, 43d General Assembly, 1883, Secretary of State Papers.

question, it would usher in "the dawn of a better day in our Southland. Then with the dead issues of the past buried in the sea of oblivion and our homes, formerly devastated and laid waste by war, built up, with the mineral resources of our country developed, with the color line obliterated, and with our many manufacturing industries, the South will move on to a grand and noble future."

The legislation he proposed would benefit all the people of the state, McElwee argued, but he was especially concerned about the needs of "the race which I love and of which I am proud of the honor of identification, and by whose votes I occupy this seat." Negroes had already made "wonderful progress" in eliminating illiteracy, he stated; they should be further encouraged by the passage of his bill. Nevertheless, the black legislator's forceful remarks failed to persuade a majority of his colleagues. His appropriation measure was tabled, 50–38; eventually a bill recommended by the Committee on Education and Common Schools, which appropriated only $3,300, was passed.[21]

In their efforts to improve the quality of education for members of their race, black representatives also backed a compulsory attendance proposal and an attempt to give Tennessee blacks greater control over their public schools. In the 1885 legislature, Representative William A. Fields, a Negro schoolteacher from Shelby County, introduced a bill that would have made school attendance compulsory for all children between the ages of seven and sixteen. Although it was defeated, Fields' measure reflected the continuing concern of Negro leaders with the educational advancement of their people. Another expression of this interest was the persistent effort of black legislators to create the position of assistant superintendent of public instruction, to be filled by a person of their race who would supervise the state's Negro schools. Representative Greene E. Evans introduced such a proposal in both the regular and extra sessions of the 1885 legislature, but neither measure passed the house.[22]

[21]Nashville *American*, Jan. 24, 1883; New York *Globe*, Feb. 3, 1883; *House Journal*, 1883, p. 397.

[22]*House Journal*, 1885, pp. 156, 401, 415, 505: 1885, 1st Ex. Sess., pp. 21, 40;

Another educational concern of Negro legislators was the disposition of black student cadets appointed to serve in the state militia. The University of Tennessee had an arrangement with Knoxville College and Fisk University which allowed black students who received appointments as state cadets to attend either of the two private Negro schools. The scholarship money granted to state cadets, usually educated at the University of Tennessee, was simply forwarded by the University to either Fisk or Knoxville College. In the mid-1880s the University revoked this agreement with Fisk University, and Knoxville College in the eastern part of the state became the only school which could receive black tuition students. In the 1885 legislature, Samuel A. McElwee pointed out that Nashville's Fisk was more conveniently located and offered better educational opportunities than the Knoxville school, and, in 1887, he succeeded in persuading the legislature to instruct the University of Tennessee trustees to resume forwarding the tuition grants to Fisk University as well as to Knoxville College.[23]

However short they fell of achieving all their objectives, Tennessee's Negro legislators made a creditable showing in obtaining appropriations for the education of Negro teachers, in opening the state institutions for the blind and for the deaf and dumb to Negroes, and in facilitating the appointment of Negro cadets with state tuition grants to Fisk University. Their efforts to gain greater control over the administration of their schools by the appointment of a black superintendent indicated both a tacit acceptance of segregation in public schools and a desire to have black schools administered by blacks.

Tennessee's black representatives also expressed concern over the predicament of black laborers in the state. In 1883, Representative John W. Boyd of Tipton County fought unsuccessfully to repeal the state's contract-labor law which made any laborer who broke a work contract or anyone who enticed a laborer away from

---

House Bill 119 and House Bill 514, 44th General Assembly, 1885, Secretary of State Papers.

[23]*Acts*, 1885, pp. 341–42; *House Journal*, 1885, pp. 382, 393; 1887, p. 783; House Joint Resolution 83, 45th General Assembly, 1887, Secretary of State Papers.

a contracted job subject to damages.[24] In the succeeding legislature Representative William A. Fields tried, with a similar lack of success, to liberalize the state law by which landlords were given a lien on the crop of tenants. Fields also attempted to obtain legislation requiring employers who advertised for hands to pay the wages stated in their advertisements. Often, laborers were recruited from long distances by notices offering high wages, only to be exploited by sharply reduced wages upon their arrival.[25]

The black legislators also worked for better state penal facilities. Thomas A. Sykes, a member of the house Penitentiary Committee in 1881, introduced a measure to purchase a site for the erection of a new penitentiary. After extensive debate of Sykes' bill, the legislature decided to set up a committee to investigate and report to the next General Assembly the cost of building a new penitentiary.[26]

Efforts by blacks to reform the state's criminal code were not as successful. In the 1881 legislature Isaac F. Norris proposed a bill to abolish the practice of requiring persons convicted of misdemeanors to work out the costs of their trials and fines, but it failed to pass. Of greater importance, Styles L. Hutchins, a black representative from Hamilton County, introduced a bill in 1887 that would have abolished the convict-lease system, confining convict labor to work on the public roads, but it, too, met defeat. Although black prisoners were notoriously abused under the convict-lease system, there is no evidence that the matter was debated as a racial issue.[27]

The black legislators of the eighties also sought to revoke state legislation banning interracial marriages and to end racial discrim-

[24]*House Journal*, 1883, pp. 379, 425; House Bill 54, 43d General Assembly, 1883, Secretary of State Papers.

[25]*House Journal*, 1885, pp. 187, 188, 232, 495; House Bill 151, 44th General Assembly, 1885, Secretary of State Papers.

[26]*House Journal*, 1881, pp. 126, 621, 712–14; 1882, 2d Ex. Sess., 10, 27, 98; *Senate Journal*, 1881, p. 671; see also Jesse Crawford Crowe, "Agitation for Penal Reform in Tennessee, 1870–1900" (Ph.D. diss., Vanderbilt Univ., 1954), 148–49.

[27]*House Journal*, 1881, pp. 548, 824; 1887, pp. 351, 401; House Bill 447, 45th General Assembly, 1st Sess., 1887, Secretary of State Papers.

114

ination in the selection of jurors. In 1881, Thomas F. Cassels created considerable turmoil in the General Assembly by attempting to repeal the antimiscegenation statute. Cassels' repeal bill would have allowed interracial marriages but explicitly prohibited interracial sex outside of marriage. Following a vigorous debate over the measure, opponents of the bill amended it to prohibit both interracial marriages and interracial cohabitation outside of marriage. Even in this form it was defeated; no doubt the white majority was satisfied with the law on the books, but the Memphis *Appeal* puckishly observed that several white legislators might have been embarrassed by the existence of a law against interracial sexual relationships outside of marriage. Efforts of black legislators to outlaw racial discrimination in the selection of jurors were also unsuccessful. Representatives Sykes and McElwee introduced bills in 1881 and 1883, respectively, to eliminate discrimination against blacks in the selection of circuit and criminal court juries, but neither of the measures received much support.[28]

In the face of mob violence against members of their race in the 1880s, Tennessee's black legislators also sought to curb lynchings and similar lawless acts. Following two particularly brutal, brazen incidents in Springfield in late 1880 and early 1881, which together involved the lynching of eight Negroes who had been accused of murdering a white farmer, the General Assembly took limited action. First, the Assembly adopted a resolution introduced by a white Republican senator from Shelby County which denounced "this violation of law as tending to subvert all government, and as deserving prompt punishment" and adjured the state executive "to use all means for the arrest and punishment of the perpetrators of this crime." With the full support of the black representatives, the legislature also enacted a Republican-sponsored law providing that "any sheriff who either negligently or willfully, or by want of proper diligence, firmness and promptness . . . allows a prisoner to be taken from his custody and put to death by violence" should

[28]*House Journal*, 1881, pp. 89, 532, 573, 723–26, 824; 1883, pp. 116, 416, 456; Memphis *Appeal*, Mar. 17, 1881; *House Journal*, 1887, pp. 204–576; House Bill 6, 45th General Assembly, 1887, 1st Sess. Secretary of State Papers.

be guilty of a "high misdemeanor," fined, removed from office, and barred from future offices. This measure passed the senate and house by the substantial margins of 18–2 and 44–7, respectively. In the same session, however, Thomas F. Cassels failed in an effort to secure legislation that would have provided state compensation to the families of the victims of mob violence.[29]

The lynching of three Negroes in West Tennessee in 1886 provoked Samuel A. McElwee to introduce a measure in the legislature in February 1887 calling for stricter penalties against lawmen who were negligent in defending their prisoners. One of the lynchings had involved a black woman jailed in Jackson for allegedly poisoning her employer. A mob of about 1,000 whites broke into the jail, apparently without opposition, seized the unfortunate woman, stripped her of her clothing, and hanged her in the courthouse yard. Her body then was riddled with bullets and left hanging above the courthouse lawn until the next morning.[30] Speaking in defense of his bill in the legislature, McElwee reviewed lynchings in Jackson, Dyersburg, and McKenzie, and indicted the "public press" of the state "for condoning, by its silence, the wrongs and outrages perpetrated upon the Negroes of the state by mob violence." After describing the gory details of the Jackson lynching, McElwee declared:

> . . . grant for the sake of argument, that these parties were guilty, does that make it right and in accord with our principles? When the citizens of Madison, Dyersburg and Carroll go to judgement with the blood of Eliza Wood, Matt Washington and Charles Dinwiddie on their garments, it will be more tolerable for Sodom and Gomorrah in that day than it will be for Jackson, Dyersburg and McKenzie . . . . I stand here today and demand a reformation in Southern society.[31]

[29]For a partial review of Tennessee lynchings, 1875–85, see the Chattanooga *Times*, Sept. 14, 1885. For accounts of the two Springfield lynchings, see the Clarksville *Semi-Weekly Tobacco Leaf Chronicle*, Sept. 17, 1880; Feb. 18, 1881; *Acts*, 1881, pp. 54, 288–89; *Senate Journal*, 1881, pp. 396, 404, 502; *House Journal*, 1881, pp. 447, 573, 786, 817.

[30]This account of the Jackson lynching is taken from the following sources: Memphis *Appeal*, Aug. 19, 1886; Robert H. Cartmell Diary, Vol. VI, Aug. 18, 1886 (Manuscript Div., Tennessee State Library and Archives); Memphis *Avalanche*, Sept. 16, 1886.

[31]Nashville *Tennessean*, Feb. 13, 1971.

Despite his emotional plea, McElwee's bill was tabled in the house, 41–36, with thirty-nine of the majority votes being cast by Democrats. Most Republicans supported the antilynching measure.[32]

The Negro members of the General Assembly during the 1880s were also concerned about the twofold problem of protecting the right to vote and of having votes fairly counted. In 1885, Representative William C. Hodge failed to obtain approval of a bill to provide for greater protection of the ballot box during and after elections. In the same session, a bill sponsored by William A. Fields that would have allowed the candidates of each party to appoint election judges also suffered defeat. In the following legislature, black representatives unsuccessfully sponsored two bills that would have made it illegal for candidates to be present at the counting of ballots. Styles L. Hutchins was more successful: he persuaded the legislature to repeal an 1883 revision of the Chattanooga charter which had made the payment of poll taxes a prerequisite for voting in city elections.[33] The poll tax provision had not been rigidly enforced, and the apparent ease with which Hutchins obtained its repeal suggests that the measure was not yet viewed by whites as a device for restricting black suffrage.

By and large, the black men who served in the Tennessee legislature during the 1880s proved to be very capable representatives. Several were men of superior education, energy, and talent. The measures they introduced, the protests they registered, and the few records we have of remarks they made indicate that they attempted to represent the interests of their black constituents by working to improve educational opportunities, labor conditions, and respect for civil rights. The grounds upon which they appealed to the white majority revealed an understanding of the political process and, perhaps, reflected the extent to which some of them shared in the moral, political, and economic assumptions of their white colleagues. The issues they raised in the legislature about racial justice did not find a receptive audience, but the

[32]*House Journal*, 1887, pp. 68, 204, 539.
[33]*House Journal*, 1885, pp. 66, 87, 236, 417, 511; 1887, pp. 187, 253, 606, 634, 939; *Acts*, 1883, pp. 315–16.

dignity, ingenuity, persistence, and skill with which several of the black legislators pursued their goals indicate that, contrary to the stereotyped portrayals of Negro voters in the white press, the black electorate produced eminently qualified officeholders. The brief and limited presence of Negroes in the General Assembly would not last through the decade. By 1889 that body would again be all white, and for more than seventy-five years it would remain unchallenged by the probing inquiry or the pointed entreaties of a black representative.

IV

Urban Reform: The Nemesis of Black Power

Lacking the power to achieve their goals in the state legislature and unable to shape the policies of the state or national Republican party, still black leaders in Tennessee did, on occasion, play crucial roles in county and municipal governments. The three largest urban areas of Tennessee—Memphis, Nashville, and Chattanooga—all had sizable black populations which, in conjunction with a faction-ridden party structure on the local level, presented Negroes with numerous opportunities to wield political influence. For a time during the eighties they exercised limited power in all three cities and won positions as aldermen, received appointments to serve as policemen and firemen, obtained an increasing number of municipal jobs, and saw improvements made in their public educational facilities. These cities provide, therefore, a fertile ground for examining the dynamic quality of black participation in politics during the decade.

The social and economic flux of the eighties was reflected in each city by the emergence of reform movements led by white businessmen, professional groups, and property owners. The reformers, depicting themselves as the "best people," declared their goals to be more efficient city government, elimination of corruption, reduction of taxes, and an end to domination of city government by machines based on boss rule and ward politics. In Nashville several Negro leaders broke with the old city boss, Thomas A. Kercheval, and joined the reformers in a successful effort to change the system of municipal government by placing it in the hands of businessmen. This movement, however, only partly deflected the hostility of white reformers toward Negro participation in the city's politics. In Memphis and Chattanooga

119

the reform movements, from their inception, sought to curtail black political power. In all three cities the reform movements significantly altered the racial atmosphere, heightened white opposition toward black political activity, and encouraged institutional changes that sharply curbed the influence of blacks in city government. Knoxville, the other major urban area in Tennessee in the 1880s, did not undergo a reform movement of the same magnitude and character as those experienced in Chattanooga, Nashville, and Memphis; therefore, it is not included in this analysis. Perhaps the smaller percentage of blacks in Knoxville's population and the ability of Democrats to win most city elections made unnecessary the centralization of local government there for partisan or racial advantage.

The municipal reform movements in Tennessee focused largely on structural changes and avoided social justice measures. They reflected the general character of urban reform movements elsewhere in the country in the late nineteenth century in that they were business oriented and concerned with efficient government. Contrary to what Samuel P. Hays describes as the norm for urban reformers of the late nineteenth and early twentieth centuries, there was no clear conflict between the political ideology and the political practice of urban reformers in Tennessee. They expressed reservations about participatory democracy and publicly espoused structural changes in city government to eliminate the political power of the uneducated, propertyless masses—especially blacks. Whatever else they were, the urban reformers were clearly partisan: they were concerned with the way Democrats—or a particular Bourbon, or New South, faction of the party—could rule the cities. In the rhetoric of the reformers, this problem was not unrelated to the question of how well the cities would be ruled. In any case, the author has accepted their identification of themselves as reformers. That their reforms often were antidemocratic and aimed at reducing the role of blacks and Republicans in city government presents the student with a paradox only if reform is construed to be the exclusive work of angels. The drive for urban reform in Tennessee carried within it seeds that germinated by the end of the decade in a statewide electoral reform movement to restrict Negro voting.[1]

On the surface, the biracial, nonpartisan reform movement that swept Nashville in 1883 portended well for race relations in the state capital. In the spring of that year the Citizens' Reform Association, headed by Arthur S. Colyar and his Nashville *American*, petitioned the legislature to amend the city charter. The legislature complied, accepting the reform guidelines proposed by the association and drafted by a young Nashville attorney, Jacob McGavock Dickinson. The reform charter reduced the size of the city council from forty-two to ten men and stipulated that each was to be elected from the city at large. The charter delegated the operational duties of the city government to a board of public works which was to be appointed by the city council.[2]

The reform charter ostensibly was designed to break up the old ward system of political patronage, improve city services, reduce taxes, and place more power in the hands of the council. The primary impulse behind the movement came from business leaders and propertyholders who resented the power wielded by lower-class elements in the community under the democratic system of ward representation. "The change proposed is a business change," declared the Nashville *American*, representing "an effort to abandon the semi-political ward system for a government run on business principles."[3]

A biographer of Arthur S. Colyar attributes other motives to the editor-industrialist's leadership in the reform campaign. Through

[1] For a general analysis of urban reform movements in the late nineteenth and early twentieth centuries see Samuel P. Hays, "The Politics of Reform in Municipal Government in the Progressive Era," *Pacific Northwest Quarterly* 55 (Oct. 1964), 157–69; see also Zane L. Miller, *The Urbanization of Modern America: A Brief History* (New York: Harcourt, 1973), 99–121. For an examination of an urban reform movement in another southern city in the late nineteenth century and its impact on black political power see Eugene J. Watts, "Black Political Progress in Atlanta: 1868–1895" *Jour. Negro Hist.* 59 (July 1974), 268–86.

[2] Chattanooga *Times*, Mar. 1, 1883; Memphis *Appeal*, Mar. 22, 1883.

[3] Sept. 23, 1883.

the centralization of city government and the election of council members at large, Colyar and his business associates, according to this author, hoped not only to exercise greater power in municipal affairs but also to use that power as a base for strengthening their position in the state Democratic party.[4] There were hints that Colyar's interest in reform also stemmed from his determination to protect the local monopoly of the Louisville and Nashville Railroad with which he was affiliated. In any case, in a convenient fusion of political self-interest and a desire for efficient city government, Colyar threw the full weight of his influential Nashville *American* behind the reform movement. In the first election to be held under the new charter in the fall of 1883, the reform-minded editor left the editorial desk and took to the hustings, speaking in behalf of the municipal ticket sponsored by the Citizens' Reform Association.[5]

The association's ticket reflected the business influence behind the reform movement. It was headed by C. Hooper Phillips, a leading Nashville merchant who was a candidate for mayor. Of the ten candidates for city council on the reform ticket, eight were prominent businessmen. The other two were Negroes who had been chosen to win black support away from the incumbent mayor, Thomas A. Kercheval, a Republican. The platform advanced by the reformers called for reduction of taxes, improved streets, a better police force, a city police court "so administered that the humblest citizen whether white or black" should have a fair trial, improvements in the city waterworks, and a better sewage system. When Colyar's use of the convict-lease system became an issue in the campaign, the reformers appended a statement to their platform declaring that all improvements in the city would be made with paid labor.[6]

Both the Citizens' Reform platform and the inclusion of two black men on the municipal ticket indicated the extent to which the success of the reformers would rest upon their ability to win at

---

[4]Thomas Woodrow Davis, "Arthur S. Colyar and the New South, 1860–1905" (Ph.D. diss., Univ. of Missouri, 1965), 327.

[5]Nashville *American*, Oct. 3, 9, 11, 1885.

[6]*Ibid.*, Sept. 22, Oct. 7, 1883.

least a part of the black vote. Constituting approximately 38 percent of the city's population in 1880, Negroes had played a crucial role in city elections since their enfranchisement in 1867. For most of the past decade they had been aligned with the ward-patronage machine run by Kercheval. The revision of the city charter had stemmed in large part from the desire of Nashville businessmen (and a Democratic state legislature) to destroy the Republican city machine operated by this "evil genius of Nashville politics."[7]

In light of this situation, the Citizens' Reform Association set out immediately to win black support. Speaking at a reform rally, Colyar dramatically underscored the importance of Negroes in the faction-ridden politics of Nashville and described the advantages that would spring from black support of the reform movement:

> The colored men of this city now have it in their power, standing firmly by those who have so long suffered under misrule, and praying for relief, to bring to a people who have been helpless great joy, and to make for themselves many friends. You have it in your power, at the approaching election, to give a longsuffering tax-ridden people relief, by condemning the mob spirit now rife all over the city, because you have the balance of power.
>
> If you, colored men, join our determined young white men and stand with them shoulder to shoulder on the day of election, you will make everlasting friends among the better class of white people.[8]

The Nashville *American* praised the two blacks on the Citizens' Reform ticket, pointing out that it "would be impolitic as well as unjust to ignore this large element of our local population." During the campaign the *American* tried to persuade blacks that they should abandon Boss Kercheval; the white reformers were in earnest, it declared, and would not desert the two blacks on the ticket. Since blacks paid taxes and were subject to city laws, the *American* reasoned, they should have representatives in Nashville's government.[9]

[7]*Ibid.*, Oct. 6, 1885.
[8]*Ibid.*, Oct. 10, 1883.
[9]*Ibid.*, Sept. 21, Oct. 7, 1883.

The two Negroes included on the Citizens' Reform ticket for the city council were Charles C. Gowdy and James C. Napier, both of whom were popular leaders in the Negro community. The twenty-nine-year-old Gowdy had worked as a drayman and was serving his third term as constable.[10] According to the Nashville *American*, he was "very popular and influential with his race, and highly respected by the whites for his integrity and conservative course." Napier, a successful thirty-seven-year-old lawyer, had accumulated substantial property in Nashville. First elected to the city council in 1878, he had done yeoman service in representing the interests of the Negro community under the Kercheval regime. Although an unsuccessful candidate for the state legislature in 1882, Napier had retained his seat in the Nashville city council and apparently worked in harmony with the city boss. In fact, when Napier had sought to be appointed postmaster in Nashville in 1881, Kercheval had written President Garfield a flowery letter of recommendation describing Napier as "a young man of intelligence and fine moral standing" who was "highly esteemed by all parties and colors."[11]

The presence of Napier and Gowdy in a white-dominated reform movement led by businessmen seeking to destroy a Republican political machine supported by the vast majority of Nashville Negroes raises several questions concerning the motives of the two black candidates. The decentralized, representative government of Nashville under the old ward system offered blacks a chance to exercise greater political influence than would the new city government with its appointive officials and centralized councilmanic elections. In all likelihood, it was far from easy for Napier, a stalwart Republican booster who had heretofore counseled blacks to remain loyal to the party, to jump the party traces and support a movement clearly led by Democrats.

A number of considerations shaped Napier's decision. For one thing, by the fall of 1883 the revised city charter was an ac-

[10]*Ibid.*, Mar. 8, 1888.

[11]Thomas A. Kercheval to James A. Garfield, Apr. 2, 1881, and Petition from Nashville Negroes to J. A. Garfield, Mar. 27, 1881; copies located in Napier Papers.

complished fact; under its provisions candidates for the council would have to run at large, an arrangement which would dilute the influence of the Negro vote. Napier may well have joined the reformers on the assumption that the only hope for Negro representation in the city government lay in such an alliance. Perhaps, too, Napier and Gowdy supported municipal reform by reason of their perception of its merits aside from any promises of political preferment. In addition, blacks had accumulated a store of grievances against Kercheval, and, even though he was a Republican, some had turned against him. Moreover, Nashville Negroes were aware that the businessmen leading the reform movement had jobs to dispense; by supporting those who had economic power, they might logically expect to be rewarded. Finally, when Napier declared during the campaign that he believed the movement would "bring the two races in the community together and let them work harmoniously for a common interest," he voiced a hope that probably impelled other Negroes to join the Citizens' Reform movement.[12]

Whatever their motivations, Napier and Gowdy linked fortunes with the reformers and accepted the task of organizing the Negro vote. Both worried, however, that their course would be rejected by the vast majority of Nashville Negroes. They were joined by another popular Negro leader, William H. Young, who worked tirelessly throughout the contest, speaking to large audiences of both races. Colyar's newspaper devoted considerable attention to the campaign work of Gowdy, Napier, and Young, carefully explaining that they had joined the reform movement without any special promises and that they represented the "best" element among Nashville's black population—an element that sought to join whites in promoting good government. The *American* presumptuously labeled Young "the colored Cicero," praising both

[12]In his study of blacks in Philadelphia in the late nineteenth century, W. E. B. Du Bois found that municipal-reform causes secured "a respectable Negro vote" even though such causes often threatened black jobs and influence in the city government. See Du Bois, *The Philadelphia Negro: A Social Study* (Philadelphia: Univ. of Pennsylvania, 1899), 382–83; Nashville *American*, Sept. 22, 29, Oct. 4, 1883.

his sharp attacks on the incumbent administration and the enthusiastic response they evoked. A few years later, when Young would employ similar rhetoric in the interest of his own congressional candidacy, the *American* would damn him as an irresponsible firebrand, but in 1883, with municipal reform at stake, the newspaper reflected that he represented "the true position of the colored citizens" and that his speeches were in "the interest of reform."[13]

In the course of the campaign the black reformers cited a number of reasons why Negro voters should support the Citizens' Reform ticket. Under the Kercheval administration several racial incidents had occurred in which white policemen had killed black men while taking them into custody. The Negro reformers claimed that Kercheval had done nothing in response to repeated black appeals for an investigation. William H. Young urged Negroes to align themselves with the business interests, since they were the ones wielding economic power, and held aloft the hope that a victory of the Citizens' Reform ticket would usher in better race relations. In any case, he asserted, the reformers had given blacks representation on their ticket; the Kercheval supporters had not. Napier expressed hope that a reform government would improve black public schools. He also stressed the fact that, if the Citizens' Reform ticket were successful, Negroes would have a greater voice in municipal government than they ever had enjoyed under the old system. One black speaker at a reform rally included among his reasons for supporting the Citizens' Reform ticket the argument that, "though elected largely by colored votes," Kercheval had "never in his messages to the city council recommended any measures for the benefit of the colored citizens of Nashville."[14]

Napier and Gowdy were justifiably concerned about the way blacks would respond to their participation in the reform movement. Although accounts of the campaign in the Nashville *American* doubtless exaggerated the coarseness and violence of black

[13]Nashville *American*, Sept. 29, Oct. 3, 1883.
[14]*Ibid.*, Sept. 22, 29, Oct. 3, 1883.

opposition to the Citizens' Reform ticket, as the campaign progressed it became clear that a large segment of the black community remained loyal to Kercheval. White leaders in the reform movement blamed campaign violence and heckling on black toughs who, they claimed, had been hired by the Kercheval forces to disrupt Negro speakers for the Citizens' Reform ticket. Speaking at a reform rally, editor Colyar urged blacks to condemn the unruly mob of Kercheval supporters because "of all the people in the world you are the most interested in a government of law."[15] A letter to the *American* from a black reformer illustrates the hostile reception that occasionally greeted black speakers for the Citizens' Reform ticket:

> Tuesday last, in the Fourteenth Ward, I was cursed to my teeth, three times violently struck with stones, my buggy was nearly torn to pieces, and I dared not speak for fear of my life, and for no other cause than that I have chosen to support the reform ticket, and am trying in a fair and gentlemanly manner to elect to office candidates who, besides being good and capable men, are fair and impartial enough to recognize on said ticket, two good men of our race, Messrs. C. C. Gowdy and J. C. Napier.[16]

Negro leaders in the reform movement condemned the "unusual, unreasonable, and shamefully unfair manner" in which the incumbent administration conducted the city canvass, and at one tumultuous meeting black and white reformers stood with arms linked to protect a Negro speaker from what an *American* reporter described as a "howling mob."[17]

The hackneyed denunciations that had previously characterized the *American's* coverage of practically all Negro political meetings were conspicuously applied only to Kercheval supporters during this campaign. Colyar, for example, described a rally held by Negroes to endorse the Citizens' Reform ticket as "remarkable in point of numbers, respectability and the intelligence which marked the proceedings."[18] Still, the editor of the *American* proceeded cautiously in wooing the black vote, paternalistically

---

[15]*Ibid.*, Oct. 7, 1883.
[16]*Ibid.*, Oct. 11, 1883.

[17]*Ibid.*, Oct. 10, 11, 1883.
[18]*Ibid.*, Sept. 29, 1883.

127

instructing Negroes in their responsibilities as citizens rather than holding aloft any promises of special favors or of racial equality.

As the campaign progressed, some white reformers apparently grew uneasy over the attention blacks were receiving in the campaign. Keenly attuned to white racial sensibilities, the *American* began to play down the significance of race, stressed the benefits of law and order that would follow a reform victory, and predicted that black voters would best guarantee lasting racial harmony by supporting the reform ticket. Through his newspaper, Colyar depicted the reform campaign as an opportunity for Negroes "to indicate their capacity for citizenship. If their suspicion of their white fellow-citizens induces them to vote against what they suppose to be the interests of their white neighbors, then they are hopelessly blind to their own interest." The election, he ominously concluded, would indicate "whether the colored voter is a freeman—capable of thinking for himself and of judging what his best interest is." If the Negro "wastes his vote to gratify his prejudices or justify unworthy suspicions," Colyar admonished, "he establishes his political ignorance beyond question."[19] By placing the Negroes' ability to vote responsibly on this basis, Colyar helped lay the groundwork for future white disillusionment with Negro suffrage.

In the ensuing election the entire Citizens' Reform ticket won. A special correspondent to the Chattanooga *Times* who observed the election remarked, "The intelligent portion of the Negro population voted and worked with the whites in the cause of reform, and their work was of much value." In fact, he reported, it was "the first time that the colored vote has been divided here." Although many had feared that the two Negroes on the reform ticket would be "scratched" by white voters, he wrote, more whites cast ballots for black candidates than ever before. "It is the first time in the history of the city government since the Negro was invested with citizenship that the whites and blacks are united," he concluded. In a like vein the Nashville *American* rejoiced that party lines had been obliterated and past racial animosities forgot-

[19]*Ibid.*, Oct. 11, 1883.

ten as the combined labor of black and white reformers had prevailed over the old municipal regime.[20]

An examination of the election returns, however, suggests that these newspaper accounts may have exaggerated the extent of black support for the Citizens' Reform ticket. In the predominantly black fourth ward, for example, Kercheval beat C. Hooper Phillips, the reform candidate for mayor, 366–285. In 1881, however, Kercheval had polled 476 votes in the fourth ward; so it is evident some blacks did indeed support the reform ticket. Both Gowdy and Napier carried the fourth ward, running ahead of the rest of the reform candidates by 50 to 60 votes, but the other eight council candidates polling the highest number of votes in the fourth ward were all aligned with Kercheval. On the other hand, not all the whites who supported the reform ticket voted for the two blacks; Gowdy and Napier ran from 800 to 1,100 votes behind the other reform candidates in the citywide balloting. In light of these statistics, it appears unlikely that black support for the Citizens' Reform ticket was as decisive a factor in the campaign as the postelection estimates indicated, although the reformers drew some blacks away from the Kercheval machine.[21]

The story of the successful alliance in Nashville between black and white reformers received publicity outside the state. A Chicago editor observed that the biracial reform movement in Nashville augured well for the future of southern politics. As soon as southern blacks found their political claims recognized by southern whites their distrust would subside and racial animosities would end, he predicted. Colyar agreed that the results of the municipal election offered encouragement for the future, for the integrated ticket had been "strongly supported by colored voters irrespective of their party bias." Nevertheless, he argued, blacks themselves largely bore the responsibility "for the closeness with which the color line has been drawn in politics." Ignoring the exception of Republican control of the city government and the

[20]Chattanooga *Times*, Oct. 12, 1883; Nashville *American*, Oct. 12–13, 1883.

[21]For a breakdown of the municipal vote by precincts, see Nashville *American*, Oct. 13, 1883.

crucial role of the black vote in Nashville, Colyar declared that the ascendancy of the Democratic party in the South had been accomplished "without the aid of the colored vote." Probably more for home customers than for outside observers, he assured his readers that southern Democratic concessions to Negroes had not been made from "partisan promptings." Instead, "Southern Democrats were voluntarily taxing themselves to support Negro education." Colyar concluded that, although southern whites did not originally "clothe the colored man with citizenship," by now they recognized his rights "under the law" and had demonstrated their "readiness to accord him the rights and privileges of citizenship."[22]

Whatever reservations Colyar had about the conclusions drawn by outsiders concerning biracial cooperation in the reform campaign, he and his associates clearly appreciated the contribution black leaders had made to the success of the Citizens' Reform ticket. Shortly after the election, a "citizen committee" presented William H. Young with a watch and chain inscribed with Young's name and the words, "From the Business Men of Nashville, Tennessee." Inside the case of the watch was a picture of Arthur S. Colyar.[23]

In the short run, Nashville Negroes reaped benefits from the reform movement—the establishment of a Negro fire company, an increase in the number of city workers, the awarding of city contracts to black bidders, and improvements in Negro school facilities represented some of the more tangible gains. To some blacks, these concessions did not go far enough. Less than six months after the election, a group of Negroes met to censure the new reform mayor for vetoing councilman James C. Napier's resolution calling for the appointment of blacks to the police force.[24]

Disagreement over the course of the reform administration did not deter some Negro leaders from again joining the effort to elect a reform mayor and city council in the next municipal election.

[22]*Ibid.*, Oct. 16, 1883.
[23]*Ibid.*, Oct. 18, 1883.
[24]*Ibid.*, Mar. 1, 1884.

The nonpartisan Citizens' Reform Association was revived in 1885 under the banner of "Business and Reform." A well-known Republican businessman, Andrew W. Wills, a former Union officer from Pennsylvania who had settled in Nashville after the war, headed the ticket, which included James C. Napier as the sole Negro candidate for the council. Arthur S. Colyar and Edward B. Stahlman, associated with the Louisville and Nashville Railroad and the Tennessee Coal, Iron, and Railroad Company, were prominent members of the executive committee of the association, provoking charges that the railroad interests were behind the reform movement and Wills' candidacy. Stahlman eventually resigned from the executive committee in an effort to dissociate the reform movement from the Louisville and Nashville Railroad interests. One of the matters of business expected to come before the new council would be a proposal to grant a Nashville right-of-way to the projected Chesapeake and Nash-ville Railroad which, if completed, would compete with the Louis-ville and Nashville line. The Nashville *American*, no longer in Colyar's hands, expressed its concern and hope that the "special interests" not be allowed to gain control of the reform movement. The *American*, now under Bourbon control, favored naming a straight Democratic ticket in the municipal election, but the supporters of a nonpartisan ticket forestalled the Democrats by holding a public rally to nominate their candidates. The *American* subsequently advised Democrats not to run a party slate.[25]

In 1884, Kercheval again sought the mayoralty and launched a vigorous attack on the incumbent reform administration, charging it with being antidemocratic, extravagant, and controlled by special interests. As in the campaign of 1883, the former city boss expressed his approval of reforms in the structure of the city government. Now taking the offensive, he employed the campaign strategy the reformers had previously used to defeat him by depicting himself as the leader of an indignant taxpayers' revolt. Kercheval condemned the reform administration for raising the salaries of city officials, for increasing the city's bonded indebted-

[25]*Ibid.*, Sept. 29, Oct. 2, 9, 11, 1885.

ness to build a new waterworks system and a bridge across the Cumberland River, and for raising the assessed value of property so that, even though tax rates had been lowered slightly, overall there had been an actual increase in taxes under the reform administration.[26]

Several Negro leaders again participated in the reform campaign. Young and Napier were joined by Thomas A. Sykes, a former member of the legislature, and George W. Bryant, a prominent Nashville minister. These black reformers, appearing jointly with whites at the reform rallies, complained that, as mayor, Kercheval had increased racial hostilities, manipulated black voters, and exploited black city workers. During the campaign Bryant labeled Kercheval "a demagogue" and accused him of trying "to pit one race against the other." He claimed that Kercheval had attracted support only from "the illiterate black man" who could be bought with "a drink of whiskey and a few dollars." On the other hand, "The Reform administration was the colored man's friend, the black minister declared"; it had "willingly" given Negroes jobs, thousands of dollars in city contracts, and equitable wages. "The best of the Negroes are going to vote with the best of the whites for Wills in this election," Bryant promised. To fulfill this promise he held out to black Nashvillians the vision of racial harmony as the reward for taking the outstretched hands of their white friends.[27] Described by the *American* as a man of "superior" intellect and "high cultivation," Bryant attracted enthusiastic coverage from the reform-minded newspaper.

To critics who said a minister should not be participating in politics, Bryant retorted, "Every good minister owes it to himself and his people to point the masses to that which will enlighten and elevate them." Further, Bryant asserted, anyone who attempted to harass him physically during the campaign would have to be carried away on a stretcher. "The time has passed," he added, "when Negroes can be bulldozed and the sooner white people find it out the better."[28]

[26]*Ibid.*, Sept. 22–25, 1885.
[27]*Ibid.*, Oct. 2–9 (N. B. Oct. 3–4, 7), 1885. [28]*Ibid.*, Oct. 3, 8, 1885.

Other Negro leaders extolled the virtues of the reform administration's racial policies, pointed out that the general improvements
in municipal services introduced by the new city government had
benefited blacks, and emphasized the inclusion of black representatives on the city council. "The reform system of government
has acted a noble part toward the colored people," observed
Joseph H. Dismukes, a local lawyer. "It has been fair to all classes
and just to the humble citizen. The colored man has received more
benefits from this form of government than from any other administration the city has ever had." James C. Napier announced that,
if reelected to the city council, he would work for continued
improvement of the streets, the sewage system, the sanitation
program, and the public schools.[29]

William H. Young and Thomas A. Sykes drew a sharp contrast
between jobs awarded Negroes under the old Kercheval machine
and those they had received recently from the reform government.
Although a Kercheval supporter in the previous campaign, Sykes
had switched to the reformers because they had given Nashville
"the best form of city government we have ever had . . . . I have
seen my people prosper under this form of government." There
was now a Negro fire company commanded by a black captain, a
Negro boss on the street construction crews, a black watchman on
the bridge across the Cumberland River, and an overall increase
in the number of Negro workers employed by the city's board of
public works. "The colored man who would go back on all that,"
Sykes continued, "ought to hold his head down in shame." Young
commended the "just policy" displayed by the incumbent administration and credited it with giving the Negro "more than was
promised him." In contrast, when Negroes had received jobs
under the Kercheval administration, he charged, they had been
paid in scrip redeemable only at exorbitantly priced stores owned
by the mayor's political supporters. If city workers had become
indebted to any of the storekeepers under the Kercheval regime,
their wages had been turned over to their creditors. Young
contrasted this with the reform administration's granting of some

[29]*Ibid.*, Oct. 3–4, 8, 1885.

2,000 jobs to Negroes and its abolition of scrip payments.[30]

White leaders in the reform campaign based their claims for black support largely upon the racial policies of the incumbent administration. Mayor Phillips pointed out that shortly after his election he had urged the city council to appoint a city judge who would be fair to Negroes and to give "the colored people of our city a fair and equitable representation" in job appointments. He boasted that his administration had given more jobs to blacks than any previous one, that it had ended the practice of paying city workers in scrip, and that when it advertised for construction bids "the poorest man in the city, white or black, has an equal chance with the richest one." The books would show that "thousands of dollars have been paid to Negro contractors." Improvements in the waterworks and in sanitation had benefited blacks and whites alike, and, unlike the old city government, his administration had employed paid laborers rather than convicts on work projects. Finally, the mayor claimed that, while his administration had lowered taxes generally, blacks had especially benefited from a reduction in license fees for drays and small businesses.[31]

The disillusionment among many blacks with Kercheval fed black support for the reform movement. In 1884 the former mayor had been elected to the state senate, where he became a central figure in a Republican effort to block a bill that would have required all Nashville voters to register and to present a registration receipt before voting. Although he had voted against the registration bill, Kercheval had alienated many Negroes by refusing to join his fellow Republican senators in what turned out to be a successful walkout to prevent passage of the bill and by condemning the Republican boycott as a "cowardly act." Since many Nashville Negroes, however, considered the Republican boycott a heroic stand which had preserved Negro suffrage, some reformers astutely focused on this incident to discredit Kercheval with his remaining black followers.

The *American* was caught in an embarrassing position by this campaign tactic; the newspaper had endorsed the registration bill

[30]*Ibid.*, Oct. 6, 1885.　　　　[31]*Ibid.*, Oct. 2, 7, 1885.

and, ironically, was forced to defend Kercheval. "It should be said," the editor, John J. Vertrees, curtly stated, "that Mr. Kercheval did his duty as a legislator in sticking to his post—which the other Republican senators did not." The fragile foundations of the nonpartisan reform alliance began to crack as a result of the registration-bill issue. The *American* had been ambivalent from the start about the nonpartisan character of the reform movement and its bid for black support; now, with the registration issue brought into the campaign, the newspaper began to assume a more partisan stance. Many Democrats had come to view a registration law as the best means of escaping nonpartisan government of the city; if the black vote were reduced, nonpartisanship could be cast aside without fear of risking Republican domination of municipal affairs. Use of the registration issue, therefore, was dangerous; it might cut into Kercheval's black support, or it might backfire and provoke a major defection of Democratic voters from the reform ticket.[32]

Indeed, on election day many Nashville Democrats who previously had supported the reform movement either stayed at home or voted for Kercheval. The Citizens' Reform ticket was defeated. The editor of the *American* claimed that the registration-bill controversy and the city administration's special interest in Negroes—especially the creation of a black fire company—had precipitated a Democratic defection from the reform movement: reform had lost its nonpartisanship and had become associated with Republicanism. It is also likely, however, that the prominence of railroad interests in the Citizens' Reform Association cooled the enthusiasm of some reformist Democrats, as did increases in the assessed value of property and taxes under the incumbent administration. A comparison of the 1885 election results with those of 1883 bears out the theory that the reform ticket was defeated by Democratic voters who simply stayed at home. While Kercheval polled only about 300 more votes in 1885 than he had in his losing effort in 1883, the reform candidate's total was approximately 1,500 less than it had been in 1883.[33]

[32]*Ibid.*, Oct. 2–3, 1885. [33]*Ibid.*, Sept. 29, Oct. 2–3, 6, 8–11, 1885.

From all indications the reform slate again attracted black support, although it certainly did not win a solid Negro vote. Election-eve prognostications that three-fourths of Nashville's Negro voters would support the reform candidate for mayor gave way to a post-election analysis which stated that "a majority of the colored voters" had cast their ballots for reform. Even this probably represented an exaggeration, for in the predominantly black fourth ward the candidates on the Kercheval ticket averaged about a 100-vote margin over the reformers. Although James C. Napier ran slightly ahead of other reform candidates in the fourth ward, he, too, was defeated. In 1883 the reform candidate for mayor had polled 285 votes in the fourth ward and Kercheval had received 366; in 1885 the respective votes were 257 and 380.[34]

Napier's defeat in the city council race was unfortunate. His service on the council had produced tangible benefits for the Nashville Negro community. Through his leadership two Negro schools had been built, one in South Nashville and another in East Nashville. He also conducted a successful crusade to have the city's Negro schools staffed with black teachers. Previously, all the black public schools in Nashville had been taught by white teachers who, Napier claimed, "were concerned primarily about the salary and were willing to teach the colored pupils if the pay was worthwhile." In his first campaign for the council in 1878, Napier had pledged that, if elected, he would endeavor to have Negro teachers placed in charge of the students; their example would provide "an incentive to colored pupils." When he relinquished his seat on the city council in 1885, all the Negro schools had black administrators as well as teachers. In addition, he had successfully promoted the creation of a Negro fire company, headed by a black captain. Despite his defeat, he continued to hold the Nashville reform movement in high regard. In 1909 he wrote to Jacob McGavock Dickinson, the white lawyer who had drafted the reform charter, stating that it "did more to unite and bring together the better classes of white and colored people than anything that has occurred since the civil war. The colored people

[34]*Ibid.*, Oct. 9, 1885.

of Nashville are still enjoying many benefits that resulted from this movement."[35]

Napier overlooked the fact that citywide voting on each candidate for the council had made it more difficult for Negroes to win election to the municipal government: Napier and Gowdy would be the last blacks elected to that body during the eighties.[36] Also, the 1885 election in Nashville offered little evidence that the reform movement had appreciably altered the voting habits of the majority of the city's black citizens, despite the presence of several prominent black leaders in the reform camp. Despite interracial cooperation in the campaign, there was no significant improvement in the racial attitudes of the city's white citizens. Indeed, some observers claimed that the few benefits bestowed upon Negroes by the reform administration had alienated many whites, who registered their protests by not voting in 1885. The Democratic reaction to the campaign's registration-bill controversy underscored the ambivalent potential of reform for Negroes. In 1883 Arthur S. Colyar had implied that, if Negroes failed to support the reform movement, they would cast doubt upon their capacity to vote. Two years later, perhaps because of the narrowness of their victory in the city election of 1883 and their disgust with nonpartisanship, a number of Democratic reformers had come to favor a voter-registration bill as part of the process of political reform and as a solution to the precarious position of the Democratic party in Nashville. On this issue, as well as others, nonpartisan reform in Nashville foundered.

The issue of municipal reform played an even more volatile role in Memphis politics during the eighties. In the wake of a steadily deteriorating financial condition and a disastrous yellow fever epidemic, the state legislature had revoked the city charter in 1879. From that time until 1890 Memphis was officially governed as "the taxing district of Shelby County," under the direction of a

[35]Undated manuscript, Napier Papers; James C. Napier to Jacob McGavock Dickinson, Apr. 14, 1909, Dickinson Papers (Manuscript Div., Tennessee State Library and Archives).

[36]J. Woolridge, *History of Nashville, Tennessee* (Nashville: Methodist Pub. House, 1890), 128–29.

board of fire and police commissioners and a board of public works. The board of fire and police commissioners had three members; originally, one of these was selected by the governor, another by the quarterly court, and the third by the voters of the district. The appointee of the governor, designated president of the board of fire and police commissioners and endowed with executive powers, functioned as the chief officer of the city. In 1882 the voters of the district gained the right to elect all three members of the board.[37]

This centralization of the local government represented the culmination of a decade-long movement to remedy the city's financial plight and to abolish the city-council form of government. A steadily mounting bonded indebtedness, a corresponding rise in taxes, and an inefficient city government had provided the ingredients for a revolt of businessmen and propertyowners against the mayor-council system with its decentralized representation by wards. A severe yellow fever epidemic in 1878 simply delivered the crippling blow to the already enfeebled municipality.[38] With its commissions and appointed executive, the new municipal government held promise of solving the acute financial and sanitary problems that had plunged the city into despair and of eliminating the patronage and graft associated with the old ward system; it also conveniently destroyed the democratic representation of blacks in the city government, thereby offering comfort to those white citizens who were concerned about the rapid demographic changes that seemed to threaten white ascendancy.

Following the 1878 outbreak of yellow fever, the population of Memphis rapidly declined from over 40,000 to less than 20,000, of which Negroes comprised approximately 14,000. Almost 70 percent of the whites who remained in Memphis during the summer

[37]L. D. Bejack, "The Taxing District of Shelby County," West Tennessee Historical Society *Papers* 4 (1950), 14 (hereinafter cited as WTHS *Papers*); Nashville *American*, Oct. 4, 1883.

[38]John H. Ellis, "Businessmen and Public Health in the Urban South during the Nineteenth Century: New Orleans, Memphis, and Atlanta," *Bulletin of the History of Medicine* 44 (July-Aug. 1970), 351–53; see also Ellis, "Business Leadership in Memphis Public Health Reform, 1880–1900," WTHS *Papers* 19 (1965), 94–95.

of 1878 died, whereas less than 7 percent of the blacks perished. By 1880 the white population had increased to 18,677, while the number of blacks reached 14,896. Memphis whites were acutely sensitive to the presence of a growing number of Negroes who accounted for approximately 45 percent of the total population by 1880.[39] Combined with the increasing bonded indebtedness, the rising tax rate, and the sanitary crisis was the view of many whites that the increased presence of blacks posed a threat to "good and efficient government." This attitude was exemplified by the businessmen who led the drive to abolish the city charter. "We have in our midst a large and controlling voting element which has but little at stake in the welfare of our city," their reform proposal stated. Their belief that government ought to be by the "best people" and by propertyowners who had a "stake in society" led them to declare boldly, "Our purpose is to remove our city government and the business from all partisan influences."[40]

Under the taxing-district system of government the local contests for the elected members of the commissions took place largely within a nonpartisan framework. At least, that was the case until 1887, when restive businessmen and Democratic leaders began a drive to displace David P. Hadden, who had served as president of the taxing district since 1882. There were diverse forces behind the attack on the Hadden administration. By 1887 the financial and sanitary problems that had provided a great part of the impetus for a nonpartisan-commission form of municipal government had largely been solved. Moreover, some elements within the Memphis business community, never a monolithic group, had begun to grumble that the strict economic policies of the taxing-district government hindered business progress. There were even some complaints about tax increases to pay for expansion of public works and sanitation improvements, and there was

[39]United States, Bureau of the Census, *Statistics of Population, 1880*, I, Table VI, 424 (Washington, D.C.: Government Printing Office, 1883).

[40]The report of business leaders calling for abolition of the city charter is found in full in Memphis *Appeal*, Jan. 12, 1875; see also Memphis *Appeal*, Oct. 3, 1884; and Keating, *History of Memphis and Shelby County, Tennessee* (2 vols.; Syracuse: D. Mason, 1888), II, 33.

growing dissatisfaction among industrialists with a privately owned waterworks that enjoyed a local monopoly and imposed steady increases in city water rates. In addition, a battle was looming over the disposition of a lucrative streetcar franchise which a group of local businessmen hoped to secure by ousting the Hadden administration. Party and racial interests also entered the picture as local Democrats began to complain that Hadden had taken nonpartisanship too far by including Independents, Republicans, and a contingent of Negro leaders in the taxing-district government. Negro commissioners had been elected on pro-Hadden municipal tickets in 1882, 1884, and 1886, and through his personal style of politics "Pap" Hadden had won substantial Negro support.[41]

The Memphis *Avalanche*, owned by Congressman James Phelan, launched the attack against Hadden in the fall of 1887, charging that the taxing-district government was antidemocratic, corrupt, and riddled with Negroes and Republicans. In the weeks preceding the municipal election of January 1888, Hadden's critics put together a Citizens' ticket to oppose his reelection. In return, Hadden's supporters advanced a People's ticket, declaring that their major objective was to preserve the taxing-district system of government. The heretofore rather placid municipal campaigns gave way to one of bitter recriminations. John M. Keating, editor and part owner of the Memphis *Appeal*, overrode the opposition of his partners and enlisted his newspaper in support of Hadden and the People's ticket. Keating charged that Hadden's opponents represented special business interests which hoped to acquire the municipal streetcar franchise and wanted to control the city by restoring the old ward system. Initially, Negroes were divided in their loyalties, but the persistent efforts of the *Appeal* to solicit black votes for Hadden and the inclusion of a Negro candidate for school commissioner on the pro-Hadden ticket paid increasing dividends. The city's leading black newspaper, the *Watchman*, endorsed the Hadden ticket: "The people,

[41]Memphis *Avalanche*, Jan. 5, 18, 1882; Dec. 15, 1885; Memphis *Appeal*, Jan. 11, 1884; Knoxville *Journal*, Jan. 10, 1886; Ellis, "Businessmen and Public Health," 361–62.

black and white, are determined to have good and efficient officers at the head of the Taxing District affairs. They believe in the present system of government, and to this end they propose to fight it out, knowing that they are in the right and will prevail. . . . [The people of Memphis] cannot afford to have our city retrograde to the old manner of government." Noting that the future of the city rested equally upon blacks and whites, the *Watchman* urged blacks to "rally and do their part in the support of a principle that is pure and honorable . . . [voting] for men who are above suspicion, who will be for the maintenance of the present form of city government, and who will administer the laws in a faithful and impartial way, to the best interest of all classes."[42]

In the ensuing election the Hadden forces triumphed, with the notable exception of the black candidate for school commissioner. The predominantly Negro fifth ward overwhelmingly supported the People's ticket; on the day after the election the *Appeal* boasted, "They [Negroes] cast a heavy vote for good government, which for them, as for all of us, has been a blessing and a reliance ever since it was established." Through their behavior at the polls Memphis Negroes had proved that "the black man, so recently but a slave, has grown to a degree of intelligent comprehension of his duty, that leaves no room to doubt his entire reliability when the public interests are at stake." The *Appeal* heaped special praise upon J. T. Turner, editor of the *Watchman* "as a leader of his race, who is not afraid to push prejudice aside and stand with the great body of the white people in their efforts for good government." The taxing district under Hadden's direction stood for government "free from all outside control, free from corporate interests," the *Appeal* continued, and the Negro voters "deserve the thanks of the white people" for their "singleness of purpose and an unalterable resolve to faithfully perform their duty."[43]

[42]Memphis *Appeal*, Jan. 1, 4–6, 1888; Memphis *Watchman*, quoted in Memphis *Appeal*, Jan. 5, 1888; Thomas H. Baker, *The Memphis Commercial Appeal: The History of a Southern Newspaper* (Baton Rouge: Louisiana State Univ., 1971), 152–53.

[43]Jan. 6, 1888.

The fight over municipal government in Memphis was largely obscured throughout the remainder of 1888 by the state and national elections. Local dissension, however, spilled over into the Democratic contest for the state legislature. When the regular Democratic convention in Shelby County nominated a slate of candidates pledged to reelect Isham G. Harris to the United States Senate, local opponents of Harris named a rival People's Reform ticket and campaigned to defeat ring politicians. The *Appeal* led the opposition to Harris and supported the bolters. The insurgent faction adopted a platform which endorsed the taxing-district government and implied that the regular Democratic legislative candidates would attempt to undermine the existing municipal government in the General Assembly.[44]

The Memphis *Avalanche*, a Harris supporter, blasted the People's Reform ticket with a steady stream of racist invective and, as the campaign progressed, raised the specter of Negro domination. A few days before the election, the *Avalanche* printed a crude political cartoon which depicted a Negro mob rampaging through the streets of Memphis with torches and guns. An accompanying article warned that blacks were arming themselves for a race war. The backers of the People's Reform ticket were to blame, according to the *Avalanche*; by their charges of election irregularities they had emboldened Memphis Negroes to armed rebellion, and "in the present emergency" any Democrat who voted the People's Reform ticket would be taking "the brutal blacks by the hand in their universal struggle with intelligence for the mastery."[45]

In response, the *Appeal* ridiculed the *Avalanche's* "lurid headlines" and its predictions of a race war: "The negroes are now more quiet and peaceful, even to the degree of apathy, than they have been during any election in many years past." The *Avalanche's* scurrilous race scare represented "the last desperate effort of the 'machine' to drive the bolters back into the ranks, to solidify the white vote in opposition to the negro vote, and to intimidate the latter by threats of death and destruction." Whatev-

[44]*Ibid.*, Oct. 18, Nov. 3, 1888.
[45]Nov. 2, 4, 6, 1888.

er other issues there may have been in the 1888 legislative campaign, by election day the race question had virtually preempted the news columns and editorial pages of both major newspapers. In this tense atmosphere, the regular Democrats carried the day, electing their entire legislative ticket.[46]

The defeat of the People's Reform legislative ticket cast ominous shadows across the political career of David P. Hadden and the taxing-district government. Early in 1889 the Memphis *Avalanche* proclaimed that increasing public sentiment in Memphis demanded a return to home rule. Continued agitation of this question during the summer resulted in an acrimonious struggle for control of the Memphis *Appeal*, whose management held divided views over Hadden and the taxing-district government. John M. Keating, a staunch Hadden supporter who had been editor of the *Appeal* since 1868, lost control of the paper to William A. Collier and his associates, fierce critics of the Hadden administration. Under its new management the *Appeal* joined the attack upon the taxing-district president. In the fall of 1889, Hadden's opponents issued a call for a Democratic convention to select a ticket for the upcoming municipal election. Hadden's supporters, on the other hand, opposed the convention and urged a continuation of the nonpartisan process of selecting municipal officers. The *Avalanche* associated the proposed Democratic convention with home rule and attacked its opponents as advocates of Negro domination of the city. "All who are in favor of a white man's government in Memphis want a convention," it claimed. In a tumultuous public convention the Democratic opponents of Hadden nominated a full slate of candidates to run against the incumbent administration in the approaching election. With both major newspapers, as well as the Democratic party machinery, aligned against them, the Hadden forces named an Independent Citizens' ticket, hoping to draw support from Independents, Republicans, and Negroes.[47]

---

[46]Nov. 2–3, 1888.

[47]Memphis *Avalanche*, Feb. 24, Nov. 8, Dec. 2, 11, 25, 1889; Memphis *Appeal*, Jan. 6, 1890.

The regular Democrats presented themselves as a mass movement intent upon the abolition of government by a syndicate and the return of municipal affairs to the people. The nonpartisan character of the taxing-district government rankled the regular Democrats, who assumed partisan politics necessary to preserve white supremacy. Following the decision to place a Democratic ticket in the municipal campaign, the *Avalanche* explained: "A majority of the Democratic voters assembled last night for the purpose of deciding the issue as to whether or not the white people of Memphis should assume absolute control of taxing district affairs." It described the action of the meeting as an effort to "enthrone the white man's party in the Democratic strong hold of Tennessee."[48] The sharp focus on race doubtless obscured other issues—home rule, taxes, public ownership of utilities, and disposition of the streetcar franchise—that divided the two groups vying for control of the municipal government.

There was another important ingredient, however, in the resurgence of local Democratic partisanship and the clear effort to draw the color line in municipal politics. Early in 1889, as a part of a general reform movement aimed at "purifying" the ballot, the legislature had prescribed a secret ballot that struck at illiterates and had passed a law that required somewhat complex registration procedures and the presentation of a certificate in order to vote. These laws represented the culmination of an effort, especially in the larger cities of the state, to reduce the number of Negro voters.[49]

During the campaign prior to the January 1890 municipal election, Hadden actively solicited Negro support and was endorsed by the local Negro press. The Citizens' Reform ticket, which he headed, charged the regular Democrats both with manipulating the registration books in the 1889 Shelby County election and with intimidating Negro voters in the 1888 state and national contests. The regular Democrats, in return, waged an unrelenting white supremacist campaign, claiming that "Pap"

[48]Nov. 7, 9, 1889.
[49]See Ch. VI.

144

Hadden was truckling to Negro voters by encouraging them to register, by promising them a fire company, and by holding forth the prospects of adding more Negroes to the police force if he were victorious. They also condemned the bolters as "pious" Independents who perfidiously used the knowledge they had obtained "while in the confidence of the Democratic party" to raise the issue of fraudulent election practices. Such tactics, warned the Memphis *Avalanche*, simply played into the hands of the enemy by "giving comfort to the white carpet-baggers and the native black Republicans" and, even worse, by furnishing ammunition to the advocates of a federal election bill.[50]

By the final days of the campaign the *Avalanche's* excited appeals to race consciousness had drawn the color line taut in Memphis politics. An election-eve pamphlet written by the Democratic executive committee hurled familiar bloody-shirt accusations at the Citizens' Reform ticket for abetting the ambition of "white carpet-baggers and black Republicans." Independent parties could not be tolerated. "There are but two parties," cried the *Avalanche*. "In the South the Democratic party stands for pure government and for white government; the Republican party represents corruption and ignorance." Race baiting reached a level unprecedented in Memphis when the *Avalanche* announced that the Democratic candidates "do not ask nor expect the votes of the negroes. They ask for white votes and they expect to get them and plenty of them."[51] Given the balanced strength of the two parties in the city throughout most of the eighties, an open rejection of black political support in earlier campaigns would have invited political suicide. With the Negro vote sharply reduced by the new state election laws, however, exploitation of the race issue apparently offered more political gain than at any time since the enfranchisement of blacks.

By the fall of 1889 one of the deterrents to a restoration of home rule—the fear that black political leverage might be enhanced—no longer existed. With the Negro vote under control,

[50]Memphis *Avalanche*, Dec. 2, 25–26, 1889.
[51]*Ibid.*, Dec. 27, 29, 1889.

the financial and sanitation problems of the city largely solved, and an incumbent administration out of favor with segments of the business community, white revulsion for the old ward system dissipated.[52] Home rule and a return to representative government were now heralded as the true American way. Indeed, the taxing-district government, which under Hadden's administration had offered limited recognition to blacks, now carried the opprobrium of undermining business interests and of weakening white supremacy by fostering Negro political ambitions.

The advocates of home rule won a complete, but narrow, victory in the ensuing election. Even in its postelection rejoicing the Memphis *Appeal* retained its race consciousness by boasting that Democrats "had not permitted themselves to go to sleep over the real question, white or black rule." Balloting was light, explained the *Appeal*, because "not many Negroes had registered . . . . Needless to say, the people seemed pleased with the new system of voting."[53] Nevertheless, the narrow margin by which the advocates of home rule had won indicated that the racist campaign tactics employed by the *Avalanche* and the *Appeal* had not convinced all whites that the real question was white supremacy, although the race issue doubtless played a crucial role in the Democratic victory.

In the fight for municipal reform in Nashville and Memphis, Negroes appeared to align themselves with the white leaders whom they thought best represented them, displaying little concern about structural changes in municipal government. To the majority of black voters, there also seemed to be little real appeal in the issues of taxation and public services. Even when these services were expanded by business-reform administrations, they seldom affected the low-tax areas of the cities, especially the Negro communities.[54] Thus, in Memphis the majority of blacks apparently voted to retain the centralized taxing-district government because its president, David P. Hadden, had given them

[52]Ellis, "Business Leadership in Memphis Public Health Reform," 103–4.
[53]Memphis *Appeal* and Memphis *Avalanche*, Jan. 10, 1890.
[54]Ellis, "Memphis Sanitary Revolution, 1880–1890," *Tenn. Hist. Quar.* 23 (Mar. 1964), 66.

patronage and representation in the city government. In Nashville, even though two blacks were elected to serve on the city council in the reform administration in 1883, the majority of black voters seem to have remained loyal to the old city boss, Thomas A. Kercheval. Many black voters in Nashville may have foreseen the effect centralization of the city government would have upon black representation, and, as a well-recognized Republican leader and a shrewd political operator, Kercheval doubtless had bound many blacks to him by personal favors during the long years of his domination in Nashville. The Negro leaders who joined the reform movement in Nashville apparently misjudged both the discontent of many black voters with the Kercheval regime and the willingness of whites to support black candidates even on a reform ticket.

Perhaps the racial implications of municipal reform were more visible in Chattanooga than elsewhere in Tennessee during the eighties. Negroes constituted approximately 40 percent of the city's population at the beginning of the decade. Because their support generally assured political success to the party that received it, Chattanooga Negroes played a conspicuous role in municipal affairs. In combination with northern industrialists who had moved to the city, Union veterans who had remained at the close of the Civil War, and native white Unionists, Chattanooga blacks helped keep the city in Republican hands for most of the period from the Civil War through the eighties.[55]

To a greater extent than in Nashville and Memphis, Negroes in Chattanooga effectively employed their numerical strength to wrest political patronage and nominations for office from the local white Republicans. Occasionally, by joining forces with restive Democrats, they increased their political leverage. In the seventies and early eighties the "intrusion" of Negroes into local political affairs had reached the point, declared Henry M. Wiltze, a contemporary Republican mayor of Chattanooga, where there were Negro fire companies, Negroes on the police force, Negroes

[55]Gilbert E. Govan and James W. Livingood, *The Chattanooga Country*, *1540–1951* (New York: Dutton, 1952), 394, 403–4.

147

on the board of education, a Negro militia company, a Negro city band, black justices of the peace, constables, deputy sheriffs, state legislators and jurors, and a Negro circuit court clerk.[56] Although blacks fell considerably short of exercising the kind of power to which their numbers should have entitled them, their participation in local government alarmed whites in both parties.

Republican dependence on the Negro vote and the shrewd fashion by which black leaders made the most of that dependence eventually provoked Democrats into trying to curb black political power in Chattanooga. What most rankled whites was the growing number of Negroes on the city police force. In the fall of 1880 the Democratic editor of the Chattanooga *Times*, John E. MacGowan, leveled a barrage against the city council for adding two Negroes to the police force. Out of ten men on the force, complained Mac-Gowan, four were Negroes, who had been appointed for "an unworthy and partisan motive." They had been hired by the "Republican party machine," the editor charged, "without the slightest reference to the fitness of them for the place, and with as little regard as possible to the rights and interests of the great body of taxpayers." There were practical disadvantages to the appointment of Negro policemen as well: "The ignorant and depraved white people who raise disturbances on the streets, promote brawls in saloons and generally misbehave themselves, regard the attempt of a colored man to exercise authority over them as abundant excuse for a fresh and violent outbreak." Thus, "a colored policeman, unless he is a very superior man, will shirk his duty, when an inferior white man would act without hesitation." Stripped of its partisan and practical veneer, however, Mac-Gowan's opposition to Negro policemen rested on a more fundamental premise: "We think we know the peculiarities of the negro character tolerably well. . . . . The negro is utterly and irretrievably spoiled by a badge of authority." In short, few

[56]Henry M. Wiltze, "History of Chattanooga" (Unpublished MS, Chattanooga Public Library), 64, 105.

Negroes had "the judgment and discretion required for such a place."[57]

In the municipal election of October 1881, M. J. O'Brien, the Democratic candidate for mayor at the same time vigorously denounced the presence of Negroes on the police force and made an opportunistic bid for black votes by claiming partial responsibility for their appointment. If Negro voters "stood by the Democrats half as faithfully as they did the Republicans," he claimed, "we would show them ten times the attention."[58] Despite his overtures to Negroes, O'Brien lost, although Democrats won three of the five city council seats that were up for election.

William C. Hodge, one of the Republicans who won a seat on the city council, had served on that body since 1878; he would be one of two Negroes elected to the state legislature from Hamilton County during the eighties. The Democrats now held a majority on the city council, but the white Republicans boycotted the council meetings in order to prevent the Democrats from filling all the city offices. The Democrats, who needed Hodge's presence in order to constitute a quorum, secured his cooperation only by appointing four Negroes to the police force. A year later, when Republicans regained control of the city council, they sought to increase their support among black voters by appointing seven Negroes to the city's twelve-man police force.[59] While these appointments of Negro policemen by both parties illustrated the importance of Chattanooga's black vote, they also aroused antagonism among reform-minded whites.

John MacGowan, editor of the Chattanooga *Times*, continued to decry the appointment of black policemen only "because of the political services rendered aldermen by the men selected, and for no sufficient fitness in themselves." His chief objection, as usual, rested on deficiencies he perceived in the Negro's character. He admitted, however, that Republicans had been no more guilty than Democrats of darkening the complexion of the police force.

[57]Chattanooga *Times*, Oct. 28–29, 1880; Oct. 7, 1881.
[58]*Ibid.*, Nov. 17, 1881.
[59]*Ibid.*, Nov. 18, Dec. 20, 23, 29, 1881.

The source of the problem, as he saw it, was the fact that no party could carry Chattanooga "without toadying to the Negro vote." The blame, therefore, lay with both parties: "Any attempt to show that special sins in courting the Negro vote of Chattanooga are chargeable more to one party than the other is an attempt to play at false pretenses."[60]

MacGowan reflected the growing dismay with which many local white citizens viewed the political situation in Chattanooga. In the spring of 1883, concerned whites initiated a drive to repeal the city charter and to turn the management of local affairs over to state officials. A bill introduced in the state legislature called for the reduction of the city to a taxing district. As in Memphis, local authority would reside in a legislative council comprised of members of a fire and police commission and a public works commission, the majority of whom would be appointed by the governor. As a further blow to ward politics, it was proposed that candidates for these posts would have to run as commissioners-at-large.[61]

In a petition read to the legislature upon introduction of the bill, the sponsors of the charter-repeal movement, describing themselves as "three-fourths of the businessmen of Chattanooga," declared that the city government was a failure. Taxes had become an "onerous burden"; streets were in a state of disrepair; and, "the most villainous wrong of all," Negroes sat on the school board. The petitioners embellished their appeal to the legislature with a description of a school visitation made by a Negro school commissioner who allegedly had "impudently" questioned "the young white lady teachers." The books required in the Chattanooga schools were declared to be "of the most ultra radical type, poisoning the minds of the children against the democratic party and its principles and practically advocating social equality with the negro." If the legislature did not grant relief, the petitioners warned, "we will soon have negro teachers over our children." Concluding, they grimly declared, "We have no prejudice against the Negroes, but dislike to be ruled and ruined by them."[62]

[60]*Ibid.*, Dec. 21, 25, 1882.
[61]*Ibid.*, Mar. 17, 1883.   [62]*Ibid.*, Mar. 24, 1883.

Backers of the charter-repeal measure publicly reasoned that its passage was necessary to destroy Republican control of the city, to halt the appointment of Negroes to public office, and to put an end to the government of Chattanooga by "a very radical, unscrupulous class of white men and subservient negroes." Local government had failed, they claimed, because a "majority of the property holders are democrats, but a large majority of the voters are radicals, and of the latter number at least three-fourths are negroes." The number of local offices held by Negroes in the city proved that the white Republicans would "make any concessions to the negroes in order to retain power," the supporters of repeal declared. One outspoken Chattanooga lawyer, championing the bill before the senate committee to which it had been referred, made no pretensions about his views of the ills which the measure would remedy: "If any of you gentlemen will come over to Chattanooga and get on a little bender we will furnish a nigger to arrest you, a nigger to lock you up and a nigger to take care of you after you get into jail."[63]

Influenced by these economic, partisan, and racial arguments, the bill passed the house and appeared to be on the way to clearing the senate when it ran into stubborn opposition. Republicans of both races vigorously opposed the measure; many Democrats recoiled from the crude partisanship of the bill's less sophisticated backers; others opposed it on principle. Halbett B. Case, the Republican senator from Hamilton County denounced the claim of local misgovernment; Edmund D. Patterson, an independent-minded Democratic senator from Hardin County, pointed out that his party would be "belying its history" by centralizing local government in the hands of the state.[64]

After several weeks of editorial silence on the charter fight, the Chattanooga *Times* denounced the bill as "an absurd jumble; contrary to good sense; subversive of the popular will." It took issue with the contention of the bill's sponsors that they represent-

[63]Wiltze, "History of Chattanooga," 130; Weston A. Goodspeed *et al.*, eds., *History of Tennessee, from the Earliest Time to the Present* . . . (Chicago and Nashville: Goodspeed Pub., 1887), 895.
[64]Goodspeed, *History of Tennessee*, 894–95.

151

ed the businessmen of Chattanooga. Part of the reason for the *Times'* outburst against the repeal of the city charter was the editor's conviction that such a move would turn control of Chattanooga over to the Bourbon wing of the Democratic party, directed by Governor Bate and Senator Harris. Rather than see this happen, the *Times* called for the formation of a nonpartisan reform organization similar to that under way in Nashville. The *Times* had followed the Nashville reform movement with interest, observing at one point that "popular suffrage" was the root of the problems confronting city governments. The remedy for this evil, Mac-Gowan now thought, would be a type of commission government supervised by local officials elected by the people.[65]

Led by Mayor Henry Clay Evans, Chattanooga Republicans drew up a petition challenging the contention that Republicans had abused their power by electing blacks to office; they also denied the charges that blacks were taking control of the school board and that black commissioners were examining white teachers. The Republicans proposed a local referendum on the repeal measure.[66]

In light of growing opposition to the radical changes proposed by the repeal measure, its sponsors were forced to moderate their position. Several compromise amendments to the existing charter received the backing of practically all Democrats, including the editor of the *Times*, and, apparently, were even endorsed by a few white Republicans. The amendments approached the problems created by popular suffrage by introducing such city voting restrictions as a comprehensive registration law and a poll tax. Another provision required each city councilman to post a $10,000 bond, thereby making it difficult, if not impossible, for poor candidates to run. Also, the amendments called for a nonpartisan school board and delegated complete authority over the city police to a commission appointed by the governor. Finally, the compromise proposals struck at the power of blacks in two of the city's wards by stipulating that all councilmen would be elected by a

[65]Chattanooga *Times*, Dec. 12, 1882; Jan. 2, Mar. 20, 26, 1883.
[66]*Ibid.*, Mar. 27, 1883.

majority vote of the entire city. A bill embodying these provisions passed the legislature in late March 1883.[67]

The measure met a mixed reception. MacGowan congratulated his fellow citizens upon securing "all the best features of the Memphis 'taxing district' scheme with few or none of its disadvantages." Its greatest asset was that it destroyed "the wretched ward system." Hearing rumors that disgruntled Republicans intended to seek an injunction to prevent implementation of the bill, the Chattanooga editor claimed that many conservative Republicans quietly approved of the reform and that dissatisfaction was confined solely to those "who deplore the prospective decapitation of the negro policemen." On the other hand, the Republican Knoxville *Chronicle* informed its readers that the amended charter of Chattanooga "took a great deal, and was intended to take all, of the power out of the hands of the people." It was "the work of our Bourbon legislature, done at the solicitation of the Bourbon faction in the Democracy of Chattanooga—the fellows who don't like 'nigger voting'." The *Chronicle* proceeded to attack the partisan provisions of the charter: the election of the board of aldermen at-large instead of by wards, the imposition of a $10,000 bond for holding office, the transfer of police control from the local citizens to the governor, and the adoption of a poll tax for voting. All of these were condemned as "expressions of Bourbon malcontent with Republican local self-government by means of free and general suffrage."[68]

Even stronger opposition to the charter amendments came from Chattanooga Negroes. They denounced any Republicans who, under the guise of nonpartisan reform, had accepted the amendments and, in preparation for the first municipal election to be held under the new system, held mass rallies where they vowed to fight the changes in city government to "the bitter end." Black Chattanoogans further demonstrated their resolve by creating an independent political organization, by undertaking a voter-registration

[67]*Ibid.*, Mar. 27–28, 1883.
[68]*Ibid.*, Mar. 31, 1883; Knoxville *Chronicle*, Feb. 21, 29, 1884.

153

drive, and by drawing up a list of candidates to support in the coming municipal election of 1883.[69]

To avoid certain defeat, the Republicans held reconciliation meetings where whites stressed the necessity of party harmony, and blacks vilified both the charter amendment and those of either party who had advocated it. It was time for Negroes "to demand at the hands of their political associates that recognition which belonged to them," insisted one black speaker. "In justice to themselves to their intelligence and their manhood," Negroes could not support for office any man who had participated in the movement to secure the passage of the charter amendment. The time had come, the same speaker proclaimed, "for the colored man to don his armor to battle for his rights as he had fought for his liberty." Styles L. Hutchins, lawyer, editor of a Chattanooga Negro newspaper, and a future state legislator, expressed no doubt but that "the compromise bill was aimed at the negro and nothing else." With this conviction, he continued, "I, as one of that race, repudiate and spurn it [the amended charter], and will use my best endeavors to defeat any man who had anything to do with passing it." Blacks insisted upon the right to name the Republican mayoralty candidate and three of the party's six nominees for city council. Their choice for mayor was a white city councilman who had staunchly opposed the charter revision. To avert the prospect of an independent ticket, white Republican leaders accepted the Negroes' choice for mayor but allowed them to name only two candidates for the council. Some white Republicans, finding these conciliatory acts too high a price for interracial harmony, threatened to bolt; meanwhile, steadily increasing black militancy insured continued intraparty hostility.[70]

MacGowan found the aggressive response of Negroes to the charter amendments "outrageously insulting." He cautioned, "These negroes will do well to pause and reflect on the probable results of their monumental impudence in 'demanding' a full half of the city government." MacGowan doubtless reflected the atti-

[69]Chattanooga *Times*, Sept. 15, 19, 25, Oct. 4, 1883.
[70]*Ibid.*, Sept. 19, Oct. 4, 7, 1883.

tudes of most reform-minded whites when he complained that blacks paid "but an inappreciable sum in the total of city taxes," that the education of their children "cost the real tax payers about ten thousand dollars a year of the school fund," that they furnished "about ninety percent of the pauperism and petty criminals," and, finally, that they "fill the jails." Notwithstanding his previous claims that the charter amendment had not been aimed at black voters, MacGowan warned that, if "a mob of ignorant negroes" gained control of the city, "the white citizens will, as one man, ask the next legislature for laws that will place the negro in the rear and keep him there." As the campaign progressed, the editor of the *Times* increasingly demonstrated the way racial fears often encroached upon the business interests of New South ideologues and urban reformers. The persistent black efforts to gain representation in the city government would force businessmen to take extreme measures, he predicted: "We say plainly that if the city must be ruled through negroes manipulated and used for the purposes of the worst demagogy, then businessmen and taxpayers generally, regardless of party belongings, will be found to accept any respectable and responsible system of government." In brief, stated the *Times*, the complete repeal of the city charter "could not so injure the credit and good name of Chattanooga as to have it go abroad that our Mayor and Aldermen are the puppets of ignorant, unscrupulous negroes, led and aided by bad white men."[71]

In the city election Democrats captured the mayor's office, but Republicans gained a majority of the city council seats; William C. Hodge, a longtime black councilman, was reelected. The campaign of racial fear waged by the *Times* apparently had little effect, and many white Republicans remained loyal to their party. When the Republicans again retained a majority of the city council in the election of 1884, many Democrats began looking about for more effective tools with which the Republicans and Negroes might be suppressed; the registration law and the election of councilmen-at-large had proved inadequate.[72]

[71]*Ibid.*, Sept. 20, Oct. 2, 1883.
[72]*Ibid.*, Sept. 26, Oct. 4, 10, 1883.

The continued success of Chattanooga Republicans fostered a revival of the movement to revoke the city's charter. With the local electoral machinery in Republican hands, Chattanooga Negroes displayed as great a propensity for registering to vote as did the whites. In 1884, for example, approximately two-thirds of the black voters registered, about the same percentage as that of registered white voters. According to local newspaper accounts, both parties engaged in fraudulent registration practices by openly paying the poll tax of prospective voters and by employing the electoral machinery to their advantage in the wards which they dominated. Another inducement to reopen the charter fight came from the steady increase in the city's Negro population. By the end of the fiscal year in 1884 Chattanooga contained 14,073 whites and 9,023 blacks; the increase during the previous twelve months had been 1,349 blacks and 1,084 whites. "If that proportion of race increase keeps up," warned the *Times*, "it will not be many years before a few white vagabonds with the solid negro element at their backs, will make the town an uncomfortable and unprofitable place of residence for white men."[73]

Prodded by these events, a group described as "the leading citizens of Chattanooga" sponsored a plan calling for radical revision of the city charter. They proposed to take virtually all power away from the mayor and city council, placing it in the hands of commissioners appointed by the governor. A bill to this effect passed the house of representatives and was introduced in the senate in February 1885. The bill's sponsors in the senate openly defended it on the grounds that it would preserve white supremacy in Chattanooga.[74]

MacGowan probably expressed the views of many white Chattanoogans regarding the renewed effort to repeal the city's charter. Although he believed Negroes were "entirely unfit to rule successfully a community of their own race or any other," he expressed strong reservations about investing the Bourbon state administration with the power to select Chattanooga officials. To

[73]*Ibid.*, Aug. 3, Oct. 4, 16, 1884.
[74]*Ibid.*, Dec. 20, 30, 1884; Feb. 14, 18, 1885.

the *Times*, repeal of the charter posed as great a danger as did the ills its sponsors sought to cure. The editor refused to accept the reasoning that, "if we dread, deprecate and would ward off bummer rule based on the votes of ignorant black men, . . . as an alternative we must be willing to accept the bosship of Bourbon bunglers of the Bate breed." MacGowan also rejected the extreme step of disfranchisement, for he professed to hope that, as Negroes acquired property and education, they would begin to divide politically "along the line which separates intelligence from ignorance." To give intelligent and thrifty black citizens a chance to act "with the patriotic, non-political white masses in municipal affairs, we would treat them with perfect justice, consideration and kindness," the editor wrote.

The sharp division in the Democratic party between the New South wing and the Bourbon faction doubtless tempered the racial attitude of the *Times* by making it impolitic to alienate all blacks. Democratic divisiveness also affected the newspaper's position on the revocation of the city charter as a means of undermining the Negroes' political influence. The *Times*, however, also balked at this revocation on the basis both of its time-honored belief in local government and of its sense of responsibility for solving the racial problem in a paternalistic fashion. In the 1885 charter fight, therefore, the newspaper warned its readers that the honor of southern Democrats was committed to the fate of six million Negroes: "They cultivate and harvest the cotton and food crops; they build and largely operate our railroads, furnaces, mills and factories; they furnish the labor which produces 90 per cent of the raw materials raised in the section. The presence of the race is a necessity to the South." Consequently, "conservative and thoughtful Democrats must see to it that the negro is made to realize his importance as a citizen; the dignity and honor of citizenship must be impressed on him by his real friends."[75]

Chattanooga Republicans sent a petition to the state legislature opposing the revocation of the city charter, and, under the steady pressure of the *Times* and other moderating elements in Chatta-

[75]*Ibid.*, Feb. 19, 1885.

nooga, the repeal bill was so amended as to place the appointive powers in the hands of the mayor rather than the governor. Even in this form it could not pass the legislature without a disabling clause which stipulated that before becoming effective, it would have to be approved by the voters of Chattanooga. In light of certain defeat, the bill's sponsors did not dare bring it to a vote; the city charter remained intact until 1889, when it was subjected to a new assault.[76]

At that time, with the legislature contemplating soon-to-be-passed statewide voting restrictions that included a secret ballot designed to eliminate illiterate voters, a more stringent registration system, and a poll tax, the Chattanooga charter was considered again. A Democratic senator from Hamilton County secured passage of a bill which redistricted Chattanooga in such a way that Democratic control of the city government would be assured. Under the provisions of the new law, city councilmen once again would be elected from their respective wards. The wards were gerrymandered, however, to give Democrats control of five, leaving the Republicans with only three. The most important racial effect of the redistricting bill was to confine blacks to the two wards where they clearly held majorities.[77] By attempting to restrict the Republicans to three wards, Democrats apparently hoped to undermine the political leverage blacks had traditionally exerted in local politics.

In defense of the measure, Senator John C. Myers, who had already introduced a strict state voter-registration law, declared, "The legislature has taken charge of Memphis and congress has taken charge of Washington because the illiterate negroes [have] become too numerous." He complained that in Chattanooga Republicans had built two schoolhouses for Negroes while white children went to school in log houses. "The republicans want to put the Negroes on top," he complained, "so they can use them for political purposes."[78]

[76]*Ibid.*, Feb. 21, 26, Apr. 5, Nov. 2, 1885.

[77]*Ibid.*, Oct. 6, 1889.

[78]*Ibid.*, Feb. 23, 1889. Myers' statement about Washington, D. C., referred to the congressional action of 1878 which set up a presidentially appointed commis-

Although the city redistricting bill, in conjunction with the new state secret-ballot law and voter-registration system, did not immediately end all Republican or Negro political victories in Chattanooga, the laws did mark the beginning of a rapid transition to Democratic rule. After wielding local political power for nearly a quarter of a century, Republicans were reduced to a minority party. From 1890 until the mid-twentieth century, they elected their candidates for mayor only twice, in 1899 and in 1915.[79]

The municipal reform movements in Tennessee during the 1880s defy simple categorization. Business-minded elements spearheaded the drive for reform in Memphis in 1879, in Nashville in 1883, and in Chattanooga in 1883 and 1885. Their efforts stemmed from partisan and racial motives as well as from a desire to reduce the rising taxes that mainly affected white propertyowners, thus creating an atmosphere favorable to business. Through centralization of city government and placement of responsibility in the hands of appointive officials, they reduced the power of lower-class voters in the cities; Negroes constituted the largest single easily identifiable group of these voters. The reformers assumed that fiscal responsibility, efficient government, and a sympathetic climate for business would flow naturally from an effective reduction in the influence of the black vote. The particular means devised to accomplish these goals depended upon several factors, of which one of the most important was the internal division in the Democratic party.

In Nashville and Chattanooga, leaders of the New South wing of the Democratic party led the drive for municipal reform. They centralized local government and eliminated the ward system but stopped short of complete revocation of their charters; they were unwilling to relinquish the prerogatives of local government by

sion form of government for the nation's capital. The three-man commission, in turn, appointed all local administrators. White taxpayers, who had blamed the District's financial problems generally upon black suffrage, applauded the abandonment of local self-government as a much-needed change which would introduce efficient and economical, although authoritarian, government. See Constance McLaughlin Green, *The Secret City: A History of Race Relations in the Nation's Capital* (Princeton: Princeton Univ. Press, 1967), 111–17.

[79]Govan and Livingood, *Chattanooga Country*, 403.

placing the power to appoint city offices in the hands of the Bourbon Democrat who then occupied the governor's office. In 1889, however, with Robert L. Taylor, who was sympathetic to the New South wing of the party and friendly to David P. Hadden, as governor, Bourbon elements in Memphis employed racist arguments to defeat Hadden and to regain home rule. At the same time, Chattanooga Bourbons secured a revised charter from a Bourbon-controlled legislature which decentralized the city government and reestablished a ward system, although the ward boundaries were drastically gerrymandered by the legislature to insure Democratic supremacy and reduce the political power of blacks.

Ultimately, the reform movements undermined the political leverage of black voters in all three urban areas and encouraged elitist sentiments that rejected continued black participation in the political process. The increasing black populations of these cities, the heightened visibility of Negroes in local government—especially in such crucial areas as the police force—and the rising political militancy on the part of Negro leaders proved to be the most dynamic features of race relations in urban politics. Whites feared that the costs of an expansion of municipal services for blacks in the form of better school, fire, police, and sanitation facilities would largely fall on white propertyowners. The reform thrust against black participation in local government, however, represented not only a conflict of economic interests between white propertyowners and blacks but also a conflict of perceptions. For the most part, the urban reform leaders in Nashville, Memphis, and Chattanooga hoped to build a favorable climate for business expansion and for security of private property; they perceived Negroes to be a monolithic threat to law and order, decency, and government by the educated and propertied. Urban reform combined with other developments to create a steadily deteriorating racial atmosphere in Tennessee at the end of the 1880s.

V

Separation Without Equality

White supremacy was the dominant characteristic of race relations in Tennessee throughout the 1880s. In spite of this fact, the decade saw important changes occur in the everyday pattern of interracial contacts; white racial attitudes assumed a protean character, forming in response to one or more of the following influences: demographic changes, the North-South dialogue, the participation of blacks in politics, Negro protests, or political contests upon which the race issue intruded. Indeed, whites did not reach a consensus about the means of maintaining their supremacy over blacks until the end of the decade.

The philosophy of white supremacy ranged across a broad spectrum of ideas.[1] Some of its advocates were negrophobes who generally professed hatred for all Negroes throughout the decade, changing only in that they became more intense and vocal as the decade advanced. Because of their essentially static racial policies, they seem to have played a peripheral role in the transitional nature of race relations during these years. Although they persistently advocated a policy of racial proscription, they were generally restrained by the threat of federal interference, the intra-party factionalism among Democrats, and the influence of southern conservatives of a paternalistic persuasion.

Most white leaders of public opinion in Tennessee during the eighties, especially newspaper editors and politicians, articulated

[1]A succinct analysis of the philosophy of white supremacy may be found in Guion Griffis Johnson, "The Ideology of White Supremacy, 1876–1910," *Essays in Southern History*, ed. Fletcher M. Green (Chapel Hill: Univ. of North Carolina Press, 1949), 124–56.

a racial philosophy of paternalism.[2] Bourbon and New South leaders shared essentially the same conservative racial philosophy, since both generally conceded that Negroes should be accorded their civil rights—the right to vote, to sit on juries, to hold office, and the right to protection of their life and property. A great many also held forth the promise that with the accumulation of property and education Negroes would progress; therefore, whites had the responsibility to teach and to lead. History, they contended, demonstrated that only under enlightened white guidance had Negroes advanced; first, under the tutelage of slavery, African "barbarism" had been reduced; then after the "hot-house" growth of radical reconstruction proved fruitless, Negroes once again had progressed under the direction of white Southerners who knew them best.[3]

For many whites the philosophy of racial paternalism was reinforced by concepts of Christian duty. Speaking before the annual assembly of the Methodist Episcopal Church, South at Monteagle, Tennessee, in the fall of 1883, Atticus G. Haygood, later a bishop in the church, eloquently expounded the doctrine that whites had a Christian duty to protect, uplift, and care for the less fortunate race.[4] Haygood assumed that such a course was not

[2]The analysis here is based on an acceptance of Woodward's view that a distinctive class of southern paternalists played a critical role in shaping white southern opinion on the race issue, and that there was a change in their racial attitudes during the late 1800s. The author departs, however, from Woodward's theory that the conservative-agrarian conflict was the primary cause of that change. According to him, as dissident agrarians attacked the moral and political authority of conservative paternalists, the latter abandoned their traditional concept of *noblesse oblige* toward blacks, and racial fears which increasingly united white Democrats were exploited to maintain conservative power. See Woodward, *Strange Career of Jim Crow*, 44, 47–59, 74–82. This view is also developed in Woodward, *Origins of the New South*, 79, 210–12, 312–49.

[3]See Johnson, "Southern Paternalism toward Negroes after Emancipation," 483–509, for the basic philosophy of paternalism. Although this analysis differs from Johnson's categorization of paternalistic ideas, the characteristics here fall somewhere between "benevolent paternalism" and "separate but equal" on Johnson's scale.

[4]For a brief critical analysis of Haygood's racial philosophy see Fredrickson, *Black Image in the White Mind*, 204–5, 207–8. See also Paul M. Gaston, *The New South Creed: A Study in Southern Mythmaking* (New York: Knopf, 1970), 125, 128–29, 134, 143–46.

only the Christian duty of southern whites, but that it represented the most practical solution to the race problem as well. His address set off a heated exchange in the *Christian Advocate,* a journal published in Nashville by the Methodist Episcopal Church, South. After a number of critics had accused Haygood of negrophilia, D. C. Kelly, a prominent Methodist minister in Nashville, defended him and his views on Christian education for Negroes. "No man treads Southern soil," wrote Kelly, "whose heart is truer to the interests of the white men of the South." The Nashville minister heartily agreed that the interests of blacks and whites in the South lay along the same "path of Christian education."[5]

To most whites, the past enslavement of blacks and their lack of education, property, and political experience rationalized the need for a policy of white paternalistic guidance. Such a policy offered progress for blacks but at a pace and in a direction dictated by whites. John E. MacGowan, the New South-oriented editor of the Chattanooga *Times,* denounced the "drooling folly of sympathetic imbeciles" who never hinted at defects in the Negro. At the same time, he labeled "all talk of a reactionary nature" as "mere incendiarism," which "provokes retorts in kind and tends to drive the negro into enmity and finally to desperation." To MacGowan, and doubtless to many other New South enthusiasts, there was only one path that offered promise: "We must go forward with the experiment of negro civilization, education, elevation." Since whites bore the responsibility for the Negroes' presence in the South, "common fairness, to say nothing of our superiority and the demands of morality and religion, requires that we shall care for their education and elevation to a plane of intelligence and conscience that will make them safe and useful citizens."[6]

To ameliorate racial tensions in the New South, southern white paternalists often invoked the image of the Old South.[7] "The duty of the white people of the South toward the negroes is plain," declared the editor of the Memphis *Appeal,* John M. Keating, an

[5]Oct. 20, 1883.
[6]Aug. 2, 1885; June 14, 1889.
[7]See Fredrickson, *Black Image in the White Mind,* 206–7.

163

ardent States' Rights Democrat who had been aligned with the Bate-Harris Bourbon machine in the mid-eighties. Keating took an interest in the Negroes' welfare throughout the decade, becoming a prominent champion of Negro uplift through education. He commended Negroes for the progress they had made in that respect, claimed that they had played an integral role in the economic prosperity of the South, and, as late as 1889, defended their right to vote. "They must be educated and Christianized, and so be fitted for the duties of life, and we must, in the spirit of noblesse oblige, bear with them, because of what they were in the past to our forefathers and what our forefathers were to them."[8]

Many conservative white paternalists, conscious, however vaguely, of class as much as race, saw themselves as representatives of a class that had a responsibility to use its power and influence to uphold a traditional set of values. Apparently they believed that the values they judged to be important socioeconomic and behavorial attributes of upper-class status—refinement and propriety in dress, speech, and mannerisms—needed reinforcement. One of the best ways to propagate the values they cherished was to reward those individuals who exemplified them in their behavior, and they conceded that some Negroes had acquired many of the values attributed to the upper-classes. Therefore, in response to the early efforts of Negroes to gain impartial access to public facilities and the determination of poorer whites to invoke the privileges of "Herrenvolk democracy" in making a racial demarcation, white conservatives sometimes advocated class rather than race as the proper basis for drawing distinctions in the use of public facilities.[9]

[8]June 11, 1889.

[9]Woodward briefly discusses the class connotations in the conservative doctrine of paternalism in *Strange Career of Jim Crow*, 49–51. For a more precise definition of this multidimensional use of the term "class," see Talcott Parsons, ed., *Essays in Sociological Theory* (rev. ed.; Glencoe, Ill.: Free Press, 1949), 69–88; see also Kingsley Davis and Wilbert E. Moore, "Some Principles of Stratification: A Critical Analysis," in *Class, Status, and Power: Social Stratification in Comparative Perspective*, ed. Reinhard Bendix and Seymour Martin Lipset (2d ed.; New York: Free Press, 1966), 47–53. The sociological term "Herrenvolk democracies" describes a biracial society in which one race tyran-

Obviously, however, whatever conservative standards of class an individual Negro might acquire, the categorization of "Negro" itself still carried a connotation of social opprobrium. Consequently, when whites sometimes stressed class differences rather than race distinctions, it did not necessarily mean that the two concepts were separated in their minds, but only that one or the other categorization was emphasized according to the nature of the situation. Apparently, they were simply saying that blacks who met their standards of deportment should not be ostracized from whites in the use of public facilities. Nevertheless, as the decade wore on, most white paternalists came to prefer separate but equal facilities. In this way they were able to rationalize the conflicts between class and caste by theoretically constructing a dual society that would allow for class distinctions within each group. This transition in paternalistic philosophy held the utmost significance in the development of segregationist ideas during the decade.[10]

During the early eighties whites also vacillated between a laissez-faire attitude toward race relations—one holding that

---

nizes another, yet preserves a democratic ideology simply by denying the subordinate race is fully human; therefore, "the people" retain both their egalitarian ideals and "the profitable forms of discrimination" against those defined as subhumans without apparent contradiction. See Pierre L. van den Berghe, *Race and Racism: A Comparative Perspective* (New York: Wiley, 1967), 17–18.

[10]The conceptual analysis in this chapter is based in part upon a typology of race relations formulated by van den Berghe in *Race and Racism* and upon a brief but thought-provoking critique of his formulation in Woodward, *American Counterpoint*, 242–60. Van den Berghe formulates two distinct types of race relations—"paternalistic" and "competitive." The former relies on social and economic (class) distances to define status; the latter depends on physical separation. According to van den Berghe, segregation is employed by the dominant race to maintain its status as the economic and social gap between it and the subordinate race narrows. The evolution of paternalistic attitudes in Tennessee in the 1880s, however, suggests that paternalism was embedded in both systems. In short, it seems segregation was employed by the white paternalists to provide a legal definition of role and status sufficient to formalize social distance; thus, though modified, the traits of paternalism could be perpetuated. Although van den Berghe sees industrialization as the dynamic force in changing race relations, the evidence in Tennessee points to other factors—politics, demographic changes, and black militancy—as agents of change.

segregation in public facilities was purely a private matter to be governed by prevailing white sentiment or the preferences of individual proprietors—and the belief that interracial use of public facilities should be settled by government regulation. By the end of the decade, for reasons this chapter will attempt to show, governmental regulation had emerged as the most popular solution.

The white paternalist sentiment at the beginning of the eighties, with its class connotations, was forcefully expressed by Judge David M. Key. Former Postmaster General Key had played a crucial role in the Compromise of 1877 by serving as the southern representative in President Hayes' Cabinet. During the eighties, as a self-styled Independent Democrat, he was a United States district judge in Tennessee.[11]

In an 1885 speech before the Tennessee Bar Association Key expounded the duties of paternalists, insisted that the law could not tolerate a racial basis of segregation that assigned all Negroes to inferior facilities, and expressed his own willingness to mingle with blacks in public facilities provided they met his standards of deportment. After romanticizing the Negroes' loyalty to their masters during the Civil War, he argued that southern whites had a "higher obligation" than mere gratitude to protect "the liberties of the weak against the encroachments and oppression of the powerful." It was not "one's duty to sit next to a colored person on the cars or at the table," but Key said that he "should prefer to sit by a genteel well bred Negro than by a dirty, filthy, disgusting white man."

Although he did not advocate it, Key did accept the creation of separate but equal facilities for blacks as a solution to what he judged to be the popular racial antipathies of lower-class whites. To him, however, the system of making distinctions in public facilities on the basis of color had "a ludicrous aspect." Blacks of property and social standing might be denied access to a first-class car on a train, but

> as long as a colored passenger occupies a servile position, he may ride anywhere. . . . Let a woman black as midnight be the nurse of a

[11]David Abshire, *The South Rejects a Prophet: The Life of Senator David M. Key, 1824–1900* (New York: Praeger, 1967), *passim*.

white child, or a man equally as dark be the servant of a white man [and] there is never the slightest objection to their having seats in the ladies car or any other. All the scents of Africa or from it are inoffensive; but let these same two persons by saving the wages earned in such service become the owners of property and undertake to travel upon their own business, and they will in many lines be turned out of the ladies car into the smoker as repulsive to those aboard the better car. Now where is the excuse for the difference in treatment? My observation has led me to conclude that those who are most horrified by the presence of the Negro and find so much that is offensive in him have very often least to boast of in the way of birth, renown, or achievement. For the life of me, I cannot see what injury a neatly dressed well behaved colored person does me by riding in the same car. And should he sit in some corner of the same dining room away from my table I cannot see why my appetite or self respect should suffer by it.

Key informed the lawyers who comprised his audience that if separate facilities were required, the law should not tolerate inequality in their character. "How those who are bound by solemn obligations to execute the laws faithfully and impartially can overlook or excuse their omissions in this respect is a matter of conscience I cannot undertake to determine." He viewed "discriminations unjustly made on the part of public common carriers" as the "detestation of the law," and if they were "tolerated anywhere," they presented dangers "to the public everywhere."[12]

A year before, in his capacity as a federal district judge in Tennessee, Key had more clearly implied that segregation on the basis of race, rather than on that of class values reflected the racial fears of lower-class whites. Upholding the canons of upper-class gentility, Key had informed a white jury in a civil rights case that he had found "those who are most sensitive as to contact with colored people, and whose nerves are most shocked by their presence, have little to be proud of in the way of birth, lineage, or achievement." In his subsequent ruling in the case Key declared

[12]David M. Key, "The Legal and Political Status of the Negro," *Tennessee Bar Association Proceedings* (Nashville, 1885), 188–95.

167

that the assignment of Negroes to separate facilities on railroads was legal, but he insisted that those "of genteel appearance, good repute, and good behavior," who had paid for first-class passage, could not be assigned to "inferior quarters in a smoking car."[13]

During the eighties the paternalistic philosophy exemplified by Key's pronouncements underwent a significant change as its adherents grappled with the tough problem of putting it into practice. The disposition of some white paternalists to emphasize class criteria as the basis for differentiation in public accommodations surfaced during a debate in the summer of 1885 over racial discrimination on Tennessee railroads. The debate was provoked when the Nashville *American* launched an attack on the discriminatory racial policies of the railroads in Tennessee, charging that Negroes were "shoved into filthy smoking cars, where decent colored women and their children are strangled by tobacco smoke and insulted by white loafers." In an effort to solicit Negro votes to revive the defunct railroad commission, the *American* championed the enforcement of the equal-accommodations law by means of a regulatory commission.[14]

In response to the *American*'s charge, New South paternalists at first adhered to a class standard. Editor John E. MacGowan maintained that "well dressed and behaved colored women" were admitted to the "ladies' car" on a majority of Tennessee railroads. At the same time he conceded that there was "too much of the shoving of colored people who pay full fare into cars hardly fit for hogs and cattle." The editor's faith in the ineluctable triumph of class, however, led him to contend that when "the colored man and woman make themselves fit to occupy refined quarters their rights are bound to be recognized." In the meantime, he suggested that railroads in the state should reduce their fares for "those required to ride in second or third class cars." Otherwise, he saw "no especial call for meddling in the matter."[15]

[13]Murphy v. Western & A.R.R. and others, 23 *Federal Reporter* 637–41 (1885).

[14]Nashville *American*, July 30, 1885, quoted in Chattanooga *Times*, Aug. 1, 1885.

[15]*Ibid.*

The Memphis *Avalanche* also challenged the *American*'s claim that discrimination against Negroes was universal on the railroads by declaring that "better" Negroes could ride in first-class cars on most of the railroads of the state. "Any respectable negro can and does ride unmolested in a first-class car," the editor asserted. In succeeding editorials the *Avalanche* joined its cross-state New South ally, the Chattanooga *Times,* in proposing that the railroads should resolve the problem by adopting two rates of fare to correspond with the class of accommodations provided. In any case, abstract philosophies and doctrines would have to give way to practical considerations, for any policy that flew in the face of public sentiment "would be a dead letter," stated the *Avalanche.* The Memphis newspaper viewed the *American*'s editorial campaign as "the most dangerous tampering with the race question we have had in Tennessee."[16]

As the *American* persisted in its editorial war against the discriminatory policies of railroads, it came under increasing fire from fellow Democrats who claimed that continued agitation of the issue would destroy racial harmony by introducing social equality. In response, the *American* made clear that its goal was separate but equal facilities.[17] This goal represented the most practical resolution of the inherent contradiction in the conservative paternalists' philosophy—their refusal to apply class criteria consistently when questions of race relations were involved. The separate but equal doctrine would allow white paternalists to retain their concern for class values and status without fear of being labeled advocates of social equality with blacks. It would free paternalists from the dilemma of antagonizing lower-class whites by recognizing upper-class values in blacks; at the same time it would allow conservatives to continue honoring the values which they attributed to class.

The emergence of the separate but equal doctrine also represented a desire on the part of white paternalists to regulate race relations through the adoption of a rule of law. Such a rule of law

[16]July 26, 28, Aug. 12, 1885.
[17]Nashville *American*, July 26, 1885.

169

would protect the "better" blacks from the crude racial prejudices of lower-class whites; it would also shield the "better" whites from the lower-class crudeness of most Negroes; and it would establish a procedure for interracial utilization of public facilities which would insure peace and harmony.[18]

As agitation of the railroad issue continued, the editor of the Memphis *Avalanche* moved toward a rigid separate but equal position. Continued failure to enforce the color line, he reasoned, would bring the better class of Negroes into conflict with the worst class of whites as they intermingled in second-class accommodations. Since this would inevitably result in violence and turmoil, separate but equal legislation should be enforced to preserve order. "The solution of the question for the present," the editor declared, "is to give to the negro, when he pays full fare, separate and equal accommodations. Any other way of meeting the question will be illusory and deceive those who attempt it."[19]

The evolution of white paternalistic thinking in the face of conflicts between class and race can also be seen in the editorial comments of John E. MacGowan. A "general sentiment" existed among "intelligent and refined" white Southerners, MacGowan commented in December 1888, "that the vulgar domineering of certain sorts of white people over the weaker race needs checking." He viewed with contempt "the white man who maltreats a decent colored man merely to exploit his superiority or display his brutal prejudices." When Negroes paid full fare, they were "entitled to its equivalent in the form of a seat as comfortable and surroundings as respectable as any other holding the same grade of ticket." If the Negro wanted recognition of his rights, stated MacGowan, all he needed to do was to "deserve it by his manners and personal condition." MacGowan's inclination to stress class distinctions in the use of public facilities, however, gave way during the eighties to a simple race standard. "The disagreeable conduct and filth of the great majority" of Negroes furnished sufficient excuse "to carriers on land [and] water, hotel keepers

[18]Chattanooga *Times*, Dec. 28, 1888.
[19]July 26, 1885.

and managers of public places, such as theaters, for proscribing them all," he eventually concluded. Indeed, by May 1889, Mac-Gowan was arguing that racial differences made "the proscription of nearly all negroes necessary, whatever we may think of the question of abstract right involved."[20]

MacGowan's shift to a policy of racial segregation represented a response to local political and social conditions. During the intra-party battle over the railroad commission, his perception of racial differences had overshadowed his concept of class as a basis for discrimination in the use of public facilities. Doubtless he realized the political danger of publicly applying class standards to whites as well as blacks. Also, the rising black population of Chattanooga probably influenced his transition to a racial standard for segregation. Moreover, the stubborn resistance of Chattanooga blacks to proposals for municipal reform angered him, as did the periodic threat of federal interference in southern race relations. "The public sentiment of the South would soon secure absolute justice and fair play for the negro were it not impeded and baffled by Northern crankery and demagogy, and negro stupidity and insolence," he declared in the spring of 1889.[21] Another impetus behind MacGowan's shift to a racial segregationist stance was provided by an incident that occurred in Chattanooga involving the efforts of local boosters to build a university in their city.

White citizens in Chattanooga had subscribed $15,000 to help finance a university the northern Methodist Episcopal Church proposed to locate in the city. Since 1880 the northern Methodists had moved to broaden their educational work among southern whites. Eager to secure the university, local white citizens had assumed that it, like Little Rock University which the Methodists had formed in 1882, would be for the exclusive use of whites. Moreover, in May 1884, the general conference of the church adopted an ambiguous resolution which stated that the administration of the schools established by the church should be left to "the choice and administration of those on the ground and more

[20]Chattanooga *Times*, Dec. 28, 1888; May 20, 1889.
[21]*Ibid.*, May 26, 1889.

immediately concerned." White Chattanoogans interpreted this statement as permission to exercise local option concerning segregation, although at the same general conference the national officials of the church had reaffirmed their opposition to the exclusion of any students from their church-supported educational institutions because of race. Regardless of the pronouncements of national church officials, local boosters of the proposed university—most of whom were members of the northern Methodist church—insisted that the school would be exclusively white, pragmatically concluding that the antidiscrimination resolutions adopted by the national church conference represented mere "abstractions . . . not intended to have a practical application." Nevertheless, when the university officially opened in the fall of 1886, several black students applied for admission, but the local board of trustees refused to admit them. The "abstract" principles of the church would be tested against the resolve of white Chattanoogans. "The rights and wrongs of the matter, constantly thrust into the discussion by sentimental people" were beside the point, declared MacGowan in a *Times* editorial. The discussion of abstractions would not alter the stubborn fact that in light of local sentiment, "the school must be all one thing or all the other—white or black." The impasse between national church officials and local white sentiment in Chattanooga was resolved in favor of the latter. The Negroes refused admission in 1886 were not enrolled and, amid a campaign led by the editor of the *Times* against the "spirit of perverse defiance" manifested by the prospective Negro students, no blacks applied for admission the following fall.[22]

In the face of the threatened breach of the color line at the University of Chattanooga, MacGowan had responded with a

[22]*Ibid.*, Apr. 12, 1883; May 28–30, 1884; Oct. 20, 1886; Mar. 4, Sept. 15, 23, Oct. 22, 1887; Memphis *Appeal*, Oct. 9, 1883; New York *Times*, Mar. 13, 1887. See also Gilbert E. Govan and James W. Livingood, *The University of Chattanooga: Sixty Years* (Chattanooga: Univ. of Chattanooga Press, 1947), 35–42. Govan and Livingood view the black attempt to enroll in the University of Chattanooga as a spurious issue raised by boosters of a rival northern Methodist university, Grant Memorial, in Athens, Tenn., in order to discredit the Chattanooga school. See *University of Chattanooga*, 46–47.

racial standard for segregation without allowances for class distinctions. He warned Negroes that continued "pushing" would bring them "sorrow and suffering beside which slavery was unalloyed bliss and heavenly happiness." He then proceeded to condemn "any scheme devised for mixing the races in schools, churches, or generally in social, religious and educational affairs" as "morally bad and physically unhealthy for the whites, and of no benefit to the blacks, but the reverse." Given "the present stage of negro development," he doubted that "such mixing will ever do, except as a theme for silly people to harp upon."[23]

As the philosophy of white paternalism gravitated toward the separate but equal principle in the state during the eighties, the character of interracial contact gradually became less fluid; by the end of the decade *de facto*, if not legal, racial segregation became a fixture of society. This is neither to suggest that all the varied customs of racial discrimination that came to be associated with the Jim Crow system at its height appeared first during the eighties, nor that most of the laws that eventually gave legal shape to the system had come into existence by the end of the decade. The evidence does suggest, however, that in Tennessee the eighties represented a transitional period during which the attitudes that lay behind the Jim Crow system were more clearly defined than they had been since the Civil War. Although it is impossible to assign any specific time to the emergence of a thoroughgoing system of discrimination based on race, several individual incidents provide some idea of what behavior was accepted as normal and what seemed extraordinary.

Some of the interracial taboos in the eighties had long been operative. Interracial dining and sex fell into this category. A black newspaper editor visiting Nashville in 1881 closely scrutinized the racial customs at Fisk University before conceding that they met with his approval: "At dinner there was no division on the color line, and this is everywhere, I believe, the crucial test." If, indeed, it represented the crucial test, then elsewhere across the state there could be little doubt about the disposition of whites toward

[23]Chattanooga *Times*, May 19, 1884; Sept. 28, 1886.

173

racial segregation. The existence of a broad policy of racial discrimination in public restaurants can easily be documented by the end of the eighties. Writing from Nashville in the summer of 1890, M. W. Caldwell, a local black correspondent to the New York *Age,* described the racial discrimination he experienced in the Tennessee capital: "I have visited several nice looking restaurants where a decent man or woman would enjoy taking a meal," but "I was simply insulted at every place." Caldwell also met the same treatment at the "large number of Soda-water fountains" where he attempted to obtain service.[24]

During a visit to Nashville in December 1889, southern novelist and civil rights advocate George W. Cable ran afoul of interracial social taboos by dining in the home of James C. Napier, a prominent black leader. Upon hearing of this incident Edward Ward Carmack, editor of the Nashville *American,* described it as an insult to the city of Nashville and a flagrant assertion of social equality. Carmack proceeded to blast Cable as a renegade who had fattened his purse with Yankee money by slandering the South. Deeply stung by this attack, and others, the southern novelist fired a reply to his accuser: "I have never in so much as a sentence, whether spoken or written, advocated any private social comingling [*sic*] of the two races. I heartily deprecate any rash experiments in that direction." Cable added that he thought the whole matter "a question of the individual conscience." Following a reception at the Napiers' home, he explained, his host and hostess "were in a dilemma between asking a white man to sit at their board and sending him away supperless," and he had invited himself to dine with the Napiers in order to remedy their discomfort. He stoutly defended his behavior, bidding any friendships such actions cost him "a regretful good-by."[25] Cable's explanation of this incident left much to be desired in the view of some blacks. The young editor of the Fisk *Herald* found it to be "astounding"

[24]Noble L. Prentis, *Southern Letters* (Topeka: George W. Martin, 1881), 42; New York *Age,* July 5, 1890.

[25]Nashville *American,* Dec. 6, 22, 31, 1889; Memphis *Appeal,* Jan. 15, 1890. See also Arlin Turner, *George W. Cable: A Biography* (Durham: Duke Univ. Press, 1956), 268–70.

that Cable thought the refined and dignified Napiers would be in a "dilemma" over such a matter. If there were any embarrassment, he added, "it must certainly have been on Mr. Cable's part."[26]

Unlike proscription of interracial dining by social custom, interracial sex was restricted by law. Interracial marriages were rigidly prohibited in Tennessee throughout the eighties, although the antimiscegenation statute forbidding extramarital liaisons was usually invoked only in cases involving black men and white women. In light of this practice, a group of Memphis Negroes formed an organization in 1889 which proposed to ask for grand jury indictments against more than fifty Memphis white men who allegedly had black mistresses.[27]

During the eighties available evidence suggests that, although emerging in an erratic fashion, segregation became more overt statewide in hotels, theaters, and public parks. A black man's success in obtaining lodging at a white hotel in Knoxville in 1888 apparently represented such an anomaly that it provoked a local editor to offer the novel explanation that the accommodations had been provided because the man was a French nobleman. In his visit to Nashville in 1890, M. W. Caldwell complained that it was "entirely out of the question for Afro-Americans to be accommodated in any hotel in Nashville." In September 1885, William H. Franklin, a Knoxville correspondent to the New York *Freeman*, expressed his resentment of the inability of Negroes to obtain adequate accommodations at hotels and public places of amusement, for by then blacks were being excluded from Memphis public parks and were being assigned to special seating in Knoxville theaters. In fact, by the mid-eighties, most areas of the state customarily confined blacks to special sections of theaters.[28]

A racial incident in a Memphis theater in March 1881 reveals that segregation was a recent innovation there. Mrs. Julia Hooks, a

[26]Fisk *Herald* (Feb. 1890), 8–9.

[27]Memphis *Appeal*, Aug. 19, 1883; Feb. 17, Sept. 18, 1884; Chattanooga *Times*, Feb. 21, 1885; Knoxville *Journal*, June 27, 1889.

[28]Knoxville *Journal*, Sept. 20, 1888; New York *Age*, July 5, 1890; New York *Freeman*, Sept. 5, 1885; Cleveland (Ohio) *Gazette*, Aug. 8, 1885; Knoxville *Chronicle*, Nov. 4, 1885.

young black teacher in the local schools, an accomplished pianist, and a socially refined woman, ran afoul of white sensibilities when she sat in a section reserved for whites. Boldly refusing to move, Mrs. Hooks was carried from the theater by two policemen and arrested for disorderly conduct. In the ensuing trial before a local magistrate there was wide disagreement about her deportment at the theater, but both sides agreed that the young Negro school-teacher had occupied a seat in a section reserved for whites. The theater manager acknowledged, however, that Negroes had not been segregated in a "colored balcony" prior to the 1881 season. Both Mrs. Hooks and other black witnesses testified that previously they had occupied seats in the main section of the theater without molestation. Even during the current season blacks apparently had been allowed to sit in the main section when the theater was not crowded; under crowded conditions whites sometimes sat in the section reserved for Negroes. The manager of the theater testified, however, that he considered any person guilty of disorderly conduct who took a seat in either section and refused to vacate it when ordered to do so by the officer on duty. Mrs. Hooks was fined five dollars.[29]

Exclusion of blacks from jury service, although customary long before the 1880s, continued to be a source of vexation to them. The state legislature debated a bill in 1883 that condemned the "willful and unjust discrimination in the selection of jurors for the various courts" in the state, but the house judiciary committee finally rejected it. According to the preamble to the bill, sheriffs across the state had systematically refused to summon Negroes to serve on juries, a practice which the bill would have classified as a misdemeanor.[30] Further evidence of discrimination against Negroes in the selection of jurors—as well as evidence that, in trials involving blacks, racially mixed or all-black juries sometimes were selected—was provided by David M. Key in his 1885 speech before the Tennessee Bar Association. Key affirmed the legal right of Negroes to sit on juries, but, he added, "the exercise of his right

[29]Memphis *Appeal*, Mar. 13, 1881; Memphis *Avalanche*, Mar. 13, 15–16, 1881.

[30]House Bill 526, 43rd General Assembly, 1883, Secretary of State Papers.

to sit upon juries, is not so generally allowed in this state." As a circuit court judge in Hamilton County in the early 1870s, Key said, he had made it a point to select black jurors in cases involving Negro defendants. At first he employed all-black juries in such cases; later, as public sentiment accepted this practice, "white jurors were sometimes mixed with colored ones in the trial of colored defendants." Key claimed that in Hamilton County and throughout most of East Tennessee the grand and petit juries had been racially mixed "for years." The federal judge cited his experience with black jurors in order to discredit white fears that the racial sympathies of black jurors would sway their judgment: "In all the cases I have tried by colored juries I have never known a defendant acquitted who ought to have been convicted, or convicted that ought to have been acquitted."[31]

Just as whites feared that the racial sympathies of black jurors would intrude upon their judgment, blacks concluded that the rulings of white judges and juries in cases involving black defendants reflected racial prejudices more than justice. "Color madness is made manifest," wrote Harry C. Smith, black editor-owner of the Cleveland (Ohio) *Gazette* in 1884, commenting on three court cases involving Memphis Negro defendants and all-white juries. Many blacks vigorously protested their exclusion from jury service, but even when a sheriff or judge risked white disapproval by appointing black jurors, the individuals selected sometimes refused, fearing repercussions from disapproving whites. The Reverend William H. Franklin, who served as a regular correspondent from Tennessee to the New York *Globe* during the early 1880s, indicted such Negroes for their "lack of moral courage." They should seize upon opportunities to serve on juries, Franklin admonished members of his race, in order to prove their capabilities, to set the precedent, and to utilize whatever influence they could to see that justice was accomplished.[32]

A firmly established segregation policy existed in state public schools throughout the eighties. Both the public school law passed

[31]Key, "Legal and Political Status of the Negro," 289.
[32]Cleveland (Ohio) *Gazette*, Apr. 26, 1884; Cleveland (Tenn.) *Weekly Herald*, July 30, 1880; New York *Globe*, Mar. 8, 1884.

by the Radicals in 1867 and that of the Redeemers in 1873 had required racial segregation in public education.[33] Segregationists viewed such laws necessary to prevent racial amalgamation and violence. Moreover, they argued, blacks also preferred separate schools. Even so, the barricades to interracial public education had to be guarded lest northern agitators or a few recalcitrant Negroes should challenge the principle of separation. Any perceived threat to the color line in public education, therefore, was almost certain to evoke white hostility: "The question of separate public schools for the two races is a social and not a political question," wrote the editor of the Memphis *Avalanche* in 1887. "Every kind of social intercourse is a step in the direction of breaking down the barriers of race—in other words towards miscegenation."[34]

Further evidence of the force of white sentiment against any possible breach of the educational color line was provided by the debate over creation of the position of an assistant superintendent of public instruction, to be filled by a Negro who would have had the responsibility of supervising the state's black schools. The position was never created, probably because of sentiment similar to that expressed by one of Governor Bate's correspondents, who feared that in the event of the white superintendent's death, the proposed Negro assistant superintendent might assume charge of the white schools. "Under no circumstances am I in favor of a black man having charge of white schools," he wrote. "I am opposed to mixed education of the races or in plainer terms I am opposed to the Amalgamation of the races."[35]

As long as racial mixing was in no way involved, most whites in Tennessee favored the education of Negroes at public expense.[36] Responsibility for the education of blacks was a duty inherent in the paternalistic philosophy most white conservatives espoused.

[33]Taylor, *Negro in Tennessee*, 178.

[34]Aug. 22, 31, Sept. 2, 25, Oct. 18, 1887; Joseph C. Kiger, "Social Thought as Voiced in Rural Middle Tennessee Newspapers, 1878–1898," *Tenn. Hist. Quar.* 9 (June 1950), 134.

[35]W. O. Peeples to William B. Bate, Feb. 5, 1883, Bate Papers.

[36]Prentis, *Southern Letters*, 77; *Christian Advocate*, Oct. 6, 1883.

It represented a moral, as well as class, obligation. Consequently, until the end of the eighties segments of the white pulpit and press upheld Negro education with evangelistic fervor both as the duty of whites and as the best solution of the problems associated with Negro transition from slavery to citizenship. Moreover, since manhood suffrage appeared to be a fixed part of the political system in the early eighties, white leaders feared that an illiterate and politically ignorant black voting population represented a threat to republican institutions. For these reasons universal public education seemed necessary, perhaps even compulsory. Many white newspaper editors dismissed speculation about the capacity of Negroes for self-government and supported Negro education, candidly revealing that their concern was rooted not in humanitarianism but in self-preservation. Educational and church leaders backed Negro education with warnings that blacks should be educated to the responsibilities of their citizenship as well as to its inherent rights.[37]

Other support for Negro education came from those whites who believed it could be utilized to produce a trained labor force for the industries of the New South. For differing reasons and with differing goals, both races embraced industrial education for Negroes. A black Memphis schoolteacher, for example, thought it represented "the lever by which the Negro race is to be lifted up." To a white Knoxvillian, however, it seemed to be well designed "to fit them [Negroes] for the pursuits they will of necessity have to follow." Whites heretofore predisposed against the idea of Negro education could join a self-styled "old planter" in Memphis in applauding the vogue for industrial training because it upheld the dignity of labor.[38]

---

[37]Memphis *Avalanche*, Nov. 17, 1880; Apr. 7, June 14, 1883; Memphis *Appeal*, Mar. 18, 1881; New York *Times*, Apr. 9, 1881; Chattanooga *Times*, June 5, 1881; Dec. 14, 1882; Apr. 21, May 30, 1883; Knoxville *Chronicle*, June 12, 19, 1881; Feb. 14, 1883; *Twenty-first Annual Report of the Freedmen's Aid and Southern Education Society of the Methodist Episcopal Church, 1888* (Cincinnati: Western Methodist Bk. Concern Printer, 1888), 54–57.

[38]Julia Hooks, "Industrial Education for Negroes," *Afro-American Encyclopedia*, comp. James T. Haley (Nashville: Haley & Florida, 1895), 170; Edmund

179

Negro colleges and universities in the state, although mainly oriented toward teacher-training and theological curriculums, rapidly moved to capitalize upon the sentiment for industrial education programs. In addition, new schools emerged that centered primarily on industrial education. This educational expansion was financed largely by the John F. Slater Fund, established in 1882 and administered under the direction of Atticus G. Haygood. During the 1880s, as a result of grants from the Slater Fund, LeMoyne Institute in Memphis, and Roger Williams University, Central Tennessee College, and Fisk University in Nashville either established industrial departments or expanded existing ones. Moreover, Howe Institute was created in Memphis in 1888 "for the academic, religious and industrial training of Negroes." The industrial training offered by these schools usually included woodworking, printing, blacksmithing, tinwork, and wagon making for men and needlework, cooking, nursing, shorthand, and typewriting for women. Perhaps the most extensive program was offered by Central Tennessee College, which by 1890 boasted of a "comprehensive" industrial training program highlighted by a new machine shop with the latest mechanical engineering equipment.[39]

The significance of industrial education in the growth of higher education among Tennessee blacks and the emergence of a favorable white attitude toward it may best be illustrated by LeMoyne Institute, founded in 1871 by a gift from Dr. Julius LeMoyne, a northern philanthropist. Operated under the auspices of the American Missionary Association, the school evoked little response from local whites until it added a "manual training department" in the early eighties. LeMoyne grew rapidly during

---

Kirke, "How Shall the Negro Be Educated?" *North American Review* 360 (Nov. 1886), 424; Memphis *Appeal*, May 31, 1883.

[39]Henry Allen Bullock, *A History of Negro Education in the South: From 1619 to the Present* (Cambridge, Mass.: Harvard Univ. Press, 1967), 124; Lucius S. Merriam, *Higher Education in Tennessee*, Bureau of Education Circular of Information, No. 5, 1893 (Washington, D.C.: Government Printing Office, 1893), 266, 273–74; Thomas O. Fuller, *History of the Negro Baptists of Tennessee* (Memphis: Haskins, 1936), 118–19; Memphis *Appeal*, Aug. 7, 1883; June 23, 29, 1888.

the decade, and its industrial program received favorable publicity in the Memphis press. John M. Keating, editor of the Memphis *Appeal*, wrote that the school'ŋ industrial program offered the key to black independence, freedom, and self-reliance. LeMoyne, as well as the other institutions of higher education across the state, continued to offer a broad liberal arts program. Only two of the eleven instructors on LeMoyne's faculty, for example, taught in the industrial department. The school maintained a library described as second to none in Memphis and conducted a public lecture series which was widely attended by members of both races. Such lecture topics as "The Detrimental Effects on American Society of Caste" attest to the existence of a strain of protest sentiment at the school.[40]

Whatever it may actually have accomplished, the vogue for industrial education in the eighties diminished, at least temporarily, white fears that education would make Negroes more contentious and less fit for their station in life. In 1890, however, a reporter for the Memphis *Avalanche* would reflect the continuing skeptical view of some whites toward Negro education by observing that, with education, Negroes lost "a certain childish unconscious freedom of manner and the insidious gnawing of ambitions and aspirations begin to eat into their minds and canker their feelings." Because of the increased interracial friction brought about by Negro education, he would note that many whites doubted "whether the education of the one race will be conducive to pleasant relations with the other."[41]

Some white taxpayers also opposed Negro education during the eighties because blacks paid but a small proportion of taxes for the support of public schools. The complaints of white taxpayers, however, never resulted in a serious movement to apportion the

[40]Merriam, *Higher Education in Tennessee*, 266, 268, 271, 279; Memphis *Appeal*, Sept. 27, 1883; Jan. 11, 1887; June 1, 1888; June 2, 1889; Memphis *Avalanche*, May 30, 1890; J. Winfield Qualls, "The Beginnings and Early History of the LeMoyne School at Memphis, 1871–1874," WTHS *Publications* 7 (1953), 5–37.

[41]Jan. 26, 1890. See also *ibid.*, June 9, 1889; *Christian Advocate*, Oct. 20, 1883.

state school fund according to the taxes paid by each race. Perhaps such sentiments were checked by the conviction that, since blacks held the right to vote, they should be educated. The absence of any movement to divide the school funds may also have been a result of the reluctance of whites to accept the class implications of such a move. "Will it be feasible to stop with the negro, or must such a policy not surely lead to the exclusion of poor whites from participation in the benefits of school funds raised by rich whites?" questioned the Chattanooga *Times*. From the perspective of the *Times*, the only way to avoid general taxation for the education of Negroes would be through disfranchisement or reenslavement—solutions which it viewed as being equally ludicrous. The *Times* warned that dividing the school fund would represent a dangerous step which, if adopted, might lead future demagogues to destroy free government by using the presumed danger of black suffrage "as an entering wedge" to "split and shiver popular government."[42]

Even in the control of their own schools, Negroes wielded little power, although they occasionally served on local school boards. When a Negro won election to the Knoxville school board in 1888, the white members of the board held secret meetings at a private residence in order to exclude him from their deliberations. Only after a court injunction prohibited such action was he able to assume his duties. Rarely did Negro leaders openly challenge racial segregation in public schools during the eighties. In a critique of the segregationist ideology in 1885, however, a black minister in Memphis personally defended the concept of integrated schools but carefully assured whites that "Negroes in Memphis were not demanding mixed schools." Negroes did need educational facilities, he declared, and it would be in the best interests of the whites to help provide those facilities. He warned that a "race of people held down, despised and kept in a state most favorable to ignorance and crime, becomes in time the cause of vexation, trouble, suffering to those by whom it is ill-treated." The hope for racial harmony lay in the willingness of men "to counsel on these

[42]Apr. 15, 1883.

grave questions," supplanting passion with reason. In 1883 dissatisfaction also was registered at a public meeting in Chattanooga at which blacks adopted resolutions complaining of inadequate public educational facilities for their children. Likewise, in September 1885 a Knoxville correspondent to the New York *Freeman* voiced his resentment of the "barbarous strains" of race prejudice. In his view, the most vicious manifestations of this prejudice were the separate public schools, the staffing of Negro schools by white teachers, the refusal of the University of Tennessee to admit Negro cadets for military training, the examination of Negroes for state normal school scholarships by white boards, and the gross inequalities in the separate educational facilities provided for white and Negro deaf-mutes.[43]

The battle over segregation in Tennessee during the eighties raged most furiously on the railroads, where interracial contacts focused attention upon the whole range of issues involved in the conflict between white assumptions concerning social prerogatives and black efforts to attain civil equality. It has been previously noted that the general practice on Tennessee railroads in the eighties was to charge Negroes first-class fare but to assign them to second-class accommodations in mixed smoking cars. This was done in violation of the 1881 law requiring railroad companies to furnish separate first-class accommodations for those Negroes who paid first-class fare. Some railroads complied with the law by maintaining a three-car passenger service, with the first designated the smoking car, the second set aside for Negroes, and the third reserved for the exclusive use of first-class white passengers. In usual practice, however, the car set aside for Negroes also was occupied by second-class white passengers whose smoking, profane language, and drinking went largely unchecked.[44] Other railroad companies, ignoring the law completely, simply assigned Negroes to the smoking car. In any case, whatever their individual

---

[43]Joel M. Roitman, "Race Relations in Memphis, Tennessee—1800–1905" (M.A. thesis, Memphis State Univ., 1964), 79; New York *Age*, Aug. 18, 1889; Knoxville *Journal*, July 11, 1889; Memphis *Appeal*, Feb. 27, 1885; Chattanooga *Times*, May 15, 1883; New York *Freeman*, Sept. 5, 1885.

[44]*Acts*, 1882, 3rd Ex. Sess., 12; Memphis *Avalanche*, July 24, 26, 1885.

policies, railroad company officials generally denied the existence of any discrimination against blacks.

Perhaps the transitional nature of race relations during the decade is best illustrated by conflicts that arose over racial discrimination in railroad passenger service. According to a black correspondent of the New York *Age*, the railroads serving Nashville adopted a policy in 1880 requiring all Negroes except servants accompanying their employers to ride in the smoking cars.[45] A year later, a group of Nashville blacks challenged this policy by demanding access to the first-class facilities on the same basis as whites. For three successive days in the fall of 1881, blacks appeared, both singly and in small groups, at the Nashville depots of the Louisville and Nashville and the Nashville, Chattanooga, and St. Louis railways, purchased first-class fares, and attempted to take seats in the ladies' cars reserved for whites. Their action was intended, in part at least, to provoke a test case, under the federal Civil Rights Act of 1875, challenging the validity of the Tennessee law that required railroads to provide segregated first-class facilities.[46]

Given the violence and enflamed white outbursts that generally accompanied such incidents later in the decade, the Nashville civil rights protestors found railway officials remarkably cautious in enforcing segregated first-class facilities. This probably reflected the officials' uncertainty about the constitutionality of the recently enacted Tennessee segregation law and their fear of successful legal action by blacks under the federal civil rights statute. Although railroad officials insisted that Negroes could not ride in the first-class coaches with whites, they thwarted the determined protestors by what amounted to a curious game of musical chairs. In one of these incidents, after all white passengers had been transferred from the ladies' coach and locked in another car, the blacks were granted the shallow victory of riding in the ladies' coach evacuated by whites. In an encounter the next day, four black demonstrators took seats in the ladies' car before any whites had arrived; whites subsequently boarding the train

[45]July 5, 1890.   [46]Nashville *American*, Oct. 1-3, 1881.

were diverted to the car usually set aside for blacks. When the blacks realized what was happening, they moved to the car in which whites were seated only to see the whites rush into the ladies' car and lock the Negroes out. What is remarkable about all this, beyond the pathos, is the fact that in none of the incidents were the black civil rights advocates violently removed from the train.[47]

Another significant aspect of these incidents was the response of H. M. Doak, editor of the Nashville *American*, who at first could find no explanation for this "unseemly agitation" other than speculation that the protestors were agents of local Republicans who hoped to impress recently inaugurated President Arthur with their "stalwart" principles. After this obviously partisan shot, the *American* further attacked the motives of the civil rights advocates by accusing them of being the dupes of lawyers who hoped to obtain payment of damages against the railroads. Finally, the editor calmly declared that the issue was "purely one of law and for the courts to determine." Thus, unlike later newspaper appeals to white public opinion as the sole arbiter of such matters, the *American* recognized the right of Negroes to seek redress of their grievances through legal processes. Mildly warning blacks that agitation was not the best way to obtain their goals, Doak turned to the law for a settlement of the issue, confident as he said, that the Tennessee separate-car law "conforms in every respect to the principle of the civil rights bill, which is not mixed but equal accommodations." When the legal rights of blacks were determined by the courts, Doak advised, blacks either would be "entitled to be protected in the result" or would "have to submit to the result," whatever it might be. In sharp contrast to the white obsession with segregation at the end of the decade, the *American* did not find the prospect of a black legal victory to be greatly unsettling in 1881. Doak predicted that, if the courts "confer upon him [the Negro] the right to any seat, provided he has paid first class fare, it will be of no more consequence to anybody than the right he has exercised for years in the street cars."[48]

47*Ibid.*, Oct. 1–4, 1881.   48*Ibid.*, Oct. 3, 5, 7, 1881.

Amid the controversy provoked by the civil rights demonstrations in Nashville, two black writers outlined to the editor of the *American* their views concerning the discriminatory policies of the railroads. One of them, a Nashville minister named William A. Sinclair, had accompanied a black woman attempting to gain access to a ladies' car at the Nashville station on October 2. After the Nashville *American* had presented its prejudicial account of the incident, Sinclair wrote to the editor complaining that the newspaper had "grossly, if not willfully and maliciously" misrepresented his motives. Racial discrimination on the railroads was immoral, unjust, and illegal, the Negro minister declared; furthermore, it was detrimental to the interests of the entire South, for it fanned intersectional and interracial discord. Like later blacks who protested racial discrimination on the railroads, Sinclair carefully distinguished between social rights and civil rights and appealed to the "better class of Southern whites" to act with a "spirit of chivalry" toward blacks.[49]

Another black correspondent to the *American* succinctly presented his understanding of the objectives of the Nashville protestors: "What we want, and all we ask, is to be accorded the same legal, not social, right that is accorded a white man or woman with the same amount of money, refinement and intelligence." He condemned the stigma of discrimination on the trains and the insults railroad officials often hurled at blacks. The issue, he insisted, was not that blacks wanted to ride with whites, but that they simply wanted access to facilities on the same basis as whites. The writer pointed out that on many trains divided cars merely represented a pretense of compliance with the law. Railroad officials often used the Negro side of such cars for maintenance and baggage purposes; the other side generally contained second-class white passengers who frequently wandered into the Negro section to smoke. Moreover, all blacks, irrespective of dress or refinement, were huddled into one section with the result that, in reality, many railroads made no distinction between first-class and second-class facilities for Negroes. To this

[49]*Ibid.*, Oct. 4, 1881.

black observer, as well as to many succeeding critics of the emerging pattern of segregation, discrimination on the railways was inconsistent with interracial contact in other aspects of southern life and with the close interracial contact that had existed during slavery. "Now, because we are free, why give us worse treatment?" he asked. It made little sense to the writer that blacks of refinement and culture received treatment worse than that accorded to servants. To those whites who thought it would be a mistake to "treat a decent negro right" for fear "others will want to be treated the same way," he replied: "All we want is the treatment we merit." Although the writer joined the editor of the *American* in regretting "agitation of this question," he believed that Negroes would prove themselves unmanly and would be unworthy of recognition "if we held our peace."[50]

The outcome of the Nashville protests was anticlimactic; in mid-October the federal district judge directed a grand jury to ignore the civil rights cases which had arisen from the three-day protests, on the grounds that a test case from Tennessee was already before the Supreme Court.[51] The brief confrontations, however, had revealed black dissatisfaction with the separate but equal concept at its origin. They also indicated that the railroad officials and the leading white newspaper in Nashville were uncertain about the ultimate triumph of Jim Crow. Although the Nashville incidents seem not to have aroused the ominous pronouncements that would accompany later segregation debates, available evidence indicates that, as the decade wore on, those railroad companies that had not previously introduced the Jim Crow car began to comply with growing white sentiment in favor of separation. The railroad line running to Nashville from Cleveland, Tennessee, for example, introduced a separate coach for black passengers in May 1888.[52]

The progression and character of racial discrimination on the railroads may be seen in the civil rights cases that were brought before state and federal courts during the decade. One such case,

[50]*Ibid.*, Oct. 6, 1881.
[51]*Ibid.*, Oct. 18, 1881.
[52]Cleveland (Ohio) *Gazette*, May 19, 1888.

involving a black woman named Jane Brown who had been removed from the ladies' coach on a train outside Memphis, was especially significant. It demonstrated that in the early eighties discriminations were likely to be defended on the paternalistic basis of class or character rather than race, and it revealed the practical difficulties involved in such discrimination. Heard in the federal circuit court of West Tennessee in October 1880, the case resulted in a decision which declared unconstitutional, insofar as railroads engaged in interstate commerce were concerned, the 1875 Tennessee statute that allowed proprietors of public businesses to deny services to any person "for any reason." In reply to the railroad company's contention that Miss Brown had been discriminated against, not because of her race, but because of "her notoriously bad character," the court decreed that railroad companies could not "put every woman purchasing a railroad ticket on trial for her virtue." The police power of public carriers was sufficient, the court added, to remove all persons whose conduct was unruly, but that was as far as it could go. The case also revealed the concern of some whites in the early eighties regarding the equality of separate facilities, for the federal district judge held that, contrary to the railroad company's claims, the car to which Miss Brown had been assigned was used as a smoking car and was crowded with passengers traveling on cheap rates. Accordingly, the court found that, since Miss Brown had paid first-class fare, she could not be compelled "to accept a seat in another car offensive to her because of smoking and bad ventilation." She was awarded damages of $3,000.[53] This decision may have spurred the state legislature to adopt the 1881 law requiring railroad companies to furnish separate but equal facilities for Negroes who paid first-class fare.

In any case, the separate but equal principle received additional judicial support in a civil rights decision rendered in 1884 by United States District Judge David M. Key. A railroad company could separate its passengers according to race, ruled Key, "but if

---

[53]Brown v. Memphis & C. R. Co., 5 *Federal Reporter* 499–503 (1885); Memphis *Avalanche*, Nov. 7, 1880.

it charges the same fare to each race it must furnish substantially like and equal accommodations."[54] The ruling of a federal district court in West Tennessee in March 1885 further clarified the separate but equal principle. A black woman who had been removed from a first-class train coach brought suit against the railroad company involved. The court did not believe that "equality of accommodation" meant "identity of accommodation" and proceeded to explain that the separation of black and white passengers on a train was "not unreasonable under certain circumstances" if "all paying the same price shall have substantially the same comforts, privileges, and pleasures." The testimony in this case reflected the fluctuation of racial customs in the eighties. Some Negroes, including the woman initiating the suit, until recently had been allowed to ride in the first-class cars.[55] By mid-decade, however, Negroes generally were being denied access to the first-class cars reserved for whites and had to accept accommodations in the racially-mixed second-class smoking cars. Railroad company officials callously labeled these cars first-class facilities and charged first-class fare for their use. Despite earlier court rulings, Tennessee courts came to accept this practice by the latter half of the 1880s. At least, such a policy was clearly upheld in a widely publicized case involving a young Memphis black woman, Ida B. Wells, whose future civil rights activities catapulted her into national prominence among Negroes as a militant crusader.[56]

In September 1883, Miss Wells, a public school teacher in Shelby County, purchased a first-class ticket on a local Woodstock to Memphis line operated by the Chesapeake, Ohio and Southwestern Railroad Company. Having taken a seat in the first-class coach, she was asked by the conductor to move to the forward car, which was occupied by members of both races.

[54]Murphy v. Western & A. R. R. and others, 23 *Federal Reporter* 637–41 (1885).

[55]Logwood and Wife v. Memphis & C. R. Co., 23 *Federal Reporter* 318–19 (1885).

[56]Alfreda M. Duster, ed., *Crusade for Justice: The Autobiography of Ida B. Wells* (Chicago: Univ. of Chicago Press, 1970), xiii–xxxii, and *passim*.

When she refused, the conductor, aided by several white passengers, removed her from the first-class car. Miss Wells got off the train and subsequently filed suit against the railroad company for not providing her with the first-class accommodations for which she had paid. This protracted case, first tried in the circuit court of Shelby County in late 1884, offers a revealing picture of the racial customs on Tennessee's railroads during the decade. According to Miss Wells' version of the incident, she had refused to move to the forward car because of the boisterous behavior of its occupants, who were drinking and smoking. She contended that the coach to which she was asked to move was not equivalent to the one in which white ladies rode because the rules against drinking were not enforced.

Railroad company officials, on the other hand, claimed that the train on which Miss Wells rode had provided three passenger cars—two first-class coaches and a car for smoking. Blacks and whites alike were allowed to sit in the front passenger car, but generally only whites occupied the rear one. According to the testimony of the conductor, Negro nurses were allowed to sit in the "white" coach—a practice which none of the white passengers who testified for the railroad company seemed to mind. The conductor acknowledged that enforcing the rules against drinking and smoking in the "mixed car" was difficult, and the combined testimony bolstered the prevailing view that it did, indeed, represent second-class accommodations. This was also the view of the Memphis circuit court judge, who held that the railroad company had not complied with the Tennessee statutes of 1881 and 1882 that required them to furnish accommodations for Negroes "equal in all respects" to those set aside for whites. The judge levied the maximum fine of $300 against the railroad company for violation of the statutes and awarded Miss Wells personal damages of $500.[57]

The case was appealed to the state supreme court, where Miss Wells' attorneys, two of whom were white, filed a brief accepting

[57]"Ida Wells v. Chesapeake, Ohio and Southwestern Railroad Company, 1884," MS court record (Archives Div., Tennessee State Library).

the principle of racial separation but insisting upon equality of accommodations. Such facilities, they argued, had not been provided by the railroad company in this instance; if the courts refused to enforce the principle of equality, they would be guilty of making a mockery of the law by pandering to popular prejudices. If a Negro had to be a servant or nurse in order to obtain first-class accommodations, they continued, blacks faced the ludicrous prospect of finding that their privileges increased as they sank lower in the social scale. Although both of Miss Wells' white lawyers proclaimed "a proud faith" in Anglo-Saxon superiority, they contended that prejudice should not be sanctioned by the courts as a "reasonable rule" of law. "We had as well say that the colored man should not be allowed to buy the best article of groceries, though he pays in full for such and we pretend to sell him only the best. Might as well say we will ask him the same price for the best and then deliver him the inferior grade."[58]

Despite testimony to the contrary, the state supreme court was not convinced that the accommodations provided Negroes in this instance were inferior to those provided for whites paying the same fare. Speaking for the court, Chief Justice Peter Turney judged the facilities accorded Negroes and whites to have been "alike in every respect as to comfort, convenience, and safety." In the eyes of the court, the railroad company "had done all that could rightfully be demanded" in order to provide "accommodations equal in all respects." The state's highest court further claimed that Miss Wells' sole intention in the affair had been "to harass with a view to this suit, and that her persistence was not in good faith to obtain a comfortable seat for the short ride." With this dubious distinction the lower court's verdict was reversed, and the earlier legal stress on equality of accommodations was negated.[59]

The transitional nature of race relations during the early eighties is indicated not only by the flexibility of practices in the use of

[58] "Chesapeake, Ohio, and S. W. Railroad v. Ida Wells, April 1885," Brief of Greer and Adams (Archives Div., Tennessee State Library).

[59] Chesapeake, Ohio and Southwestern Railroad Company v. Wells, 85 *Tennessee Reports* 613–15 (1887).

public facilities but by the way in which blacks responded to discriminations they confronted. Without evidence to the contrary, it appears that most Negroes acquiesced, at least publicly, to white prescriptions concerning interracial etiquette. Still the fabric of race relations during the decade was interlaced with a thread of black activity protesting those practices which blacks considered either illegal or unprecedented. Sometimes protest came in the form of eloquent statements decrying the whites' equation of black rights with social equality. Occasionally, it was expressed dramatically in personal acts of defiance. Whether premeditated or kindled by a surge of anger, frustration, and resentment, these breaches of the racial mores by Negroes aroused white hostility and, at times, resulted in violence. Individually and collectively, through newspapers, social organizations, loosely organized protective associations, and political rallies, some Negroes challenged the emerging system of discrimination. Ironically, one effect of this protest activity seems to have been to speed the formulation of a sweeping legal and practical code of racial segregation.

The way in which most whites tended to link social equality with civil rights reflects the ambiguity of paternalistic thought during the decade. Black leaders labored diligently, although unsuccessfully, to refute the contention that interracial mingling in the use of public facilities would usher in social equality. On several occasions during the early eighties, Benjamin A. Imes, a black Congregationalist minister in Memphis, wrote lengthy letters to the *Appeal* attacking the assumptions, logic, and motives behind the confusion of civil rights with social equality. In the first place, Imes insisted, social equality—association with whites in private social activities or even on a personal basis in public facilities—was not a goal of blacks. The white assumption that mere association with blacks in the use of public facilities represented an intrusion into their own private social lives was not logical. Imes pointed out that in some northern states the two races shared accommodations on the railroads, worked together, and held similar political offices without altering their social relations in any way. In those states where interracial marriages were permitted, he claimed, there was less "illicit amalgamation" than in the states prohibiting such unions. The equation of social equality with racial intermingling in the use of public facilities was unsound because it was not applied to whites of questionable character in the South. Whites of every class often mingled indiscriminately in public facilities without the assumption of social equality, the black minister argued, "yet if even the most decent black man is granted similar or equal privileges and accommodations in public places, it is social equality." To Imes, and doubtless to most other blacks, the anguished cries of whites insisting upon the necessity of preserving social distinctions between the genteel folk and the unwashed masses simply masked irrational race prejudices. Whites should acknowledge the real issue, Imes stated, and "fairly come out and say, 'We hate men whom the Creator has given a dark skin, and for that reason, no matter what their condition or character in other respects, we propose to retain the negro as a target for our abuse.' " If the issue were stated in plain words, he continued, whites might disabuse themselves of the notion that blacks wanted social equality and openly admit to opposing all measures looking toward the freedom of Negroes and to the protection of their rights as citizens. Why shouldn't whites simply say "we want to hear of no proposition by which he [the Negro] shall be given simple justice?"[60]

In his attacks on racial segregation Imes also pointed out that social equality could not be enforced by law and that, in any case, "race instincts" would "guard and direct the social relation." Racial pride among Negroes, he insisted, would be as active a deterrent in preventing social equality as it would be among whites.[61] He challenged the notion that the segregationist ideology was based either on Christian principles or on natural law. Its defenders, he wrote, had marshaled the forces of God and history to justify discrimination on the basis of race:

> They hold up the Anglo-Saxon in his greatness and superior achievements on every field. They glean from history the record of race

[60]Memphis *Appeal*, Jan. 16, 1880; Dec. 9, 1883.
[61]*Ibid.*, June 16, 1880.

conflicts in which it is shown that barbarous and semi-barbarous peoples have enslaved the negro race, how they have manifested their race antipathies, in which the weak inevitably fall before the strong. And this we are asked to accept as the logic of the Creator's design in causing men to differ in color and natural aptitude and condition of life.[62]

How different all this was from "the spirit of the gospel," the black minister complained.

Other Negro leaders observed a sharp distinction between white sensitivity to racial intermingling in public and the private associations of individual whites with individual blacks. "I frequently, yes every day, see colored nurses kissing white children in the presence of their parents," wrote M. W. Caldwell from Nashville in 1890. "I observe white ladies sitting with colored coachmen every day in the streets of this capital city on their carriages and buggies."[63] The implication of Caldwell's observations was that white fears concerning social equality were not really based on the belief that private interracial associations would naturally follow public intermingling; rather, whites apparently feared they would not be able to control blacks with whom they came into contact through the integration of public facilities.

Sometimes black leaders made accommodationist pronouncements to allay white fears while simultaneously urging blacks to adopt self-help policies and develop racial pride in response to white discrimination. Frequently, such tactics for dealing with white prejudices were combined with angry protests against existing discriminations. At a Chattanooga meeting in 1883, for example, Negroes condemned "invidious distinctions" on railroads and in public entertainment facilities as "wrong in principle, injurious in practice and wholly at variance with the most advanced civilization and culture of the nineteenth century." In the wake of this oral protest, they encouraged blacks to employ a self-help philosophy and called upon members of the race to

[62]*Ibid.*, Feb. 27, 1885.
[63]New York *Age*, July 5, 1890.

avail themselves of every opportunity for education. They pointed out the need for a local black newspaper, urged the establishment of a library and reading room in order to use their leisure time more profitably, and called for more public meetings of an educative nature where hygiene, morality, nutrition, and temperance might be discussed. In addition, they resolved "to give the widest possible publicity to every act of flagrant injustice perpetrated upon our people." This was to be done, "not with the view of fanning the flames of race strife," but "to enlighten public sentiment." The fusion of protest, self-help, and accommodationist sentiments became complete when the same group of blacks, paying tribute to those whites both North and South who "dared to speak out" in defense of Negro rights, stated their desire for friendly relations with the white people. They also favored "prudential concessions" on both sides in matters that did not involve "the compromise of principle," and, in view of the fact that the two races were "destined to live side by side" with interests "inseparably linked," they invited "a freer interchange of opinion" to help both races "become more thoroughly acquainted with each other."[64]

A black critic of segregation in Nashville, M. W. Caldwell, employed a similar combination of tactics, advising blacks to unite in opposition to discrimination and to organize and pool their resources in order to fight for their rights through the courts. Submission to one outrage served only as "an inducement for the whites to impose another" which, he warned, without black opposition "they will certainly and surely do." The best remedy for the black man's plight rested in the adoption of a self-help philosophy. Caldwell called upon members of his race to "form companies, enter into all kinds of business, trust each other, stick by each other." He optimistically predicted that, by following such a course, Negroes would counteract the prejudice against them.[65]

A Memphis organization, the Negro Mutual Protective Associa-

[64]Chattanooga *Times*, May 15, 1883.
[65]New York *Age*, July 5, 1890.

tion, adopted resolutions in the spring of 1887 proclaiming that Negroes had "a duty to pursue and to claim the full rights and privileges which pertain in common to the citizens of a great republic." Just as slavery "was deep rooted and remorseless in its creation of submission on the part of the slave so do we find caste prejudices and distinctions fastened in the minds of many of the white race." This accounted "for the frequent exhibitions of childish fear lest the negro shall gain a footing of social equality with his unwilling white neighbor." These black citizens took the upper-class white paternalists seriously when the latter talked about the responsiblities of "culture and intelligence"; they pointed out that these very qualities should enable whites "to distinguish between social relations and those rights and privileges which men may share in common, with no reference to the social status of any." The social-equality arguments which were applied to restrict black civil rights were not used against the poorest and most illiterate whites, unless their conduct or appearance in some way rendered them personally obnoxious. Was it not time, the resolutions continued, "to allow prejudices and caste distinctions to give way to nobler and more humane sentiment?" The Negroes who framed these resolutions pinned their hopes upon the ability of "cultured and intelligent" whites "to rise above the narrowness which may characterize the minds of the masses."[66]

Other Negro leaders chose not to await the transformation of white sentiment by the passage of time. Like M. W. Caldwell, Nashville correspondent to the New York *Age*, they encouraged blacks to emulate whites by fighting for their rights with whatever means they had. "When any man stands in your pathway to success knock him out," urged Henry C. Smith at an African Methodist Episcopal Church conference in Memphis in 1884. These remarks had been provoked by criticisms leveled at Smith, a Democrat, by Bishop Henry M. Turner of the A. M. E. Church, an outspoken advocate of Negro emigration.[67] Smith made it clear

[66]Memphis *Appeal*, Apr. 19, 1887.

[67]For an analysis of Turner's emigrationist views, see Edwin S. Redkey, *Black Exodus: Black Nationalist and Back-to-Africa Movements, 1890–1910* (New Haven: Yale Univ. Press, 1969), 24–26.

that he thought Negroes should utilize the courts to counteract unjust discriminations, but, under Turner's prodding, he advised the Negro churchmen that, if they were thrown off a train, they should "grab the nearest white man and pull him with you. The white man has risen step by step from the barbarian," Smith continued, "and his passage is red with the blood and smoke of battle." He added that America was his country as much as it was any white man's, and, in a comment doubtlessly aimed at Bishop Turner's much-publicized emigrationist views, he maintained that he intended to remain in America and fight for his rights.[68]

The feelings of the vast majority of Negroes about racial discrimination must remain a matter of speculation, but even the white newspapers of the era contain sufficient evidence of protest to warrant several conclusions. First, some Negro churchmen, educators, and politicians maintained a steady criticism of existing racial discrimination; they drew a distinct line between social equality and civil rights, repeatedly emphasizing that they desired the latter and not the former; and because they saw the attitudes of poorer whites as the greatest threat to their rights, they appealed to upper-class whites to moderate the racial antagonisms of the white masses. Negro leaders also turned to self-help and racial unity as a means of achieving civil equality and eventual full participation in American life. Finally, in the face of heightened sectional animosities in the late 1880s and of a growing white reaction to their assertiveness, some Negro leaders attempted to assure southern whites that blacks held goodwill toward the South and hoped to achieve racial harmony, but not at the expense of a permanent caste system. Often, all these tactics were employed simultaneously by the same individuals or groups.

Race relations in Tennessee underwent a profound change during the 1880s. By the end of the decade flexibility had largely given way to rigidity in interracial contacts, white attitudes had become more fixed, blacks more bitter, and the margin for variety in interracial associations narrower. As blacks and whites came into impersonal contact in railroad cars, theaters, hotels, parks,

[68]Memphis *Appeal*, Nov. 19, 1884.

197

and other public facilities, racial tensions mounted. Agricultural depression and blighted dreams of general prosperity based on industrial plenty also subtly but surely narrowed the racial tolerance of New South prophets. Class characteristics, the touchstone of a paternalistic society in which whites were relatively sure of their economic and social status, gave way to race as a clear criterion for public distinctions. The dynamic ingredients in this change were partly demographic, partly political, and partly ideological. The increasing black population in urban areas, the growing militancy of some Negro leaders, factional disputes within the Democratic party, the black effort to separate civil rights and social privileges, the withdrawal of federal guarantees against racial discrimination after 1883, and the inherent inconsistencies within the white conservatives' paternalistic philosophy all contributed to the steady deterioration in race relations during the decade.

VI

Sources of Opposition to Negro Voting

Within a period of a few months in 1889 two Tennessee Civil War veterans addressed attentive West Tennessee audiences comprised of their former comrades-in-arms. Although one spoke to a group of Union veterans at a Memorial Day ceremony in Memphis and the other to a reunion of Confederate veterans in Fayette County, they dealt with the same topic. Perhaps, it was a fitting symbol of national reconciliation that the two speakers urgently attacked what they perceived as a common enemy facing southern society—black political power. However divided these two men had been in their concepts of nationalism in 1861, they now largely agreed that Negro suffrage had been an unsuccessful experiment that imperiled the way of life they both had fought to preserve. Both speeches evoked enthusiastic responses from the white citizens of West Tennessee.

The speaker at the 1889 Memorial Day ceremony in Memphis was "Colonel" T. B. Edgington, a former Union officer who had settled in Memphis after the war. As a past commander of the local chapter of the Grand Army of the Republic, a lawyer, and a Democrat, Edgington had been invited to make the principal speech at the ceremonies honoring the Union war dead. Ironically, Negroes not only provided the subject matter of Edgington's address but also comprised a large part of his Memorial Day audience.[1] Edgington voiced a position against Negro suffrage that had gradually become commonplace among most whites—whether Union army veterans who had remained in the South, native Unionists, or former Confederates. First, he said it

[1]Memphis *Avalanche*, June 3, 1889.

was time for the soldiers who had survived the war, rather than the politicians, to consider the purposes for which they had fought and their comrades had died. Although their sacrifices had brought freedom for the slaves, they had not fought to allow blacks, through sheer numbers, to rule over those who possessed nearly all the property and intelligence of the South. Even the Union soldiers whom they were gathered to honor had not given their lives in the late war to overthrow white supremacy, he exclaimed: "Listen attentively for the faintest whisper that comes from these graves and you will hear no syllable of approbation of this overthrow of the white race and destruction of all its dearest aspirations and hopes." Second, Edgington warned of an "irrepressible conflict between white suffrage and negro suffrage." Dreams of dividing the black vote were "utopian," he declared, for racial unity would prevail over "the influences of both property and intelligence" as determinants of voting behavior. The third of Edgington's points was perhaps the most curious. The South, he declared, was on the brink of immediate peril. "Race prejudice and passion" among Negroes could be fomented and encouraged at any time by unscrupulous, self-seeking white demagogues. The foe now confronting the South was not "a line of glistening bayonets" but an "impending destiny." White Southerners, he cautioned, "Jonah-like" were "looking into the open mouth of the Ethiopian fetish."

Edgington did not advocate the complete disfranchisement of blacks but advised only restrictions "of such a character as to remove the fear of negro supremacy." He would allow "a responsible class of colored voters" who would not conspire with "irresponsible and lawless whites" to continue voting. In short, Edgington presented white Tennesseans with a simple choice: to prevent Negro domination, they would have to change existing suffrage laws or resort to extralegal devices. With "proper limitations on negro suffrage," he assured his audience, whites could resolve all other issues of economic and social importance and become the bulwark of the American defense against the corro-

200

sive forces of anarchism and socialism.[2]

Three months later at a reunion of Confederate veterans, Josiah Patterson, a Memphis lawyer and former state legislator, drew virtually the same bleak picture of the evils of Negro suffrage. In the early 1880s Patterson had championed Negro voting, eloquently articulating a vision of racial harmony based on a biracial political alliance of Bourbon Democrats and Negroes.[3] When he spoke to the Confederate veterans in the late summer of 1889, however, he depicted a South on the brink of disaster because of Negro voting. Patterson had come to see black suffrage as a threat to law and order, white supremacy, and economic prosperity. "Every social disorder in the South," he now charged, "grows out of the efforts of the negro to assert that control in government which he is taught to believe he is entitled to by reason of mere numerical strength." As long as the Negro had hope that he might receive assistance "in asserting himself" there would be racial tension and trouble. Patterson's earlier effort to forge a biracial Democratic political alliance in Shelby County not only had failed to dislodge the majority of blacks from the Republican party but also had aroused the opposition of many whites. Perhaps this experience had led him to conclude that Negroes would be controlled by "race instincts" in politics, and that they would "stand together to a man"; accordingly, the two races could never be expected to "distribute themselves between political parties." Negroes would continue to vote solidly Republican against the best interests of southern whites. In the face of the threat to white supremacy Patterson now visualized arising from black suffrage, he urged whites, if necessary, to resort to a "higher law," using any means necessary to insure their domination. The perpetuation of civilization, commerce, and godliness depended upon it, for "Heaven itself would place its seal of disapproval on the political supremacy of the negro in a single Southern state."

Patterson's attack on Negro suffrage combined paternalism

[2]*Ibid.*   [3]See Ch. 1.

with a keen appreciation for intersectional politics. Carrying the white paternalistic perspective to its logical conclusion, he claimed that the "happiness, contentment and prosperity" of blacks depended upon white domination. Even white Northerners, having come to see that "superior intelligence and manhood" [whites] should rule, would no longer intervene to force Negro suffrage upon the South. Thus, he added, a major obstacle to a resolution of the race problem had been removed. With southern whites left free to solve the race problem, white supremacy would not have to be secured by fraud and violence; instead, it could be maintained by "the endowments which God and civilization have given the white race." There would then dawn upon the South "an era of unsurpassed prosperity."[4]

The speeches of Edgington and Patterson tapped a vast reservoir of opposition to black voting. By the late 1880s many white Tennesseans reasoned, simply, that whites should govern because they held the great majority of property and education. To the critics of Negro suffrage, black voters seemed to pose a threat to white control because, whatever their property and educational attainments, Negroes voted by a racial standard. The growing political unrest among blacks indicated that they would not be content with a few minor offices and insignificant appointments; rather, they wanted to be represented in government on a numerically democratic basis. Although some whites advocated using any means necessary to prevent blacks from exercising the kind of power such representation would give them, most proponents of Negro disfranchisement argued that fraud and violence could be circumvented by finding some legal way of eliminating blacks from the political picture, especially in light of the increasingly sympathetic understanding of northern whites.

Edgington had "fired a shot," a writer to the editor of the Memphis *Appeal* predicted, that would "be heard throughout the length and breadth of the land."[5] The editor of the Memphis *Avalanche*, grandiosely describing the speech as "the most remarkable utterance on the race question which has ever been

[4]Memphis *Appeal*, Sept. 12, 1889.
[5]*Ibid.*, June 4, 1889.

made," agreed that the many dangers inherent in Negro voting made it necessary for whites to avert black domination by some scheme of disfranchisement: "There was no more fitting place to warn the people of the danger to the republic than among the graves of its defenders." The *Avalanche* expressed confidence that the "public mind" was ripe for a discussion of a solution to the race question. Edgington's speech, therefore, representing as it did "the orderly arrangement of the chaotic thoughts of uncounted thousands," would stimulate "thousands more who have never thought seriously of the question before" to "take it up in earnest."[6] The editor of the Memphis *Appeal* wrote that every Tennessean should "feel a sense of grateful obligation" to Patterson for "conclusively" demonstrating "the necessity of white supremacy in the South."[7] The Clarksville *Chronicle* credited the Memphis orator with "clearing away the mist that overshadows the race question" and "pointing a clear way to a peaceable, and its only peaceable solution."[8]

The enthusiastic response to these two speeches—one by a carpetbagger and the other by a former rebel—reveals that by the end of the 1880s there was serious public discussion of legal ways to restrict Negro suffrage. A convergence of forces after 1885 had increased white hostility toward black voting and had reduced previous barriers to Negro disfranchisement.

One manifestation of the growing white resentment toward Negroes in politics was the rapid white disillusionment with education as a solution to the race problem. Most white politicians, newspaper editors, and business leaders in Tennessee—Democrats and Republicans alike—considered education and propertyholding to be prerequisites for a responsible electorate. They shared with northern liberals this time-honored concept of democracy, which rested on a wealth of philosophical and practical arguments.[9] Acting, therefore, on the assumption that

<hr />

[6]June 3–4, 6, 1889.
[7]Memphis *Appeal*, Sept. 12, 1889.
[8]Quoted in *ibid.*, Sept. 18, 1889.
[9]John G. Sproat, *"The Best Men": Liberal Reformers in the Gilded Age* (New York: Oxford Univ. Press, 1968), 253–57.

Negro suffrage was an unalterable fact, most whites had come to view public education as the necessary means of preparing a largely propertyless and illiterate voting population to exercise their political rights. This view was based on the hope that, among other things, the public education of blacks would reduce their tendency to vote as a bloc, thus allowing whites to divide politically over economic and social issues without fear that this division might give blacks the balance of political power. As it became apparent that public education would not immediately disrupt the loyalty of the vast majority of Negro voters to the Republican party, an increasing number of whites began to look for a means of eliminating blacks from politics.

This change in white attitudes reflected both bitterness and fear. Commenting on the efforts the South had made to provide public education for Negroes, the editor of the Memphis *Avalanche* saw growing white skepticism concerning "the efficacy of education as a means of solving the [race] problem." Southern whites were no longer "sitting up at night . . . devising means to raise money to endow schools for the education of the negro," he declared. Instead, "they are restlessly employed in searching for some means to make him a nonentity in politics."[10] A white farmer in Middle Tennessee expressed similar sentiments in a letter to the Nashville *American* in the summer of 1890. "Education," he claimed, "does not make the negro a better voter." Whether "educated or uneducated," it was "as certain as death and the tax collector" that when the Negro needs help he "will go to his white neighbor to get it," but "so surely as election day comes so surely will he vote against the interests of that white neighbor unless paid to do otherwise."[11] A writer to the Memphis *Appeal* viewed the plea for Negro voting restrictions made by T. B. Edgington as an "infinitely more sensible and harmless" remedy to the race problem "than the one proposed by those who seem to regard the education of the negro as a panacea for all the ills, social and political, present and prospective, incidental to a conflict of

[10]Aug. 27, 1890.
[11]Aug. 18, 1890.

204

races." However "ameliorating" the influence of education might be upon society generally, "it is undeniably true that the most clamorous and aggressive negroes where the race question is involved, will be found amongst those best educated."[12] Not only was education unlikely to resolve racial conflict in politics, according to this view, but also it would lead inevitably to increased hostilities.

Adding to white resentment of Negro suffrage were white temperance crusaders who, like embittered state-credit men earlier in the decade, blamed their defeat in the statewide prohibition referendum of 1887 upon Negro opposition. "I don't suppose there were a hundred negroes who voted for it, they were almost solid against it," John H. Henderson, a white Franklin lawyer who had worked hard for prohibition, confided to his diary.[13] John MacGowan explained the defeat of the Prohibitionists in similar terms: "The colored voters have been hired with whiskey and money to vote against the proposed amendment."[14] The editor of the Nashville *American* echoed MacGowan's sentiments, as did Oscar P. Fitzgerald, editor of the *Christian Advocate*, which was published in Nashville by the Methodist Episcopal Church, South. To Fitzgerald the election revealed two "undeniable" facts: "First, that a decided majority of the white vote of Tennessee was for prohibition," and second, "that the Negro vote was almost solid against prohibition." The "liquor men in Tennessee," declared the *Advocate*, owed "their temporary escape to the black voters they sent to the polls, inflamed with whiskey, fed with their money, and wearing their badges." The "moral of this fact," the editor implied, was that black voters represented an obstacle to Christian reform.[15] In an 1890 speech to The National Reform Association in Washington, D. C., entitled "the Southern Race Problem," Fitzgerald presented another indictment against black voters. Citing whiskey as the chief cause of racial strife in the

[12]June 4, 1889.

[13]Entry of Sept. 30, 1887 (Manuscript Div., Tennessee State Library and Archives).

[14]Chattanooga *Times*, Oct. 2, 1887.

[15]Nashville *American*, Oct. 17, 1887; *Christian Advocate*, Oct. 8, 1887.

South, he complained that, in the referendum on prohibition in Tennessee, "there was no end to Negro votes on the wrong side . . . . From early morn to dewy eve they poured in upon us in a continuous stream." That was proof enough for Fitzgerald that Negro voting had "not worked satisfactorily to any party or to either race."[16]

The frustrated white Prohibitionists who blamed black voters for their defeat exaggerated white votes for the amendment and apparently overlooked the real contributions that Negroes had made in behalf of their cause. Local and national black leaders had worked in the Tennessee crusade to cultivate Prohibitionist sentiment among the masses of their people. Joseph C. Price, president of Livingstone College in North Carolina, attracted large crowds comprised of both races as he toured the state advocating prohibition. Price's constant theme was that prohibition would exercise a conservative influence upon blacks by fostering self-help, education, propertyholding, and church attendance. What was more important, he argued, black support for prohibition would improve racial harmony and demonstrate the error of "those who opposed the granting of the franchise to the negro" on the grounds "that we would not vote on the side of reform and patriotism."[17] Thus, by tying black suffrage to support for reform, Price inadvertently left blacks vulnerable to ensuing white charges that the defeat of prohibition proved the moral irresponsibility of Negroes and their incapacity as voters.

Black support for prohibition also came from church leaders, college students, and newspapers. Bishop Henry M. Turner of the African Methodist Episcopal Church urged blacks to purify themselves of sins prevalent among whites, such as drinking whiskey, thereby demonstrating their virtue. Black Women's Christian Temperance Unions were joined by Negro students and teachers from Knoxville College and from Fisk, Central Tennessee, and Roger Williams universities in Nashville in propagandizing and

[16]*Christian Advocate*, Apr. 19, 1890.

[17]Knoxville*Journal*, Sept. 13, 1887; Memphis *Avalanche*, Sept. 26, 1887; Paul E. Isaac, *Prohibition and Politics: Turbulent Decades in Tennessee, 1885–1920* (Knoxville: Univ. of Tennessee Press, 1965), 36.

agitating for the adoption of the amendment. The editor of the Fisk *Herald,* for example, viewed prohibition as "the greatest issue that has been before the American people since the manumission of the seven millions." Moreover, blacks submitted petitions to the state legislature, organized county temperance alliances, and wrote letters to newspapers favoring the prohibition amendment.[18]

It is impossible to determine the actual racial breakdown in the vote on the prohibition amendment. In the predominantly black wards of Nashville and Memphis, however, the referendum was defeated 499–176 and 534–367, respectively. Nevertheless, many of the predominantly white wards in the two cities also returned sizable majorities against the amendment, and it failed, 5,440–4,074 in Nashville and 6,621–2,389 in Memphis. The prohibition measure suffered defeat in all five West Tennessee counties where blacks had outnumbered whites in the census of 1880, but it was also defeated in six West Tennessee counties in which blacks had constituted less than 20 percent of the total population in 1880.[19]

In short, the election returns indicate that the majority of blacks may have voted against prohibition but, apparently, so did the majority of whites. Through their oversimplified analysis of the vote, those white Prohibitionists who blamed their defeat upon black voters helped infuse the movement to restrict Negro voting with a moral impulse.

The defeat of the prohibition referendum reinforced the conviction of John MacGowan that a reform of the election laws was needed. In the aftermath of the election, he noted that his Chattanooga *Times* had urged voting reforms earlier, only to meet the stiff opposition of Republicans who feared such laws would reduce the black electorate. "Now some of these same politicians are dismally howling over alleged frauds committed by this same

[18]Memphis *Appeal,* Nov. 1, 1887; Knoxville *Journal,* May 1, 1887; Sept. 30, 1888; Isaac, *Prohibition and Politics,* 36; Fisk *Herald* (Sept., Oct. 1887); *Senate Journal,* 1887, p. 234; Chattanooga *Times,* Apr. 26, 1886; May 21, 1887; New York *Freeman,* July 16, 1887.

[19]Nashville *American,* Oct. 1, 14, 1887; Memphis *Appeal,* Sept. 30, 1887.

class of people," he asserted. MacGowan doubted, however, that "this dose of their own medicine would have a salutary effect" upon Republicans who had supported prohibition. The upcoming presidential election probably would see "the criminal use of the negro at the polls next year on a larger scale than ever was seen in Tennessee," he warned.[20]

Another irritant that aroused fierce resentment among whites was the insistence with which some black leaders demanded political patronage and federal intervention to protect black voting rights. With Republicans in control of the presidency and both houses of Congress after the 1888 national elections, there was real fear of federal legislation to protect voting rights. Black efforts to secure such protection heightened Democratic anxieties. For example, an appeal by Memphis Negroes to President-elect Harrison for political patronage and federal protection of the ballot provoked a quick response from the Memphis *Avalanche*. With most of the institutions, property, and resources in the South belonging to white people, the editor asked, did blacks really expect whites to turn the government over to their direction? "The pretensions of so-called 'leading colored men,' and their radical backers, to control matters and assert themselves in a country where the great bulk of their race own nothing, have no interests, and show no disposition to acquire any," he stated, "exhibits a degree of colossal assurance which reaches the sublime." Fear that blacks might succeed in winning federal support prompted the editor of the *Avalanche* to applaud voting restrictions in Tennessee as a necessary precaution against federal intervention. The *Avalanche* admonished West Tennessee Democratic leaders who were meeting prior to the extra session of the legislature in February 1890 to examine any revisions the voting laws might need "from the standpoint of our homes and our home government."[21]

Black appeals to Washington for suffrage protection provoked Jacob McGavock Dickinson to advise Negroes during the Tennes-

[20]Oct. 7, 1887.
[21]Memphis *Avalanche*, Feb. 24, 1889; Memphis *Appeal*, Feb. 17, 20, 1890.

see centennial celebration in 1896 that "the day has passed when you can look to outside power to push you to a position which you can neither achieve nor maintain." Dickinson had played a prominent role in centralizing the Nashville city government in 1883 at the expense of black representation. He now paternalistically urged Negroes to strive to elevate themselves through "industry, economy, integrity, the practice of social virtues and fidelity to the demands of useful citizenship." Until they had spent "many years of training for the duties of citizenship," he assured them, they would "enjoy more liberties and blessings" by placing themselves under Anglo-Saxon control than they ever could hope to enjoy under a government of their own.[22]

In addition to the fear of federal intervention, there were other forces that increased white hostility toward Negro voting. Foremost among these forces in Tennessee was the political leverage of blacks in the municipal politics of Memphis, Nashville, and Chattanooga. White urban reformers viewed propertyless black voters as tools of Republican or "nonpartisan" machines, and blamed black voters for the inefficiency and corruption of city government.[23] In the wake of the national and local elections of 1888, urban newspapers in Nashville and Chattanooga launched an electoral reform movement by focusing attention on fraudulent voting practices in those cities. In both places Negroes were singled out as the prime source of political corruption. "To say that the Negro race in its present condition is fit for self-government," the Nashville *American* editorialized, "would, in our opinion, be all else than truth." Even if it were conceded that Negroes were capable of self-government, the *American* insisted, they were incapable of governing the white race. The crucial question, therefore, was "how to so regulate matters that the two races so essentially different [might] live under the same laws and under the same flag in peace and harmony." During the weeks following the election of 1888, the *American* conducted an exposé of fraudulent voting practices that it attributed to Negroes in that election.

[22]MS copy of speech delivered at Nashville, June 1, 1896, Dickinson Papers.
[23]See Ch. IV.

Each account was followed with a plea for a voter-registration law.[24]

The *American* alternated between stigmatizing Negro voters as a peculiar source of corruption in politics and vilifying them because of presumed deficiencies in their character. Negro voters, according to its logic, were "just the kind of men to be blind, obedient and unthinking tools in the hands of smart, unscrupulous and designing demagogues." The Negro voted "blindly, stupidly, passionately as the dupe of knaves who play upon his prejudices, his credulity and his unfathomable ignorance." In any case, if Negroes could not protect their right to vote against the encroachments of whites, the editor of the *American* curiously reasoned that they were "not very safe voters anyway." According to the *American's* formulations it was unnecessary to search for the dishonest voter because "the color of his face proclaims the presence of one who has a vote to sell for a few cents or barter for a few drinks of whisky." It was not simply a class deficiency that kept blacks from voting rationally, for the white voter, "however poor and ignorant, knows that there is an immeasurable distance between him and the Negro, and he feels that the practice of 'selling votes' is peculiarly a mark of Negro depravity and baseness." The most pressing question facing Southerners, therefore, was "whether an inferior race shall by mere force of number rule over a superior race."[25]

By 1887, John MacGowan of the Chattanooga *Times* had turned from optimistic assessments concerning the beneficial effect education would have on Negro voters to a blanket indictment of them as "the fraudulent voting class in all our cities." If the South hoped to retain law, order, and civilization, he declared, "the supremacy of intelligence and morality" must be maintained. The South would not submit "to the domination of an element totally unfit, morally and intellectually, for the functions of government." During the weeks preceding and immediately following the fall elections of 1888, MacGowan waged a campaign similar to that of

[24]Nashville *American*, Dec. 6, 1888; Jan. 19, 1889.
[25]*Ibid.*, Jan. 23, Apr. 19, 21, 1889.

the Nashville *American*, stigmatizing Negro voters as a peculiarly corrupt element in city politics. The *Times* charged that hundreds of black Georgians were imported into Chattanooga on election day to cast Republican votes. Moreover, the conduct of blacks at the polls was "disgraceful in the highest degree." To prevent these fraudulent practices, MacGowan advocated an educational qualification for voting, at the same time urging that adequate provision be made for universal public education.[26]

In Memphis, the battle over home rule carried with it a drive to limit the political power of blacks—power that had been reduced when, in 1878, control of the local government was transferred to the governor and the legislature. Now, in the municipal elections of 1888 and 1890, home rule was a fiercely fought issue, especially because a return to self-government could have brought an expansion of black political power. Memphis had gradually regained a measure of local control as a taxing district headed by an elected president. To beat incumbent David P. Hadden, who favored continuation of the taxing-district government, his opponents would have had to satisfy whites that home rule would not benefit the large black population of Memphis. This they had been unable to do, and, although cunningly accusing Hadden of courting Negro votes, they had failed to dislodge him in the election of 1886.[27] Switching tactics, the advocates of home rule thereupon supported state electoral reforms that were intended, in part at least, to control the urban Negro vote. In December 1888, and again early in 1889, the Memphis *Appeal* endorsed the Australian ballot and voter registration as much-needed reforms in Tennessee.[28] After the 1889 state legislature adopted voting restrictions aimed largely at blacks, the advocates of home rule in Memphis could press for local self-government without risking white control.

In the movement to erect legal barriers against black voting in Tennessee, a prominent place must be accorded white urban reformers in Memphis, Nashville, and Chattanooga. In these

[26]Mar. 30, 1887; June 1, Oct. 1, 10, 24, Nov. 4, 6, 8–9, 22, 28–30, Dec. 18, 1888.
[27]Memphis *Avalanche*, Feb. 24, 1889.
[28]Dec. 13, 1888; Feb. 8, 1889.

211

cities the class interests of white propertyholders and business-minded city boosters, together with racist assumptions about black voting behavior, made voting restrictions aimed at blacks appear to be a logical progression in the drive for good government.

Democrats from the heavily black-populated counties of West Tennessee also played an important role in the drive for the adoption of restrictive voting laws in 1889 and 1890. Indeed, a recent student has argued that "upper-class, black-belt, conservative politicians led the movement in Tennessee."[29] A Democratic legislator revealed something of the extent of the influence of black-belt party leaders when he wrote Governor Robert L. Taylor during the summer of 1889 claiming that the election laws had been "forced upon us by our West Tennessee friends."[30] West Tennessee Democrats were certainly not alone in advocating restrictive voting laws, however.

Each segment of the Democratic party in Tennessee joined in the movement for restrictive-voting legislation. Governor Taylor, whose administration leaned toward the New South-industrialist faction in dispensing patronage, provided executive leadership for the movement by urging electoral reform. New South-oriented newspapers, like the Chattanooga *Times* and the Memphis *Avalanche*, joined Bourbon journals in demanding restrictions on Negro voting. In fact, the state voting laws were adopted in a New South atmosphere that equated the public welfare with business interests and with both political and economic stability. Moreover, the occasional competition for the Negro vote between agrarian and industrial-oriented factions in the Democratic party

[29]J. Morgan Kousser, "Post-Reconstruction Suffrage Restrictions in Tennessee: A New Look at the V.O. Key Thesis," *Political Science Quarterly* 88 (Dec. 1973), 676. Kousser assigns responsibility to black-belt aristocrats for leading the disfranchisement movement throughout the South. He also contends that the movement to restrict suffrage in Tennessee typified what happened in other southern states; i.e., it succeeded only after intimidation, fraud, and violence had already reduced Republican support. See *ibid.*, 656–57, 674, 675–76; see also Kousser, *The Shaping of Southern Politics: Suffrage Restriction and the Establishment of the One-Party South, 1880–1910* (New Haven: Yale Univ. Press, 1974), 6–7, 107–9, 243–44, 246–47.

[30]W. J. Whitthorne to Robert L. Taylor, July 29, 1889, Taylor Papers.

and the way by which each attacked the other for soliciting that vote invariably resulted in the paradox of increased hostility from both sides toward black suffrage. It is hard to tell exactly what role the rising agrarian element in the state legislature played in adoption of the restrictive-voting laws. Leaders in the agrarian movement in Tennessee did not threaten to breach the color line by forging a biracial political alliance during the eighties, but of the 132 members of the legislature in 1889, 52 have been identified as members of the Farmers' Alliance; notable among them was Benjamin J. Lea, the speaker of the senate. Although members of the Alliance did not dominate the leadership of the legislature in the 1889–90 General Assembly, they supported the voting laws with greater consistency than did non-Alliance Democrats.[31] In the final analysis, urban and black-belt Democrats from each faction of the party were in a position to enact suffrage reforms for a combination of partisan, racial, and so-called progressive reasons.

The arguments in favor of Negro disfranchisement in Tennessee, as throughout the South, encompassed a broad range of racist dogma. They also touched upon complicated economic and social realities that raised fundamental questions about age-old tensions between property rights and individual rights in the democratic process. Earlier in the eighties many whites had struggled to accommodate the prevailing laissez-faire individualism with their convictions concerning innate racial differences. They briefly considered the idea of interracial competition on an individual basis but then rejected it in favor of the concept of a dual society allowing for racially separate but equal class and individual distinctions. Before the end of the eighties, however, most whites accepted racial categorizations which lumped all Negroes together at the bottom of the social ladder. In short, most whites had

---

[31]Hart, "Bourbonism and Populism," 193–97, 204, 206. Examination of the state newspaper published by the Tennessee Alliance during the eighties, the *Weekly Toiler*, provides no evidence that the members of the Alliance held racial attitudes different from those of the majority of whites. See the *Weekly Toiler*, 1888–1890. Hart, "Bourbonism and Populism," 180–83, arrives at a similar conclusion.

come to view the black voter as irresponsible, gravely threatening the interests of the white propertyholder, large or small. Suppression of Negroes politically, therefore, was necessary in order to preserve the white man's property. This concept was a central ingredient in the campaign for Negro disfranchisement. "When men's property, their peace and all that they hold dear, are endangered," wrote Edward Ward Carmack, editor of the Nashville *American*, "they will defend them, no matter in what form the aggression may come—whether as a highwayman with a bludgeon or a negro with a ballot."[32] Based on the perceptions that the white majority held concerning black voters, cultural ethnocentrism, and economic self-interest, and buttressed by the conclusions of science, these views came to exercise a compelling influence in Tennessee politics.

Nowhere was the growing white hostility to black voting in Tennessee reflected more clearly than in the pronouncements of the leading Democratic newspaper in the state, the Nashville *American*. In several editorials devoted to the race issue following the Democratic triumph of 1890, Carmack expressed some of the most extreme anti-Negro sentiment contemporarily disseminated in the Tennessee press. To Carmack, the Republican party represented "the densest ignorance" and "the basest passions," and was in "league with 'conjure' bag doctors and rabbit-foot 'hoodoos.'" It "sought to give over as prey to negro barbarism the land which our fathers wrested from the Indian savage." Carmack urged the constitutional disfranchisement of Negroes even if it meant a loss of representation in Congress. The extension of suffrage rights to them had been "a blunder and a crime" because of their recent emergence from "ages of barbarism and centuries of slavery." In a ringing assertion of Anglo-Saxon superiority, he judged the white man's right to govern to be "the growth of a germ which existed among our ancestors at the time of Christ"; on the other hand, "the African race" never had "a gleam of light across its dark history and . . . had within itself no promises or possibili-

[32]Nashville *American*, May 8, 1883; Apr. 25, 1889.

ty of progress. It was a race without history, without ideas and without hope."[33]

The practical effect of this attitude had been revealed by one of Carmack's contemporaries a few months earlier when MacGowan of the Chattanooga *Times* responded to a letter asking him to explain the Democratic party's position on Negroes in politics. There was little place for Negroes in the Democratic party, replied MacGowan; it had become the white man's refuge because of the Republican willingness to cater to blacks. Acknowledging that in sections of the South blacks could not vote, or, if voting, were "counted out," MacGowan added that any other course "would cause financial ruin, destroy civil government, bring in anarchy." Suppression of the Negro vote was not "a party measure"; it was done as "a necessity to decent political and social conditions." Whether Democrat or Republican, MacGowan advised, the white race would control southern politics, for whites would never "permit a race or class destitute of all training, as well as of natural aptitude for political affairs to control."[34]

The idea that Negroes had no business in politics found reinforcement in many white churches. The Reverend R. A. Steel, pastor of the McKendree Methodist Episcopal Church, South, of Nashville, was particularly vocal in making pronouncements from the pulpit relegating Negroes to their "proper role in society." Steel claimed black political power would result in the destruction of civilization. The Negro problem should be left to the white South, he asserted, where moral and religious forces could be relied upon to reach a safe solution. This was "God's plan of progress." He assured his congregation that Negroes were "coming more and more to realize that . . . they have nothing to gain from politics," and that, if left alone, they would "quietly and wisely" acquiesce "in the inevitable supremacy of the whites."[35]

[33]*Ibid.*, Nov. 11, Dec. 24, 1890.
[34]Aug. 5, 1890.
[35]*Nashville City Directory*, 1890 (Nashville: Marshall & Bruce, 1890), 548, 759; Nashville *American*, July 29, 1890.

As white hostility toward black voting surged in Tennessee, the barriers that had previously blocked legal efforts to restrict Negro voting crumbled.[36] Throughout the early eighties most southern whites had assumed that northern control of the federal government made Negro suffrage a permanent reality. Consequently, attempting to minimize its influence, they forged political alliances with responsive blacks, centralized local governments to check black political power, and, on occasion, resorted to fraud, intimidation, and violence. In the late eighties, however, some white leaders began to perceive a change in northern liberal sentiment on the race question. Throughout 1889 and 1890 Democratic newspapers in the state kept their antennae trained on the northern press and frequently published excerpts reflecting disillusionment with Negro voters and growing sympathy for the racial attitudes of southern whites. In a series of editorials in January and February 1889, for example, the Memphis *Avalanche* focused its attention upon a feasible resolution of problems presented by Negro suffrage. The *Avalanche* attributed the rising interest in the "negro problem" to northern perplexity over the question of Negro suffrage in the South. Because northern Republicans finally had realized that they could not further "help the negro," the editor of the *Avalanche* suggested that southern whites could now take the initiative in resolving the race problem.[37] A few months later the editor of the Memphis *Appeal* made a similar observation. "The Northern people are beginning to understand the relative social and political positions of the white people and the negroes in the South," he wrote.[38] In late 1890, John MacGowan approvingly quoted a northern Republican editor who had concluded that northern concern for the political rights of blacks was misdirected. Northerners were simply acknowledging, stated MacGowan, what white Southerners had long recognized—that to "intrust

[36]In *Strange Career of Jim Crow*, 69–82, Woodward describes the erosion of "restraining forces" which had previously checked the South's capitulation to "extreme racism." According to him, the retreat of northern liberalism and conservatives' use of the race issue to beat down agrarian radicalism resulted in a sharp decline in paternalism and produced a wave of racism that led to rigid segregation and disfranchisement.

[37]Jan. 15–16, Feb. 12, 19, 1889.   [38]May 24, 1889.

either local government or the choice of national representatives in the hands of a negro majority" would mean "bankruptcy, disorder, and, if persisted in, the fall of the white to the social and moral level of the black race."[39]

Ironically, it probably was the adoption of voting restrictions in northern states that provided the immediate stimulus for the enactment of restrictive-voting legislation in Tennessee. Democratic newspapers in the state closely followed the passage of a statewide Australian-ballot law in Massachusetts in May 1888, and the adoption of a similar bill by the New York legislature in 1888 and again in 1889, although Governor David B. Hill of that state vetoed the bill on both occasions. By the end of 1889, nine nonsouthern states had adopted the secret ballot: Massachusetts, Connecticut, Indiana, Michigan, Minnesota, Missouri, Montana, Rhode Island, and Wisconsin.[40]

In brief, the Australian system required the state to print and distribute uniform ballots which listed the candidates either by office or by party columns. Also required were physical facilities enabling the voter to cast a secret and independent ballot. Only two of the first ten states to adopt the law allowed party symbols to be printed by the names of the candidates, thus making it easier for illiterates to select the candidates of their choice. As a result, in most states where it was adopted, the secret ballot entailed a modified educational qualification by making it difficult for illiterate voters to distinguish among the maze of candidates usually listed by office on their ballots.[41]

This point was not lost upon advocates of electoral reform in Tennessee who cited the Australian-ballot legislation of northern states, especially that of Massachusetts, as justification for the adoption of voting restrictions at home. This tactic allayed white fears of federal interference. It also bolstered the growing convic-

[39]Dec. 22, 1890.

[40]Joseph B. Bishop, "The Secret Ballot in Thirty-three states," *Forum* 12 (Jan. 1892), 592; L. E. Fredman, *The Australian Ballot: The Story of an American Reform* (East Lansing: Michigan State Univ. Press, 1968), 38–46.

[41]Bishop, "Secret Ballot," 592; Fredman, *Australian Ballot*, 43, 46–47; Kousser, *Shaping of Southern Politics*, 52–53.

tion that the secret ballot represented an acceptable means of eliminating illiterate voters, of whom blacks constituted the most easily identifiable group. In fact, many white electoral reformers had come to view the problem of illiterate voters in terms of race rather than class. Certainly any effort to disfranchise illiterate voters would fall most heavily on blacks. According to the census of 1880, 71.7 percent of the blacks over ten years of age in Tennessee were illiterate; the corresponding figure for whites was 27.3 percent; by 1890 illiteracy in the same age group had fallen to 54.2 percent of blacks and 17.8 percent of whites. In Tennessee and some northern states both early advocates and opponents of an Australian-ballot law alike viewed it as a means of imposing an educational qualification for voting.[42]

When the Tennessee legislature convened in Nashville in January 1889, several Democratic newspapers across the state published laudatory accounts of the Australian-ballot laws recently implemented in Louisville, Kentucky, and Massachusetts, as well as the one then under consideration by the New York legislature. "This is one way of providing for an educational qualification without a decrease in representation," observed the Memphis *Avalanche*. "And yet no objection could be made to it, since numerous Northern states are adopting it for themselves." The *Avalanche* "heartily" recommended that the Tennessee legislature eliminate illiterate voters by adopting the Australian ballot, since it met "all the requirements of the Southern problem better than any other plan which has been suggested." Similarly, following its approval by some northern states, the Memphis *Appeal*, an early champion of the Australian ballot, pressed with renewed vigor for its adoption, along with a voter-registration bill in Tennessee.[43]

[42]United States, Bureau of the Census, *Abstract of the Eleventh Census, 1890* (2d ed., rev. & enl.; Washington, D. C.: Government Printing Office, 1896), 64–67; Fredman, *Australian Ballot*, 43–45, 47–49, 51; Kousser, *Shaping of Southern Politics*, 52–60, 111.

[43]Memphis *Avalanche*, Jan. 16, Feb. 12, Mar. 12, 1889; Memphis *Appeal*, Nov. 14, 1886; Dec. 13, 1888; Feb. 8, June 3, 1889. See also the Nashville *American*, Jan. 12, 22, 1889.

The secret ballot and the requirement of registration for voting would eliminate white, as well as black, voters. Before Democratic leaders in the state dared to adopt either an Australian ballot or a voter-registration law they had to solve this dilemma. "Any attempt to compel the plain people of the villages, smaller cities and country precincts to register as a condition precedent to voting will be fiercely resented," MacGowan of the Chattanooga *Times* warned. He feared that a statewide voter-registration law would "make the majority party intensely unpopular." If fathered by a Democratic legislature, such a proposition might "anger to the point of irreconcilability thousands of ignorant white Democrats, and make them Republicans." Consequently, MacGowan suggested that, since the major voting problems—blacks going to the polls in large groups and their showing greater independence—were largely urban phenomena, suffrage restrictions should be limited to the major cities. This scheme, while presenting a handy device for controlling the black vote, would at the same time reduce the risk of alienating rural white voters.[44] Democrats in the 1889 legislature adopted precisely this formula by confining the secret-ballot law to the four major urban areas of the state—Chattanooga, Knoxville, Nashville, and Memphis—and to the entire counties of Davidson and Shelby, within which the latter two cities were located. This selective application of the law reflected both the efforts of its backers to appease those Democrats who shared MacGowan's fears and the extent to which urban Democrats like MacGowan provided much of the impetus behind the movement to restrict black voting in Tennessee.

The primary obstacle to the adoption of voting restrictions in Tennessee, however, was the two-party system that survived in the state throughout most of the eighties. Until 1888 Republicans generally held from 35 to 40 percent of the seats in the state senate and from 35 to 50 percent of the seats in the state house of representatives. As long as they maintained at least one-third of the members in either house, Republicans could block suffrage restrictions that would fall heavily on Negro voters simply by

[44]Dec. 29, 1888; Mar. 16, 1889.

boycotting legislative sessions in order to prevent a quorum. In 1885 they utilized this means of blocking a bill which would have required voters to register and, furthermore, to present certification of registration. The debates on the 1885 measure are significant in that they foreshadowed later developments. Democratic advocates of the 1885 registration bill employed racial arguments in behalf of the measure and supported it as a deterrent to fraudulent Negro voting. "The negro voters are as much alike as two black-eyed peas, and it is a notorious fact that in the larger cities they vote early and often," the Memphis *Appeal* declared. It further claimed that, in every important election in Tennessee, Republicans brought Mississippi and Arkansas Negroes into the state to vote their ticket.[45]

The Republican Knoxville *Chronicle*, however, labeled the 1885 registration bill a crude partisan device intended to check the steady growth of the Republican party in the state. Under the camouflage of voting reform, it charged, Democrats intended to disfranchise a large percentage of the black voters in order "to keep the Democratic party in power." Republicans insisted that a registration system administered in the partisan interests of Democrats would, instead of reducing corruption, "authorize fraud by law under a pretense of honesty." For proof of this contention they ironically pointed to the abuses that had existed in the registration system instituted during the administration of Republican Governor William G. Brownlow.[46] A leading East Tennessee Republican, Roderick R. Butler, who would be elected congressman from the First District in 1886, succinctly summarized his party's opposition to the registration bill: "With a registration bill they [the Democrats] could defraud the colored voters in Memphis, Nashville, Chattanooga and Knoxville." Since these cities had

[45]For the party composition of the state legislature during the 1880s, see the following: 1881—Memphis *Appeal*, Nov. 7, 1880; see also White, *Messages*, VI, 639; 1883—Chattanooga *Times*, Nov. 10, 1882; 1885—extrapolated from Memphis *Appeal*, Jan. 6, 1885; 1887—White, *Messages*, VII, 234; 1889—Memphis *Appeal–Avalanche*, Nov. 15, 1890; Memphis *Appeal*, Apr. 10, May 15, 19, 1885.

[46]Apr. 7, 17, 21, May 30, June 5, 1885.

become centers of Republican strength, Butler continued, "something had to be done to give them to the democracy."[47] The 1885 fight over the registration bill convinced the Knoxville *Chronicle* that, if the Democrats ever gained sufficient power in the legislature, they would both adopt a registration law and enact legislation making the payment of poll taxes a suffrage requirement. Finally, by 1889, with their power in the legislature reduced to only 9 of 33 seats in the senate and 29 of 99 in the house, the Republicans would be unable to forestall the adoption of election laws that even further undermined their strength by reducing the number of black voters.[48]

Disillusionment with education as a curative for the color line in politics, the displaced aggressions of white temperance crusaders, the growing militancy of black leaders in demanding political equality, the threat of federal protection of voting rights, and the urban political power of blacks all helped create a white reaction against Negro voting in Tennessee. Nevertheless, it was the change in northern liberal sentiment concerning the race question, the adoption of voting restrictions in northern states, the diminished white apprehension that voting restrictions might weaken the Democratic party by disfranchising whites as well as blacks, and the heavy majority Democrats held in the legislative session of 1889 that set the stage for the restriction of Negro voting in Tennessee.

Although Tennessee's voting legislation of 1889 and 1890 did not eliminate Negro voters as thoroughly as did the more proscriptive legislation of Mississippi in 1890, South Carolina in 1895, and Louisiana in 1898, it foreshadowed the trend toward the disfranchisement of Negroes within a framework of legality and reform.[49] The impact of the new voting laws eclipsed black

[47]Bristol *Courier*, quoted in the Memphis *Avalanche*, Aug. 7, 1885.
[48]Knoxville *Chronicle*, May 18, 1885; Memphis *Appeal–Avalanche*, Nov. 15, 1890.
[49]For a general discussion of the restrictive-voting legislation in other southern states, see Woodward, *Origins of the New South*, 275, 321–49; *Strange Career of Jim Crow*, 83–86; and Kousser, *Shaping of Southern Politics*, 83–103, 123–38.

political influence and marked an important turning point for Negroes in Tennessee politics. Better than half a century would pass before they regained the position in state politics that they had occupied in the eighties.

VII

Suffrage Restriction and the Decline of Black Political Influence

The state legislature convened in January 1889 with Democrats holding better than a two-thirds majority in each house. Leaders in both parties anticipated changes in Tennessee's voting requirements. Thus it came as no surprise when Democratic Governor Robert L. Taylor, in his opening address to the Fifty-sixth General Assembly, urged the adoption of a "well devised registration law" and called for legislation to implement the dormant state constitutional provision making payment of the poll tax a suffrage requirement. Shortly after the organization of the legislature, Democratic leaders moved swiftly to marshal support for a revision of the election laws. Despite vigorous opposition, a party caucus eventually endorsed a voter-registration bill and a secret-ballot proposal. At the same time, the caucus clearly revealed its partisan intent by also endorsing a scheme to gerrymander the Third Congressional District, which had been carried by the Republicans in 1888.[1]

After its endorsement by the Democratic caucus the registration bill sailed through the legislature on a strictly partisan vote. It was sponsored by Senator John C. Myers, a thirty-eight-year-old lawyer from McMinnville, a Prohibitionist, and a staunch Democrat. His bill gave the governor the authority to appoint registration officials, ended registration twenty days before the date of the election, and required presentation of a registration certificate at the polls before the prospective voter could cast a ballot. Democrats easily beat down Republican-sponsored amendments to blunt the effect of the Myers bill and then used their clear control

[1]White, *Messages*, VII, 289, 295; Nashville *American*, Feb. 20, Mar. 19, 21, 1889.

223

of the legislature to extend the bill's provisions to all cities, towns, and voting districts with 500 or more voters, rather than the 2,000 or more originally stipulated. In a final effort to forestall adoption of the Myers bill, Republican legislators offered their own registration measure. It would have given the county courts, rather than the governor, the power to appoint registration officials, and it called for a less detailed examination of prospective voters than did the Myers bill. This tactic, like the earlier Republican amendments, met swift defeat.[2]

Shortly after the Myers bill was introduced, Senator Joseph H. Dortch of Fayette County fanned the partisan flames in the legislature by sponsoring a secret-ballot law modeled after the Australian-ballot system. Senator Dortch was part-owner and editor of the Somerville *Reporter and Falcon* in Fayette County and chairman of the county's Democratic executive committee.[3] His secret-ballot measure would apply to Shelby and Davidson counties and to the cities of Knoxville and Chattanooga—all areas with a sizable black vote. The controversy over the Dortch bill turned upon a provision that prohibited assistance to illiterate voters in marking their ballots. Republicans and a few Democrats insisted that the bill was unconstitutional because it indirectly imposed an educational qualification on voting. The state constitution explicitly forbade any restrictions on adult male suffrage other than those imposed for criminal offenses and a provision, unenforced since 1873, making the payment of a poll tax a voting requirement. When opponents of the Dortch bill sought to amend it in order to provide assistance for those voters who could not read their ballots, a sharp debate followed.

Senator Dortch, with the assistance of his two colleagues from Shelby County and the speaker of the senate, Benjamin J. Lea, led the fight to defeat the amendment. Dortch complained that permitting illiterate voters to receive aid struck at the main safeguard of the secret ballot and that, in the interest of the Democratic

[2]For a biographical sketch of Myers, see Nashville *American*, Jan. 5, 1889; *Senate Journal*, 1889, pp. 42, 47, 51, 80, 414–20, 602, 621, 645–52; Nashville *American*, Feb. 20, Mar. 19, 29, Apr. 3, 1889.

[3]Nashville *American*, Jan. 5, 1889.

party, the bill should be preserved intact. Lea, a former attorney general of the state, Confederate veteran, and Haywood County lawyer, revealed the identity of the illiterate voters about whom he was concerned by asserting that it had reached the point in Tennessee "where Negroes were bought and voted by the hundreds." Their bloc vote, he warned, posed a grave threat to white control. At least one Democratic senator, however, argued that the measure would be politically inexpedient. Apparently he feared that it might antagonize the many illiterate whites who would be equally affected by its provisions. "The party that puts this bill into the laws of Tennessee," he declared, "hangs a millstone about its neck." Nevertheless, the major impact of the bill obviously would fall on blacks since, according to the census of 1890, 54.2 percent of the state's black population over ten years of age was illiterate compared to 17.8 percent of the whites.[4]

During the heated legislative debates on the Dortch bill the Democratic press in Nashville and Memphis applied steady pressure to secure its passage, voicing progressive concern over honest and orderly elections as well as employing partisan and racist arguments. The Nashville *American* urged all Democrats to stand by the party caucus's endorsement of the secret ballot, defending it as a measure that would "at once introduce clean methods into politics and prove of immense advantage to the Democratic party." The Memphis *Avalanche* specifically identified Negro voters as a grave threat to good government and viewed support for the Dortch law as a blow to black political influence. To carry Shelby County in the past, the editor complained, Democrats had been "compelled to do an amount of work not known in any other state." The nature of at least part of that work was then explained: "A man who persuades a negro to leave town a day before the election is a hero. A man who persuades one to stay away from the polls is a public benefactor." Support for the law was also equated with party self-interest. The *Avalanche* argued that Democrats should take advantage of the largest

[4]Memphis *Avalanche*, Mar. 29, 1889; Chattanooga *Times*, Apr. 3, 1889; Nashville *American*, Jan. 5, 1889; Census Bureau, *Abstract of the Eleventh Census, 1890*, 66–67.

majority they had enjoyed in the General Assembly since the war and strike a blow at Republican strength in the state. "Shall we use this or fritter away a golden opportunity?" it asked. Without the Dortch bill, the editor cried, Shelby County would be lost to the Republicans: "Ask anybody who is familiar with the politics of this county, and he will say give us the Dortch bill or we will perish." The newspaper warned that any Democrats who refused to abide by the decision of the party caucus to support the bill were assuming "a grave responsibility" which might jeopardize their careers. Could they "afford to desert the best interests of the Democratic party and to turn over Shelby County bound hand and foot to the venality and corruption of Negro rule?"[5]

While it was attuned to the partisan advantages the Dortch bill offered, the Memphis *Appeal* contended that the measure also would end electoral corruption, provide the voter with security to cast an independent ballot, and encourage "decency, order and peace at the polls." In short, it would dignify the voting process by eliminating "the negroes who stand about and hinder elections." To those who questioned the constitutionality of the educational qualification, the *Appeal* and the *Avalanche*, as well as the Nashville *American*, skirted the issue by pointing out that northern states had taken the lead in passing similar legislation. Tennessee was simply in the vanguard of a growing national reform movement.[6]

In the face of the urgent prodding of the Democratic newspapers, the constraining influence of the caucus, aggressive leadership in the General Assembly, and the lobbying activities of a prominent delegation of Memphis citizens who descended upon Nashville during the debates, the Dortch bill was pushed through the legislature in April. Anthony Walsh, one of the Memphis lobbyists, was interviewed in the *Avalanche* following the bill's

[5]Nashville *American*, Mar. 27, 29, 1889. The Democratic caucus had endorsed the Myers and Dortch bills on Mar. 18, 22–11. See Nashville *American*, Mar. 19, 21, 1889; Memphis *Avalanche*, Mar. 26, Apr. 1, 1889.

[6]Memphis *Appeal*, Mar. 17, 1889. For similar expressions, see *ibid.*, Mar. 13, 22, 26, 29, 1889; Memphis *Avalanche*, Mar. 26, 1889; Nashville *American*, Mar. 27, 1889.

adoption. "It makes Tennessee Democratic," he exulted, "and it ends Republican attempts to ride into office in Shelby County by bribery and by stirring up the negroes." Democratic newspapers shared his exuberance. The editor of the *Avalanche* predicted that the law would "bear hard upon the Republicans in the counties to which the law applies, and where they have been accustomed to drive the ignorant masses of their party to the polls like pigs and vote them solid." A Democratic newspaper in Chattanooga joined in the praise for the Dortch bill because it would "keep those not capable of reading or writing from voting. That class is not composed, as a rule of property holders." Senator Dortch's leadership in the passage of the law catapulted him into the first rank of Democratic gubernatorial candidates for 1890. There were even rumors that he might contest the Tenth District congressional seat of Democrat James Phelan, owner of the Memphis *Avalanche*.[7]

In addition to passing the registration law and the secret ballot, Democrats in the 1889 General Assembly also took steps to counteract anticipated congressional action on the supervision of national elections. Speaker of the Senate Benjamin J. Lea of Haywood County successfully sponsored a separate-ballot-box law which set aside one polling booth to be used in voting for national officers and another for state officers. The object of the bill, according to Senator Lea, was to remove the election of governor and state legislators from the supervision of federal officers. The means by which Democrats had won control of Haywood County in 1888 doubtless gave Lea a compelling reason for wishing to evade federal supervision of local elections. Like the two previously enacted election laws, the Lea bill passed the legislature by a strictly party vote.[8]

To complete their blueprint for electoral reform, some Democratic leaders in the legislature also hoped to make payment of the poll tax a voting requirement. The Constitution of 1870 included a

[7]For the activities of the Memphis lobbyists, see the Memphis *Avalanche*, Apr. 4, 6, 1889; unidentified Chattanooga newspaper quoted in the Memphis *Appeal*, Mar. 1, 1889.

[8]*Acts*, 1889, pp. 437–38; Chattanooga *Times*, Mar. 31, 1889.

poll-tax provision, but in 1873 the legislature had repealed the enabling act which provided for payment of the tax as a voting qualification. As Democratic legislators gathered in Nashville for the opening session of the General Assembly, many of them included the poll tax among the electoral reforms they thought desirable. Shortly after the legislature convened, Democratic Representative J. D. Pearson of Madison County introduced a bill in the house reinstituting payment of the poll tax as a suffrage qualification. One scholar has attributed the sudden interest in poll-tax legislation to growing demands for additional funds for the public schools, claiming that "it is difficult to connect the poll tax with Negro suffrage." The basis for this argument rests on the fact that poll taxes went into the education fund. Any measure that would encourage payment of the tax, which seems to have gone largely uncollected because it was not a voting requirement, obviously would augment the school fund. Indeed, available records of the debates over the poll tax in the regular session of the 1889 legislature reveal that its supporters offered only two defenses for the measure in the house: it was required by the state constitution, and it would increase the school fund. The existence of widespread opposition to the poll tax among whites, however, probably explains the reticence of Democratic supporters of the measure.[9]

Opponents of the poll tax in the house broadened the scope of the debate by insisting that it would impose an unconstitutional property qualification for voting, would provide numerous opportunities for corruption, would give rich candidates an advantage, would increase taxes, would disfranchise "a large portion of the people of Tennessee," and would discriminate against the poor; furthermore, it was wrong in principle, "wholly un-American," and "a direct stab against our free institutions." While many Democratic legislators feared the poll tax would arouse poor white hostility and be detrimental to the party, Republicans damned the measure as a partisan device.[10]

[9]Nashville *Banner,* Jan. 5, 1889; *House Journal,* 1889, p. 24; Frank B. Williams, "Poll Tax as a Suffrage Requirement," 78, 86, 90.

[10]At least partial coverage of the house debates on the poll tax are found in

The introduction of the poll-tax measure in the legislature occurred in an atmosphere marked by growing white disillusionment with universal manhood suffrage, especially that of Negroes. In the press, the most enlightened contemporary discussions of the need for voting reforms viewed literacy and property qualifications as desirable suffrage requirements which would eliminate irresponsible voters who presumably had neither a financial stake in good government nor a rational concern for public issues. White proponents of voting reform usually, but not always, identified blacks as the irresponsible voters about whom they were most concerned. They explicitly equated tax paying with responsible voting and categorized Negroes as propertyless nontaxpayers. They assumed, sometimes explicitly and sometimes not, that reducing the number of Negro voters would help secure that good government which, by their definition, necessarily meant government by whites.[11]

The poll tax ran aground in the 1889 legislature, however, on the shoals of Democratic fears that it would encourage corruption by enabling wealthy candidates to bribe voters by paying their poll taxes, and, perhaps more significantly, that it would disfranchise poor whites and precipitate a reaction against the Democratic party. It was narrowly defeated in the house and died in committee in the senate. The editor of the Memphis *Appeal*, doubtless reflecting the disappointment of many of the bill's boosters, blamed the failure of the measure on the opposition of Republican legislators who had "largely profited by the colonizing of negroes." The Republican use of the Negro vote should have supplied Democrats with "a controlling reason for the passage of the bill." In any case, the editor found consolation in the passage of the Dortch, Myers, and Lea laws: "The purity of the ballot, the honor of the State and the safety of the liberties of the people appeal with

---

Nashville *American*, Mar. 12, 1889; Memphis *Appeal* and Memphis *Avalanche*, Mar. 12, 1889; see also *House Journal*, 1889, pp. 473, 476, for explanations of votes on the measure.

[11]Memphis *Appeal*, Mar. 12–13, 17, 26, 29, 1889; Memphis *Avalanche*, Mar. 26, 29, Apr. 1, 4, 6, 1889; Chattanooga *Times*, Apr. 3, 1889.

trumpet-tongued earnestness for these measures as necessary and essential safeguards of the public welfare."[12]

The first test of the new election laws came in the municipal elections in Chattanooga in October 1889. Soundly defeated in the legislature, Republicans sought federal and state court injunctions to block implementation of the Myers and Dortch laws in Chattanooga, but both United States District Judge David M. Key and the state chancery court judge in Chattanooga, William H. DeWitt, denied the authority of their respective courts to interfere in that city's election. Judge DeWitt declared that "some of the provisions" of the Dortch Act went "to the verge of constitutional power, if not beyond it," but it was his opinion that the constitutionality of the election laws should be settled by the state supreme court. Judge Key, although also disclaiming any power to issue an injunction, expressed his personal opposition to the Dortch law. It "ties chains around the feet and arms of free men," he stated. Though Key conceded that he thought the implied literacy requirement in the Dortch law clashed with provisions in the state constitution, he claimed that there was no practical way the federal district court could enforce an injunction against the election laws, even if it were granted.[13]

The new voting laws did not have the impact in the Chattanooga election Democrats had desired. With the local electoral machinery in the hands of a strong Republican organization, a large number of blacks complied with the new registration law. Republicans won both the mayor's race and a majority of seats on the city council. Democrats may have been lulled to sleep, as MacGowan of the Chattanooga *Times* had speculated, by assuming that there would be a "sweeping reduction of the negro vote under the provisions of the Dortch bill."[14] In any case, the Chattanooga experience revealed that the secret-ballot and registration laws

[12]Memphis *Appeal* and Memphis *Avalanche*, Mar. 12, 1889; *House Journal*, 1889, pp. 472–73; *Senate Journal*, 1889, p. 485.

[13]Memphis *Avalanche*, Sept. 25, 1889; Knoxville *Journal*, Sept. 29, 1889; Chattanooga *Times*, Oct. 6, 1889.

[14]Knoxville *Journal*, Oct. 11, 1889; Chattanooga *Times*, Oct. 7, 1889.

did not drastically damage the Republicans where they controlled the election machinery.

Succeeding elections between October 1889 and January 1890, held under the new registration and secret-ballot laws in Knoxville, Nashville, and Memphis, however, gave Democrats cause for rejoicing. In its first municipal election after the new registration and ballot laws became effective, Knoxville, situated in a strong Republican county, elected a Democratic mayor. Democrats had usually carried the city during the eighties, and apparently the election laws worked to their advantage chiefly by reducing the total vote. The Knoxville *Journal* claimed that not more than 60 percent of the qualified voters had registered and that less than half of those had actually cast ballots. A candid headline in the Nashville *American* revealed the partisan expectations of Carmack, the editor, regarding the new election laws: "Knoxville Election—The Dortch Law Works Like a Charm—A Democratic Victory."[15]

Prior to the municipal election in Nashville, the Memphis *Appeal* reported that 4,000 voters, "mostly negroes," had neglected to register and were, therefore, disfranchised. "The negroes seemed generally indifferent or were prejudiced against the system," the *Appeal* explained. "The elimination to so large an extent of the element of ignorance from the vote will doubtless prove a good thing for Nashville." The failure of such a large number of Nashville Negroes to register provided the editor with "further evidence of the negro's lack of comprehension of the voting privilege and also his disposition to inaction when free of the place-hunting politicians and the 'inducements' of election day."[16] About 1,800 Negroes were registered; between 400 and 600 voted, the Memphis *Avalanche* estimated. The Memphis press closely observed the Nashville election for some indication of what might be expected in Memphis. The editor of the *Avalanche* noted that the election laws were not rigidly enforced in

[15]Memphis *Avalanche*, Oct. 10, 1889; Knoxville *Journal*, Jan. 19, 1890; Nashville *American*, Jan. 19, 1890.

[16]Memphis *Appeal*, Sept. 20, 1889.

Nashville. Apparently, such was not the case in the subsequent election in Memphis; following the Democratic victory there, the editor of the *Appeal* described the effect of the new voting system: "The Negroes as a rule were slow, and in the main took unkindly to the new conditions upon which a ballot could be cast."[17]

The first trials of the new election laws seemed to indicate that they were advantageous to the Democrats in those areas where the two parties were evenly balanced or where the Democrats already held the majority. In Chattanooga, however, where Republicans clearly were in the ascendancy, the election laws did not produce a political revolution.

Democrats were generally satisfied with the new voting procedures, although their trial in the municipal elections revealed mechanical defects that had to be ironed out. Some Democrats continued to insist that the Dortch law should be amended to provide illiterates assistance in marking their ballots; others wanted both the registration law and the secret ballot extended throughout the state. To clarify the matter of the election laws and to resolve other pressing concerns, Governor Taylor called an extra session of the legislature for February 1890. He recommended that the registration and the Australian-ballot laws be made applicable throughout the state.[18]

A few days before the extra session of the legislature convened, West Tennessee Democratic legislators held a meeting to assure full party support for the revised versions of the election laws. Among those present at the Democratic conclave was "Colonel" T. B. Edgington of Memphis, an outspoken advocate of Negro disfranchisement. He opened discussion of the voting laws by stating, "Some restraint should be put on the negro vote and if the Dortch bill has that effect, I am in favor of it." Edgington,

[17]*Ibid.*, Jan. 11, 1890; Memphis *Avalanche*, Oct. 11, 1889.

[18]For an example of a defect, consider the following: the Dortch law required election officials to collect and cancel registration certificates, but the polling places for state and national elections were to be separated; therefore, upon surrendering his registration certificate at one of these sites, the voter technically would be disqualified from casting his ballot at the other. Memphis *Avalanche*, Feb. 20, 1890; Chattanooga *Times*, Oct. 9–10, 12–13, 19, 1889; White, *Messages* VII, 324–25.

however, vigorously opposed the disfranchisement of "a single white man." Another delegate fervently expressed his belief in the principles of the Democratic party and, with apparent reference to the new voting proposals, announced his willingness to support "anything to put it [the Democratic party] in power and keep it so." Although several delegates at the meeting resurrected the question of a poll-tax law, none took a forthright public stand in favor of such a measure.[19] In this meeting, as in previous discussions of restrictive-voting legislation, the secret-ballot and registration laws were defended as necessary for independent voting and honest elections without reference to the race issue. In most cases, however, blacks were singled out whenever any specific group of voters was mentioned as threatening these principles.

The efforts of West Tennessee Democratic leaders to unite the party behind the new election laws proved successful. When the extra session of the legislature convened, a Democratic caucus endorsed both revised versions of the Myers, Lea, and Dortch laws and the controversial poll tax. The extent of Democratic unity was revealed when the editor of the Chattanooga *Times*, shedding his earlier reservations about the constitutionality of the voting laws, enthusiastically endorsed educational and property qualifications as obstacles to Negro voting. The first bill introduced in the house of representatives called for payment of a poll tax as a prerequisite for voting. Democratic legislators enlisted a wide range of arguments in its behalf: the need to augment the sadly deficient school fund; the idea that only taxpayers should vote; the view that the Constitution of 1870 made it mandatory; the partisan advantage it would give their party; and, finally, the hope that it would help preserve white supremacy by disfranchising Negroes. By a large party vote, Democrats overran Republican opposition and rammed the poll-tax bill, as well as revised versions of the registration, the separate-ballot box, and the Australian-ballot laws, through both houses.[20]

[19]Memphis *Appeal*, Feb. 17, 20, 1890.

[20]Memphis *Avalanche*, Mar. 2, 1890; Chattanooga *Times*, Feb. 2, Mar. 4, 1890; Memphis *Appeal*, Feb. 27, 1890; Nashville *American*, Feb. 27, 1890; Nashville *Banner*, Feb. 28, Mar. 10, 1890; Knoxville *Journal*, Mar. 2, 1890; *House Journal*,

The small minority of Republicans in the legislature again futilely attempted to obstruct, or weaken, the new voting laws. They sought to moderate the effect of the secret ballot upon illiterate voters through an amendment requiring the initial of the candidate's party to be printed on the ballot; another amendment would allow illiterate voters to receive assistance in marking their ballots. They also tried to give the county court, rather than the governor, the power to appoint commissioners of registration under the Myers bill and to allow registration to continue until the day before the election. When all else failed, they attempted to render the Dortch and Myers bills obnoxious by extending their provisions throughout the state. Despite Republican denunciation of the measures as "direct stroke[s] at the rights and privileges of the poor and uneducated class" and as partisan creatures of the Democratic caucus, the new Dortch and Myers bills emerged from the legislature intact.[21]

The secret-ballot law of 1890 was virtually the same as the one passed by the 1889 legislative session. Under the provisions of the revised Dortch law the official ballots listed the names of candidates in alphabetical order under the office for which they were running. The order in which the offices were printed could be varied, and the ballots carried neither party symbols nor other party identifications of the candidates. These provisions almost certainly were designed to make it difficult for illiterates to vote. A section making it a misdemeanor for anyone to "attempt to aid any voter by means of any mechanical device, or any other means whatever," unless the voter was blind or otherwise physically disabled, also discouraged illiterates from voting.[22]

The new version of the Myers law established even more complicated procedures for registering to vote than the original had contained. Its provisions now applied to any city, town, or voting district with a population of 2,500 or more. It empowered

---

1890, 1st Ex. Sess., 13, 28, 99–100, 101–3; *Senate Journal*, 1890, 1st Ex. Sess., 52, 59, 62, 66.

[21]*Senate Journal*, 1890, 1st Ex. Sess., 57–62, 68; *House Journal*, 1890, 1st Ex. Sess., 102–3.

[22]*Acts*, 1890, 1st Ex. Sess., 50–59.

the governor to appoint three commissioners of registration for each county in which the law was applicable. The county commissioners then appointed the registrars for each city, town, or civil district having sufficient population to fall within the provisions of the act. Registration of voters was to close at least twenty days before the election. Upon the request of the registrar, a prospective voter was required to state his age and place of residence (including district or ward, road or street, house number or a description of its location). If the registrant did not own his home, he had to furnish the name of the owner. He also might be required to state his length of residence in the state, district, or city; his marital status; his vocation; his place of business, or where, and by whom, he was employed. If the applicant was a newcomer, he had to identify his previous place of residence. If the applicant did not supply all this information satisfactorily, the registrar could refuse to accept him. In that case the prospective voter could request that his application be reviewed by the commissioners of registration in his county. Although the commissioners of registration were required to provide a certified list of the registered voters to the officials at each polling place, the voter still had to present his certificate of registration in order to cast a ballot.[23]

The poll-tax law vaguely required the prospective voter to furnish "satisfactory evidence" to the election judges that he had paid his two-dollar poll tax for the preceding year. Such a provision gave the judges considerable latitude in deciding what constituted sufficient proof of payment.[24]

Through the Lea law, which was also slightly revised to eliminate procedural complications, Democratic leaders hoped to avoid federal interference in local elections. In state elections, therefore, the registration system, the secret ballot, and the poll tax could be administered safe from the prying eyes of federal election supervisors. In a reference to possible congressional action instituting the federal supervision of national elections, the editor of the Memphis *Avalanche* described the Tennessee voting laws as

[23]*Ibid.*, 50–66.
[24]*Acts*, 1890, 2d Ex. Sess., 67.

"the only means of defense against the desperate assaults of the rule-or-ruin Republican majority in Congress."[25]

The strong protest leveled at the election laws by the Republican minority in the legislature foreshadowed a stiff barrage of criticism from other party leaders. In their assault on the voting measures of 1889 and 1890, Republicans combined constitutional and moral protests with enlightened self-interest. Contrary to Democratic boasts, Tennessee did not stand in the front ranks of a progressive electoral reform movement. Republicans maintained that, in truth, the new voting laws, by giving Democrats firm control of the election machinery, so complicated and regulated the voting process that Negroes would be largely disfranchised.

The Knoxville *Journal*, whose response to the election laws probably reflected the views of most Republicans, scoffed at Democratic claims to be interested only in election reform. From the *Journal*'s perspective, Democrats had devised suffrage regulations solely "to get a good many negroes out of the way," to insure Democratic control of the election machinery, and to serve "as an engine of fraud and oppression." Now, no matter what steps Congress might take to supervise national elections, the *Journal* complained, the Lea law would give Democrats a free hand to manipulate local election returns as they had in Brownsville and Haywood County in 1888. Furthermore, the poll tax invited partisan discrimination, warned the *Journal*, by allowing Democratic election judges to determine what constituted "satisfactory evidence" that a prospective voter had paid the tax.[26]

The *Journal* also condemned the modified educational requirement in the Dortch law as an unjust blow against Negro illiteracy. Less than thirty years earlier it had been "a misdemeanor with heavy penalties to teach that class of voters to read whose disfranchisement was the prime motive for the passage of the Dortch law." In light of both the poor record of the Democratic legislatures on public education and the opposition of many Democrats to federal aid for education, the *Journal* labeled the

[25]Feb. 28, 1890.
[26]Oct. 11, Dec. 27, 31, 1889; Mar. 2, 13, 21, July 17, 24, Aug. 13, Oct. 14, 18, Nov. 19, 1890; see also Nashville *Banner*, Feb. 28, Mar. 10, 1890.

adoption of a thinly veiled literacy test as "a species of tyranny, brutal in its character." The Republican newspaper dismissed Democratic arguments that, since the Tennessee Australian-ballot law had been modeled after the Massachusetts law, it should be above suspicion. The dissimilarity of public educational facilities in the two states made any comparison irrelevant, the editor stated.[27] Obviously, the white Republicans' concern over just treatment of Negro voters did not necessarily reflect their racial altruism. The Republican party needed black voters and would defend their franchise as long as their votes retained political significance.

Indeed, prior to the elections of 1890, Republican leaders conducted voter-registration campaigns and organized night schools to teach illiterate Negroes how to distinguish the names of Republican candidates on the ballots. In fact, the success with which Negroes managed to register and vote in the municipal elections of late 1889 and early 1890 may have induced the Democrats to add the poll tax to the list of voting requirements in the extra legislative session of 1890.[28]

The August 1890 county elections presented the first major test of the new voting laws. In Shelby, Davidson, Hamilton, and Knox counties, where the full impact of the suffrage regulations fell, there was an overall decline in voter turnout; the Negro vote suffered especially heavy losses. "The smallest vote on record" was polled in Shelby County, declared the Memphis *Avalanche*, where Negroes were "conspicuously absent from the polls." Democrats carried wards and districts that had been Republican strongholds for twenty-five years. Attributing the meager black vote to the secret-ballot law, the *Avalanche* claimed it not only discouraged most blacks from going to the polls but also invalidated the votes of many others who had marked their ballots incorrectly.[29]

"There was a light vote polled and it was wonderfully Democrat-

[27]Knoxville *Journal*, Apr. 9, Oct. 9, 11, 14, 1889; Jan. 26, 1890.
[28]*Ibid.*, May 5, 1889; Chattanooga *Times*, Apr. 2, May 19, 1890; Memphis *Avalanche*, Aug. 7, 1890.
[29]Aug. 8–9, 1890.

ic," declared the Nashville *American,* praising unreservedly the effect of the new election laws in Nashville and Davidson County. Few blacks had registered, fewer had paid their poll taxes, and still fewer had voted. Four black candidates for minor offices in Davidson County met crushing defeats. Among them was the well-known James C. Napier, respected leader among Nashville Negroes. In a bid to become circuit court clerk Napier received only 38 votes in the predominantly black fourth ward of Nashville and 280 votes in the entire county. Black voting majorities in two Nashville wards were wiped out, and, although blacks constituted 35 percent of the male voting-age population in Davidson County, the 2,615 registered Negro voters now comprised only 21 percent of the total. These statistics tell only a part of the story, for only about one-half the registered voters in Davidson County actually cast ballots in the August elections; the percentage of registered Negroes who voted was much lower than that. The Nashville *American* had a handy explanation for this turn of events in local politics: "Intelligence armed with a paper ballot did battle with ignorance and fanaticism, and won hands down, and that was all." The Democratic editor's appreciation for the Tennessee Australian-ballot law reached the sublime: "A clarion voice echoed from vale to hill top, from gutter to citadel, and said: This country shall not be ruled by men who are not sufficiently intelligent to read names printed in capital letters and make a crossmark opposite those for which they desire to vote." He construed the election results to mean that "popular indignation had branded the seal of infamy deep upon the name of republicanism in Davidson County."[30]

For the first time since the Civil War, Hamilton County Democrats swept the local elections in a straight party fight which the Chattanooga *Times* described as "a Waterloo for the Republican

---

[30]Nashville *American,* Aug. 8–9, 1890; Nashville *Banner,* Aug. 8–9, 1890. Nashville registration figures for the 1889 city election are found in the Nashville *American,* July 6, 1890; for the Aug. 1890 election, see *ibid.,* July 13, 1890. Registration statistics for Davidson Co. in Aug. 1890 are found in the Nashville *Banner,* Aug. 8, 1890. For percentages of voting-age population, both white and black, see *Eleventh Census, 1890,* Pt. I, Population, 781.

party." The *Times* attributed the victory to "the righteous Dortch and registration laws," which it credited with preventing a large number of Negroes from voting. A black observer in Chattanooga stated that at least 50 percent of Chattanooga's black voters had been unable to mark their ballots accurately under the secret-ballot law. In Knox County, the only other place in the state where all the election laws applied, Republicans attributed their defeat to "the lightest vote ever polled," which they blamed on the poll tax and the Australian ballot. Election reports from other counties indicated that, where the registration and Australian-ballot systems did not operate, the poll tax alone barred many members of both races from casting ballots.[31]

The full effect of Tennessee's new voting laws upon the two parties in the state and upon the racial composition of the state's electorate awaited the November elections. The 1890 gubernatorial campaign was complicated both by the entrance of the Farmers' Alliance into state politics and by the prospect that Congress might pass a bill providing for federal supervision of elections. After a bitter wrangle in the state Democratic convention in July, John P. Buchanan, president of the Tennessee Farmers' Alliance, emerged as the party's nominee for governor. Buchanan had defeated two other prominent candidates, Josiah Patterson of Memphis and Jere Baxter of Nashville, who respectively represented the Bourbon and New South wings of the party. To muddle the political picture even more, in July the lower house of Congress passed a federal elections bill which called for the appointment of federal supervisors in congressional and presidential elections. Quickly dubbed the "force bill" by its critics, this measure assumed great importance in the election of 1890. Although the Republican gubernatorial candidate, Lewis T. Baxter, announced his opposition to the federal elections bill, the Republican state convention endorsed it but ambiguously excluded the endorsement from the party's platform. The Democrats made political capital out of the Republican endorsement of the mea-

[31]Nashville *American*, Aug. 8, 1890; Chattanooga *Times*, Aug. 8, 1890; Knoxville *Journal*, Aug. 8, 1890.

sure, hoisting the specter of Negro rule if it should become law. The federal elections bill, however, doomed Republican fortunes in November far less than did the recently enacted state election laws. Nevertheless, reaction to the federal elections bill did intensify racial animosities that already had been aroused by the electoral reform movement of the previous winter and spring. Using the federal elections bill to strengthen Democratic unity, drawing from the organized support of the Farmers' Alliance, and capitalizing upon the new election laws, Buchanan swept to a decisive victory.[32]

The results of the November elections surely confirmed even the most optimistic Democratic expectations concerning the effectiveness of the Australian ballot, registration, and poll tax in reducing the black vote. Following the election, the Knoxville *Journal* estimated that, of a black voting population in Tennessee roughly estimated at 100,000, only about 25,000 had actually voted in the recent contests. As the black vote declined, Republican strength outside East Tennessee rapidly waned. In the five counties of the Tenth Congressional District in which blacks constituted a majority of the voting population, Republicans suffered staggering losses, polling only about 20 percent of the vote. The Republican vote in these counties dropped to 50 percent of what it had been in 1886, the last off-year election, and to a startling 15 percent of what it had been in 1880.[33]

In Haywood County, where Democrats had resorted to armed intervention in 1888 to oust the Republicans from power, the Republican vote fell to only about 20 percent of what it had been in 1886. In Memphis and Shelby County, Republicans amazingly polled only about 9 percent of the votes they had garnered in the

[32]Hart, "Bourbonism and Populism," 211–40; James A. Sharp, "The Entrance of the Farmers' Alliance into Tennessee Politics," ETHS *Publications*, No. 9 (1937), 77–92; Margaret E. Holloway, "The Reaction in Tennessee to the Federal Elections Bill of 1890" (M.A. thesis, Univ. of Tennessee, 1970), 11–14, 27–35, 38–40, 75–112, 119–20; Miller, *Official Manual*, 278–80.

[33]Nov. 13, 1890; Tennessee's black males over 21 numbered 92,462 in 1890; see *Eleventh Census, 1890*, Pt. I, Population, 781; White, *Messages*, VII, 232–34; for county-by-county returns of the 1880 governor's election see the Nashville *American*, Nov. 6, 1882.

preceding state election. Although 12,590 voters—7,583 whites and 5,007 blacks—had registered in Shelby County before the November election, only 5,256 ballots were cast in the governor's race there. Of these, the Republican candidate received only 729 votes. A much greater proportion of blacks than whites who registered failed to vote. In Memphis, Democrats swept two predominantly Negro wards which traditionally had been Republican; in one, although 352 blacks had registered, the Republican gubernatorial candidate received only 52 votes; in the other, where 357 blacks had registered, he tallied a mere 28 votes.[34]

The results of the November elections in Nashville and Davidson County revealed the same bleak picture for Republicans and Negroes. As in Memphis, Republican losses in Nashville came largely from a precipitous drop in Negro voting. The number of black registered voters in November was only about one-half what it had been in August. While 9,738 of the approximately 26,000 males of voting age in Davidson County were Negroes, only 1,283 of the 8,187 registered voters were Negroes. Again, the registration figures are only partially enlightening; in one predominantly black ward in Nashville slightly less than 50 percent of those who registered actually voted. Similar reports came from Chattanooga and Hamilton County. There, however, the Republicans managed to survive a 44 percent decrease in votes from those of the previous gubernatorial election, carrying the county for Lewis T. Baxter with a plurality of 613. The new election laws also entered into the defeat of Henry Clay Evans, Republican candidate for Congress in the Third Congressional District. Evans discounted suggestions that his support of the federal elections bill had cost him the election. Instead, he pointed to the Dortch law as having "prevented the negroes of the city from asserting their rights at the polls." Significantly, though, Democrats in the 1889 General Assembly had gerrymandered the Third District, removing three Republican counties and adding one Democratic county. This new align-

[34]White, *Messages*, VII, 233; Miller, *Official Manual*, 278–80; Memphis *Appeal*, Oct. 26, Nov. 6, 1890; Nashville *American*, Nov. 25, 1890; Memphis *Avalanche*, Nov. 6, 1890; for registration statistics of Memphis and Shelby County see Memphis *Appeal*, Oct. 26, 1890.

241

ment combined with the new election laws and the unpopularity of the federal elections bill to assure Evans' defeat.[35]

In Knoxville and Knox County observers estimated that only about 400 of a black voting population of 2,824 cast ballots in the November elections. Democrats took two seats in the General Assembly from Republicans, and the Republican gubernatorial vote in the county fell about 50 percent below that of 1886 and approximately 60 percent below the 1888 figure. The Knoxville *Journal* attributed these reductions to the new election laws. On the basis of the decline in the Republican vote in Knox County and throughout East Tennessee it seems that the new election laws cut the Republican vote of both races. The Republican vote for governor in East Tennessee as a whole in 1890 dropped approximately 35 percent from that of 1888, while the corresponding Democratic vote there declined only about 23 percent.[36]

Existing statistics reveal a sharp decline in Negro voting from the December 1889 to the August 1890 elections; the November 1890 contest shows a further cut. Enactment of poll-tax legislation by the extra session of the legislature in March 1890 largely explains the drop in Negro voting between the December 1889 and the August 1890 elections, but reasons for the decline between August and November are more complex. Republicans apparently made few efforts in November either to organize or to educate black voters. Also, increased racial tension caused by controversy over the federal elections bill may have discouraged some blacks from voting, and doubtless both the sharp reduction in the Republican vote in August and the lily-white sentiment in Republican ranks cast a pall over whatever hopes blacks had of using the Republican party as a vehicle for exercising political power. By November many blacks who had cast ballots in August apparently decided that there was little reason to vote. A stricter enforcement of the new suffrage laws in the state elections of November also

[35]*Eleventh Census, 1890*, Pt. I, Population, 781; Nashville *American*, Oct. 28, Nov. 5–6, 25, 1890; Nashville *Banner*, Nov. 6, 10, 1890; Miller, *Official Manual*, 279; Chattanooga *Times*, Nov. 6, 1890; Knoxville *Journal*, Nov. 9, 1890.

[36]Knoxville *Journal*, Nov. 22, 1890; Chattanooga *Times*, Dec. 3, 1886; *Eleventh Census, 1890*, Pt. I, Population, 782; Miller, *Official Manual*, 257, 278.

probably had an effect. As in earlier elections, some blacks voted Democratic, although the declining vote of that party does not reflect a large influx of voters. By the end of the decade the black vote had been cut to a fraction of its former strength. This was not exclusively a result of the secret ballot, registration, and the poll tax. Political apathy, accommodationist sentiment, concentration upon economic self-help to the exclusion of politics, white intimidation and fraud, and increasing racial tension in the Republican party also took their toll.[37]

Democrats, understandably, were jubilant about the impact of the new suffrage laws. Carmack, editor of the Nashville *American*, praised the laws for having "dignified and rendered decent in a large measure the process of suffrage in Tennessee, which could not be said of it when the old crowd of negroes and ruffians were permitted to gather about the polls with their reeking smells and coarse profanity." Robert H. Cartmell, a Madison County farmer, may have expressed the majority sentiment among Democrats on the value of Tennessee's new voting laws when, after casting his ballot in the county elections of August 1892, he wrote, "The man that can't read will have some difficulty in fixing up his vote. Few negroes voted today" because they had "failed to register or had not paid their poll tax." Cartmell heartily approved of the law requiring payment of a poll tax for voting. "Under [the] present system," he explained, "a man's vote is worth something and is not killed by a no. [number] of ignorant negroes. White folks ought to govern the country and they will." Following the trial of

[37]Nashville *American*, July 21, 1890; Meier, *Negro Thought in America*, 26–41; William R. Moore to H. Clay Evans, June 28, 1890, Scrapbooks, II, 1888–90, Evans Papers (Public Library, Chattanooga, Tenn.); Isaac F. Norris to Leonidas C. Houk, Jan. 22, 1889, Houk Papers. In a Dec. 1973 article Kousser, examining the long-range effect of the suffrage laws of 1889–90 upon blacks in Tennessee politics, employs quantitative analysis of state voting statistics in the late 19th and early 20th centuries to argue that the secret ballot, registration law, and poll tax were major reasons for the sharp decline of blacks in state politics. See "Post-Reconstruction Suffrage Restrictions in Tennessee," 655–83. This analysis reinforces my own earlier interpretation that the suffrage-reform movement, rather than black apathy, signally reduced black participation in state politics. See Joseph H. Cartwright, "The Negro in Tennessee Politics, 1880–1891" (M.A. thesis, Vanderbilt Univ., 1968), 215–28, 234–35, 239–44, 257.

the election laws in 1890, the Nashville *Banner* surveyed their effect upon Negroes: "The election laws in Tennessee, twice tested this year, have effectively disposed of the negro vote." Although the poll-tax requirement had disfranchised many whites, the *Banner* observed that it had been "more signally suppressive of the negro vote." In view of all this, the editor offered a succinct judgment: "The Dortch law and poll tax law solve the race problem in so far as the elections system is concerned."[38]

With the adoption of an Australian-ballot law that deliberately prohibited assistance to illiterate voters in marking their ballots, Tennessee became one of the first southern states after the Civil War to institute a modified educational qualification for voting. South Carolina had adopted the first legal scheme to eliminate illiterate voters with its famous 1882 eight-box ballot and registration laws. Florida joined in the adoption of legislation designed to restrict black suffrage with the passage of a registration law in 1887 and both an eight-box-ballot law and a poll tax in 1889. Although North Carolina passed a voter-registration law in 1889 which, according to a recent student, was "specifically aimed at reducing the Negro vote," it required far less information from applicants than did the Tennessee law. Neither poll tax nor literacy tests came to that state for another decade. Georgia had instituted a cumulative tax in 1877 requiring payment of each year's poll tax after that date but did not adopt a registration law aimed at Negroes until 1894. Professor Charles E. Wynes, a student of race relations in Virginia, labeled an 1893 Australian-ballot act adopted in that state "a modified disfranchising law based on literacy." Unlike the Tennessee version of the Australian ballot, however, the Virginia law allowed illiterate voters assistance in marking their ballots.[39]

[38]Nashville *American*, Aug. 10, 1890; Robert H. Cartmell, Diary, Aug. 4, 1892; Nashville *Banner*, Nov. 11, 1890.

[39]See Tindall, *South Carolina Negroes*, 68–70; Kousser, *Shaping of Southern Politics*, 48, 50, 65, 87–103; Logan, *Negro in North Carolina*, 58–59; C. Vann Woodward, *Tom Watson: Agrarian Rebel* (New York: Macmillan, 1938), 275–76; Wynes, *Race Relations in Virginia*, 51, 52; Stephenson, *Race Distinctions in American Law*, 324–25.

Contemporary observers did not miss the significance of the Tennessee precedent. The Memphis *Appeal* exulted that Tennessee had been "the first Southern State and the second in the United States to take a position so advanced."[40] The success with which the new voting laws reduced Negro voting in Tennessee led some Democrats to recommend them as a solution to the race problem in other southern states. Following the municipal elections of 1890, the Memphis *Avalanche* analyzed the advantages Tennessee's Australian-ballot law offered for insuring Democratic control and white supremacy in the South. "From Memphis as a center," the editor rejoiced, "the *Avalanche* hopes to see the principal features of the Dortch law spread throughout the South. It has been tried and not found wanting."[41]

The deliberations of the Mississippi constitutional convention in the summer and fall of 1890 offered the Democratic press in Tennessee an early opportunity to publicize the value of the state voting laws. The Memphis *Avalanche*, which had spearheaded the drive for the adoption of restrictive-voting legislation in Tennessee, bluntly observed that the purpose of the Mississippi convention was "to find some means of preventing the negro from voting—means which can be used without a resort to violence or an infraction of the laws of our common country." With this goal in mind, the Nashville *American* thought it pertinent to survey the attitudes of the convention delegates toward the adoption of the Australian ballot. The Chattanooga *Times* went a step further and commended the Tennessee version of the secret ballot to its Mississippi neighbors: "The Mississippi constitutional convention will do wisely if it adopts the modified and perfected form of the Australian ballot law, known hereabout as 'the Dortch bill'." This, together with a poll tax, would insure white control of Mississippi, suggested the *Times*. The Memphis *Appeal* also recommended Tennessee's new voting laws to those Mississippians who were struggling to find a satisfactory means of curbing the black vote. The Australian-ballot law, the registration law, and the poll tax,

[40]Mar. 12, 1890.
[41]Memphis *Avalanche*, Jan. 23, 1890.

wrote the *Appeal,* provided "a virtual educational and property qualification" for voting. With these measures, the "ignorant negro" could be disfranchised, advised the Memphis editor, without any of the "objectionable features of a specific law on the subject." For proof, the *Appeal* directed the attention of Mississippians "to the efficacy of the Australian ballot system, with a poll tax adjunct, as demonstrated in the recent elections in Shelby County, Tennessee."[42]

Following the sweeping Democratic victories in Tennessee in the November 1890 elections, the Birmingham *Age Herald* observed that Tennessee's Australian-ballot law seemed "to be an excellent institution for securing fair elections and Democratic majorities" and urged the forthcoming Alabama legislature to adopt it. The Memphis *Appeal-Avalanche* joined the Birmingham newspaper in urging other southern states to heed the success of the Tennessee voting laws in disfranchising Negroes and advised that they "should take this lesson home to themselves and learn from it that they have the remedy in their own hands for all the political ills that threaten them. Mississippi has already acted and Arkansas should follow suit."[43]

Josiah Patterson, congressman-elect from West Tennessee's Tenth District, spoke at a Democratic rally at Pine Bluff, Arkansas, following the November elections. Patterson, who had helped launch the state drive for the adoption of Negro disfranchisement legislation, had recently won a seat in Congress after waging a vigorous white supremacy campaign. According to the Memphis press, Patterson instructed his Pine Bluff audience how their state might permanently eliminate "the constant menace of negro domination" by wise legislation similar to that in vogue in Shelby County and Tennessee." The Memphis *Appeal-Avalanche* commended Patterson for having "sounded the necessity and shown

[42]*Ibid.*, Aug. 27, 1890; Nashville *American,* Aug. 17, 21, 1890; Chattanooga *Times,* Aug. 27, 1890; Memphis *Appeal,* Aug. 9, 21, 1890.

[43]Quoted in the *Appeal-Avalanche,* Nov. 10, 1890; see also *ibid.*, Nov. 9, 1890. The *Appeal,* owned by William A. Collier, purchased the *Avalanche* on November 7, 1890. The new *Appeal-Avalanche* was edited by Gus C. Matthews. See Baker, *Memphis Commercial Appeal,* 156–59.

the way," and the newspaper informed its Arkansas readers that, in light of the successful test of the laws in Tennessee, Patterson could "speak with confidence on the subject." The people of Arkansas should take his advice by adopting a measure "similar to the Dortch law, modified, if necessary, to suit and serve local exigencies," advised the *Appeal-Avalanche*. This action would "render it physically impossible for the ignorant hordes of the black counties to become Goths and Vandals, and swoop down mercilessly upon the intelligence of the community and imperil or destroy white supremacy."[44]

Nowhere was the forlorn status of Negroes in Tennessee politics by 1890 reflected more dramatically than in the Republican party. In the state Republican convention of that year, the small band of black delegates found themselves excluded from the committees and completely disregarded in the nominating speeches. There was an absence of the usual token seconding speeches by prominent Negro politicians. Noticeably lacking were the blandishments of white Republican leaders, reminding Negroes of the blessings they had received through their loyalty to the Republican party. Finally, Negro orators were allotted no time to pay their characteristic tribute to the party of emancipation. Moreover, the eclipse of Negro political influence in local Republican organizations was evident in the party's county conventions in the spring of 1890. The situation in Middle Tennessee's Wilson County appears to have been typical: "The party in this county in all its conventions is usually dominated by the colored element, but on this occasion the white brother got in his work, and to a certain extent shelved the gentlemen in black." In the Davidson County Republican organization, where blacks once had exercised a potent influence, they now played only a peripheral role. The few active black politicians remaining in Nashville's Republican party by 1890 were largely minor federal officeholders who had been relegated to menial tasks in the postal service or the Internal Revenue Department. For example, Thomas A. Sykes, a former

44Memphis *Appeal–Avalanche*, Nov. 15, 1890.

247

member of the legislature from Davidson County, was now an elevator operator at the customs house.[45]

The Republican party's disregard for blacks stemmed in part from the furor created by the debate on the federal elections bill. Lily-white sentiment in the party also made its mark. Expectations that the black vote would be reduced sharply by the new election laws provided further political justification for ignoring Negroes. Without federal interference the black vote faced certain contraction, but state white Republican leaders were divided over the federal elections bill. They had to decide between boldly defending Negro suffrage, even to the extent of calling for federal intervention, or acquiescing to the racial climate of 1890, thus writing off the bulk of the black vote. After some vacillation and a few outbursts from such old Republican stalwarts as William R. Moore of Memphis, the party attempted to dissociate itself on the state level from the debilitating race issue. Lewis T. Baxter, the party's gubernatorial candidate in 1890, and Jack W. Baker, chairman of the state executive committee, both publicly opposed the federal elections bill.[46]

If, as their advocates declared, the Australian ballot, registration, and the poll tax were designed to secure the purity of elections, they failed to accomplish the desired goal. Shortly after the application of the registration law in the Memphis municipal elections of 1890, the Republican Knoxville *Journal* complained, "The registrars represented only a single faction and a single shade of public opinion." The *Journal* accused the registrars of "notoriously" abusing their legal responsibilities and of engaging in "the most shameful frauds and the most audacious violation of the spirit and letter of the law." According to this Republican newspaper, the Democratic registrars had arbitrarily turned many qualified voters away, although those "favorable to the faction in

[45]Nashville *American*, June 8, 13, 1890.

[46]T. C. Muse to Leonidas C. Houk, Jan. 15, 1890; William R. Moore to L. C. Houk, Sept. 29, 1890; John C. Houk to L. C. Houk, Aug. 4, 1890; Jack W. Baker to L. C. Houk, Sept. 21, 1890, Houk Papers. Holloway, "Reaction to the Federal Elections Bill," 13, 15–17, 19, 31–33, 40–41.

power" were registered without question. The *Journal* labeled the registration "a farce."[47]

In the wake of the August elections, other charges of flagrant violation of the new election laws came from Democrats as well as Republicans. In addition to fraudulent registration practices, there were reports of illegal distribution of blank poll-tax receipts, use of counterfeit receipts, and widespread disregard of the Dortch secret-ballot law by many election officials who simply marked the ballots of illiterate voters. Another device for allowing illiterate voters to cast a ballot was a pasteboard stencil cut in such a way that an illiterate voter might mark the preferred candidates. The ingenuity of party workers in circumventing the secret ballot was best illustrated by a scheme in which a blank ballot would be stolen from the polling booth, taken to party headquarters, and marked by a party official. It would then be given to an illiterate voter who would cast that ballot, returning the blank one he had received at the polls to party officials to be marked and given in turn to someone else. Newspaper accounts indicated that gross violations of the election laws also occurred in the November elections. Again, the laws most often abused were the Australian ballot and the poll tax.[48]

The testimony of election officials, voters, and party workers appearing before a committee set up to investigate voting returns in the 1894 gubernatorial election supplies impressive evidence that Tennessee's new suffrage laws had been violated since their enactment. The frauds uncovered by the investigation encompassed an ingenious variety of devices for evading the voting laws: ballot-box stuffing, intimidation of voters, fraudulent counting of ballots, fraudulent registration practices, illegal distribution of poll-tax receipts, and disregard of the poll-tax laws. In violation of the Australian-ballot law, some election officials marked the ballots of illiterate voters and discarded the ballots of others.

[47]Dec. 31, 1889.

[48]Chattanooga *Times*, Aug. 6, 8, Nov. 4, 1890; Nashville *American*, Aug. 7, 10, Nov. 4, 1890; Memphis *Avalanche*, Aug. 7, 1890; Nashville *Banner*, Aug. 7–9, 1890; Memphis *Appeal*, Nov. 6, 1890.

Election judges often represented only one party. In several cases, illiterate and incompetent Negroes were put up as Republican election judges by Democratic officials simulating a concern for fairness. In light of these electoral practices, the testimony indicated that some Republican voters, especially Negroes, who managed to register, to pay a $2.00 poll tax, and to read well enough to mark their ballots, still faced the prospect of having their ballots either discarded or counted for the Democratic ticket. If they dared question the activities of white election officials, they risked the fate of the unnamed black Memphis political leader who, according to an account in the Democratic Memphis *Appeal*, in the November 1890 election "received a sound thrashing from the Sheriff for his impudence."[49]

Confronted by laws that imposed both an educational qualification and a tax on the right to vote and that generally placed the election machinery in the hands of Democrats, it is not surprising that many Negroes came to view voting as a futile enterprise. Weakened by the "force bill" (federal elections bill) controversy, vulnerable to the charge that it catered to Negroes for its own political aggrandizement, and rent by internal strife between lily-whites and those who advised cooperation with blacks, the state Republican party by 1890 offered Negroes little protection against the partisan implementation of the new election machinery.

The response of black leaders to the new election laws varied. Many black leaders in Tennessee had long advocated reforms to purify and elevate the voting process. Black members of the state legislature during the eighties had introduced and supported bills to guard against fraudulent election practices and to insure an honest count of the ballots.[50] Some blacks even had supported educational and property qualifications for voters that would be applied impartially to both races. A lyceum debate among Knox-

---

[49]*Contest for Governor: Complete Proceedings of the Joint Convention and the Investigating Committee* (2 vols.; Nashville: Paul, 1895), I, 52–53, 87–88, 91–92, 96–97; II, 104–7, 119, 121–22, and *passim*; Memphis *Appeal*, Nov. 5, 1890.
[50]See Ch. III.

ville blacks in the spring of 1889, for example, ended with the "sentiment of the audience" favoring an educational qualification for voting. A student at Fisk University in Nashville, writing in the school newspaper in 1890, applied traditional conservative arguments in maintaining that government should be directed by educated taxpayers. He declared universal suffrage to be "impracticable and a down right failure" and pointed to "the thriftless and heterogeneous elements of all creeds and climes, unable to support themselves in their own countries, strangers to the spirit of our institutions," who were "pouring in upon us by untold thousands, and without one dollar at stake to remind them of the right conduct of the ballot." Another writer in the Fisk *Herald* advised "the rational and liberty loving people of Nashville" that Negroes regarded the matter of illegal voting "with far more seriousness, to say the least, than many of those Democratic Apostles in our legislature who loudly preach 'purity of the ballot.' " Yet another Fisk student condemned corruption in elections and called for a general reformation, under federal supervision, to "purify the ballot."[51]

Most blacks, in fact, regarded federal supervision as the *sine qua non* of any meaningful election reform. In any case, Negroes joined white Republicans in imputing partisan and racial intentions to the Democratic legislators responsible for Tennessee's voting legislation. William H. Franklin, a black minister in East Tennessee, wrote the New York *Age* that the adoption of the restrictive-voting laws in Tennessee represented the Democratic party's "zeal and determined purpose to defraud and discriminate against the Negro." Although he denounced the Tennessee legislature for displaying "a partisan, a selfish, and a malignant spirit," Franklin said that he opposed neither an educational qualification for voting nor a registration law, if they "originated from proper motives and were rightly constructed." The laws passed by the Tennessee legislature, however, "sprang from wrong motives and were drawn in the wrong spirit." Franklin urged Negroes to "know

[51]Knoxville *Journal*, Apr. 14, 1889; Fisk *Herald* (Feb. 1890; Feb. 1889; Aug. 1890).

their rights" and to have "the courage to demand and to defend them."[52]

Some Negroes prophesied that the new election laws would stimulate black literacy and that it would not be long before every Negro voter in the state would be able to read his ballot and vote intelligently. "What was intended for his evil will result in his good," declared Franklin in the *Age*. He also predicted that Negro education would eventually moderate the effect of the laws but, at the same time, advised court action and federal supervision of elections to overcome the partisan implementation of the measures.[53] Any expectations Negroes may have had about counteracting the effect of Tennessee's voting laws through advances in education or federal intervention must have been jolted by the political contests of 1890.

Despite the bleak picture that faced Negroes in Tennessee politics by the end of 1890, there were still black leaders who refused to concede political rights. James C. Napier, a Nashville lawyer whose career was enmeshed in black Tennessee politics throughout the late nineteenth and early twentieth centuries, never wavered in demanding full political equality for Negroes. A popular speaker, Napier delivered a number of addresses to a variety of black organizations—addresses in which he, like Booker T. Washington with whom he was closely associated, urged the moral and economic uplift of his people through the dignity of work. His sentiments regarding black political rights, however, were direct and unmistakable. To those whites who urged blacks to renounce politics in order to effect an era of racial harmony in the South, Napier responded: "To ask that we do this is like asking that a man surrender his weapon in the very presence of danger and in the face of his foe. We shall never consent to this nor to relinquishing the hold we have on any other element that constitutes citizenship in this country." If blacks should "ever lose any of these," he continued, "it must be after all opposition on our part shall have been exhausted and overcome. We must be over

[52]New York *Age*, Apr. 20, June 22, 1889.
[53]*Ibid.*

powered and they must be wrested from us and even then our consent can never be obtained to such action."

Blacks posed no threat to white society, Napier asserted; they desired neither domination of it nor social equality within it. What the black man wanted was to contribute his share toward building up the South and its people, white and black: "In accordance with the laws of his country he asks for equal conditions, equal opportunities and equal rights." If the Negro did not respond in anger on each occasion when these were denied, "his inner manhood, though in tones unheard by human ears, is bound to cry out," Napier stated. He expressed his faith that these cries would someday "be heard and heeded." Until then, the Negro's "Christian spirit and fortitude" might enable him to bear infringements upon his rights, "but nothing can ever lead him to believe that they are right or just." Although "the hand of prejudice" might "retard his progress for a time," and might even "prescribe a channel for the operation of his movements, for the exercise of his joys and pleasure," the time would come when "the spirit given him by his Creator will free itself from these bars and he will stand out a full fledged man."[54]

Napier's eloquence, however, could not surmount the barriers that had been erected to black political equality by the late nineteenth century. To assume that Negro participation in Tennessee politics declined primarily because of apathy does not give proper significance to the changes that had occurred in the electoral process and in racial attitudes in the state by 1890.[55] It is true that long before 1890 some blacks had given up voting through mere indifference, but many others found the secret ballot, the poll tax, partisan registrars, economic intimidation, violence, and corruption of the voting process to be either insurmountable obstacles or simply too great a price for casting a ballot.

[54]Undated typescript, Napier Papers.

[55]Corlew concludes that apathy and disappointment among blacks over their failure to obtain offices "had a much greater effect" on reducing the number of black voters than did the voting restrictions adopted in 1889–90. See "Negro in Tennessee," 144–45.

VIII

Conclusion

⊂⊃

The striking characteristic of relations between blacks and whites in Tennessee during the 1880s is the rapid manner in which interracial contact in politics and public facilities disintegrated and voices of moderation gave way to hostility, fear, and distrust. A variety of forces contributed to this change. At the outset of the decade the prevailing mechanistic concept of individual progress somewhat tempered racist views and left many whites with excessively optimistic notions about the ease and speed with which the race question could be resolved. This optimism rested largely on the belief that many blacks would quickly attain the standards of propriety, education, work habits, and property ownership revered by white conservatives; that black voters would soon divide along economic lines, with many joining the southern white majority in the Democratic party; and that distinctions in public facilities could be based on class values rather than on a racial standard. Most whites also believed that blacks would accept token political equality—the right to vote—without pushing for a proportionate influence in the determination of policy and leadership.

During the eighties the white attitude toward black voters shifted from benign paternalism to overt hostility, contributing substantially to the marked deterioration of race relations. Through the first half of the decade Bourbon Democrats avidly courted black support, partly to offset opposition from New South industrialists within the party, partly to win power in areas of heavy black population, and partly to broaden their political base by including a group of voters who were assumed to be a permanent part of the electorate and to share Bourbon desires for economic stability and racial harmony. Competition for black voters encouraged a conciliatory racial climate, offered blacks opportunities for elected office and patronage, fostered black aspirations for full participation within both parties, and, ironically, itself soon became a major cause of racial tension.

The battle for black votes also fed Democratic intraparty strife, and when black support for either the Bourbon or the New South faction fell short of expectations, the vision of interracial politics blurred. Sharply divergent political expectations between blacks and whites within both parties provided much of the grist for interracial discord during the decade. Indeed, by the end of the eighties disillusioned whites in both factions of the Democratic party, as well as a growing number of Republicans, were determined to crush black political influence.

The inability of the vast majority of blacks to eliminate, in two decades, the disparities between the races in education and property that represented, in part, the legacy of two and one-half centuries of slavery, reinforced white reservations about black voters and offered whites convincing proof that a fundamental conflict in the self-interest of the two races existed.

The conviction of white urban reformers that Negro voters imperiled good city government, the conclusion of white Prohibitionists that their cause had been defeated by black voters, and the threats of federal interference in the election of national officials provided further incentives for restricting black voting. Even more important was the continued political influence of blacks in the state's major urban areas, as well as in the heavily black-populated parts of West Tennessee, and the continuing insistence of some blacks upon full participation in party deliberations, equitable representation in government, a proportionate share of political patronage, and a recognition of their civil rights by the party receiving their votes.

Through their support of the Republican party in the eighties, black voters helped maintain a viable two-party system beyond the middle of the decade and reinforced the vested interest of Republicans in defending black voting rights. Most white Republicans hoped to retain black support but believed their party should divorce itself from the race issue as much as possible. In any case, Republican leaders assumed that Negroes would continue to support the Republican party, but the traditional stereotype of black voters as pliant, trusting political tools in the hands of white Republican bosses is not supported by the evidence in Tennessee. If the majority of Negroes continued to vote Republican, it does not appear to have been a blind act on their part; rather it seems to have represented a calculated political decision based on the historical stance of the two parties on emancipation and civil rights, a desire for federal patronage, and a belief that, in the long run, black progress would best be assured through Republican success.

For the most part, at least in their public pronouncements, black leaders in Tennessee were optimistic about the future. They assumed that continued educational and economic progress among members of their race would eventually solve most racial problems. Working within the political structure to improve their status, they employed traditional means of influencing public policy. In retrospect, it seems apparent that voting, by itself, was not the key to black advancement in the 1880s. Although their increased participation in state politics brought certain opportunities for Negroes in terms of limited patronage, a few elected offices, and, perhaps, even some success in influencing the civil rights policies of the major parties, it did not result in blacks exercising the power to control many of the institutions that directly affected their lives on the local level, such as schools, courts, law-enforcement agencies, and city and county governments. Although blacks did have a limited influence on local government, they were not able, through the ballot, to win adequate protection of their civil liberties; in the long run, they lacked even the power to defend an unfettered suffrage.

During the eighties many whites began to fear that widespread black participation in politics would transform the political parties, radically alter local and state government, impede the growth of business, and drastically change racial traditions. Whatever the grounds for these perceptions, in those Tennessee areas where Negroes participated in local politics on an extensive basis in the

257

eighties there is little evidence that they represented a threat to traditional property rights or to the prevailing concepts of limited government and individualism.

Blacks did challenge white efforts to formalize segregation. Whether segregation laws in Tennessee represented an attempt to institutionalize traditional racial customs or constituted a departure from previous patterns of behavior cannot be fully answered on the basis of this study. It seems likely that the emergence of Jim Crow was a blend of both. In any case, most whites viewed the efforts of blacks to obtain impartial access to public facilities as a desire for social equality and, therefore, a threat to traditional racial mores. The evidence, on the other hand, indicates that blacks insisted upon making a distinction between civil rights and social equality, only desired access to equal facilities in public accommodations, did not assume that interracial mingling in public facilities would lead to private social relationships with whites, and showed little inclination to challenge segregation in public education.

The crucial question regarding race relations in the eighties was whether state and local government would be employed largely to further the economic and social interests of one race, or whether both races would continue to compete for power in a relatively open political system. Unfortunately, before the decade ended the former decision had prevailed. This represents one of the many tragedies of race relations in the 1880s. The sharp blow struck at black political power through the adoption of restrictive-voting legislation completed the destruction of an effective two-party system and removed the Republican party's vested interest in acting as an institutional brake on exploitation of racial animosities. The choice made in the eighties gave rein to the intimidation and hostility which often would make later Negro attempts at voter registration acts of nearly revolutionary proportions. Even the passage of federal voting-rights legislation and the Supreme Court rulings of recent years, although a beginning, have not fully counteracted the black legacy of political powerlessness, cynicism, alienation, and despair engendered by more than seventy years of forced segregation and virtual disfranchisement.

Recent gains in black civil rights and increases in the number of blacks holding public office in the South generally have been measured by the standards of that long era of disfranchisement. There is, however, an earlier model, not to be forgotten, which once seemed to hold faint but encouraging promises of biracial politics and interracial tolerance. The story of race relations in Tennessee in the 1880s provides more than a contrast to the inflexible standards of racial discrimination and general disfranchisement that came later; it also serves as a reminder of how rapidly race relations can change, of how tenuous and fragile are the bonds that constrain misconception, fear, and hatred.

Bibliography

PRIMARY SOURCES

Manuscripts

Alumni Records. Oberlin College Archives.

Bate, William B., Papers. Governors' Papers. Tennessee State Library and Archives.

Cartmell, Robert H., Diary. Tennessee State Library and Archives.

Champion, S. A., Papers. Tennessee State Library and Archives.

"Chesapeake, Ohio, and S. W. Railroad v. Ida Wells, April, 1885." Brief of Greer and Adams. Tennessee State Library and Archives.

Cleveland, Grover, Papers. Library of Congress.

Dickinson, Jacob McGavock, Papers. Tennessee State Library and Archives.

Evans, Henry Clay, Scrapbooks. Chattanooga Public Library.

Fussell, Joseph H., Collection. Tennessee State Library and Archives.

Harding-Jackson Papers. Tennessee State Library and Archives.

Harris, Isham G., Papers. Tennessee State Library and Archives.

Harrison, Benjamin, Papers. Library of Congress.

Hawkins, Alvin, Papers. Governors' Papers. Tennessee State Library and Archives.

Henderson, John H., Diary. Tennessee State Library and Archives.

Houk, Leonidas C., Papers. Lawson-McGhee Library, Knoxville.

"Ida Wells v. Chesapeake, Ohio, and Southwestern Railroad Company, 1884." Manuscript court record. Tennessee State Library and Archives.

Jackson, Howell E., Papers. Tennessee State Library and Archives.

Key, David M., Papers. Chattanooga Public Library.

Napier, James C., Papers. Fisk University Library.

Secretary of State Papers. Records of the General Assembly of the State of Tennessee, 1881–1891. Tennessee State Library and Archives.

261

Taylor, Robert L., Papers. Governors' Papers. Tennessee State Library and Archives.

Wiltze, Henry M. "History of Chattanooga." Unpublished manuscript. Chattanooga Public Library.

Official Records and Documents

UNITED STATES

Biographical Directory of the American Congress, 1774–1971. Washington, D.C.: Government Printing Office, 1971.

Bureau of the Census. *Abstract of the Eleventh Census, 1890.* 2d ed., rev. and enl. Washington, D.C.: Government Printing Office, 1896.

———. *Compendium of the Tenth Census of the United States, 1880.* Washington, D.C.: Government Printing Office, 1885.

———. *Compendium of the Eleventh Census of the United States, 1890.* Washington, D.C.: Government Printing Office, 1891.

———. *Eleventh Census of the United States, 1890.* Washington, D.C.: Government Printing Office, 1890.

———. *Negro Population, 1790–1915.* Washington, D.C.: Government Printing Office, 1918.

———. *Statistics of Population, 1880,* I. Washington, D.C.: Government Printing Office, 1883.

———. *Tenth Census of the United States, 1880.* Washington, D.C.: Government Printing Office, 1880.

Merriam, Lucius S. *Higher Education in Tennessee.* Bureau of Education Circular of Information, No. 5, 1893. Washington, D.C.: Government Printing Office, 1893.

Richardson, James D., ed. *A Compilation of the Messages and Papers of the Presidents, 1789–1897,* IX. Washington, D.C.: Government Printing Office, 1898, 10 vols.

TENNESSEE

Acts of the General Assembly of the State of Tennessee, 1865–91.

Annual Report of the State Superintendent of Public Instruction, 1881–91.

Biennial Report of the Bureau of Agriculture, Statistics and Immigration, 1889–90. Nashville: Albert B. Tavel, 1891.

Biennial Report of the Commissioner of Agriculture, Statistics, Mines and Immigration, 1879–90. Nashville: Tavel & Howell, 1881.

Contest for Governor: Complete Proceedings of the Joint Convention and the Investigating Committee. 2 vols. Nashville: Franc M. Paul, 1895.

Journal of the House of Representatives of the State of Tennessee, 1870–91.

Journal of the Proceedings of the Convention of Delegates Elected by the People of Tennessee to Amend, Revise, or Form and Make a New Constitution for the State. Nashville: Jones, Purvis, 1870.

Miller, Charles A., comp. *The Official and Political Manual of the State of Tennessee.* Nashville: Marshall & Bruce, 1890.

Milliken, W. A., and John J. Vertrees. *The Code of Tennessee: A Compilation of the Statute Laws of the State of Tennessee.* Nashville: Marshall & Bruce, 1884.

Senate Journal of the General Assembly of the State of Tennessee, 1870–91.

Shannon, Robert J. *Public and Permanent Statutes of a General Nature, Being an Annotated Code of Tennessee.* Nashville: Franc M. Paul, 1896.

Thompson, Seymour D., and Thomas M. Steger. *Statute Laws of the State of Tennessee.* St. Louis: W. J. Gilbert, 1873.

White, Robert H., ed. *Messages of the Governors of Tennessee,* 8 vols. Nashville: Tennessee Historical Commission, 1952–.

JUDICIAL DECISIONS

Brown v. Memphis & C. R. Co. 5 *Federal Reporter* 499 (1885).

Chesapeake, Ohio and Southwestern Railroad Company v. Wells. 85 *Tennessee Reports* 613–15 (1887).

Chesapeake, Ohio and Southwestern Railroad Company v. Wells. 4 *Southernwestern Reporter* 5 (1887).

Logwood and Wife v. Memphis & C. R. Co. 23 *Federal Reporter* 318 (1885).

Murphy v. Western & A. R. R. and others. 23 *Federal Reporter* 637 (1885).

Robinson and Wife v. Memphis & C. R. Co. 109 *U. S. Reports* 3–4 (1883).

Newspapers

Bolivar *Bulletin*, 1880–83.

Chattanooga *Times*, 1880–91.

Christian Advocate (Nashville), 1880–91.

Clarksville *Semi-Weekly Tobacco Leaf Chronicle*, 1880–91.

Clarksville *Weekly Chronicle*, 1880–87.

Cleveland (Ohio) *Gazette*, 1883–91.

Cleveland (Tenn.) *Weekly Herald*, 1880–83; 1887–91.

Fisk *Herald*, 1887–91.

Greeneville *Herald*, 1881–85.

Hickman (Co.) *Pioneer*, 1880–82.

Jackson *Afro-American Sentinel*, Oct. 11, 1890.

Jackson *Sun*, Jan. 1880–Sept. 1881; Mar. 17, 1882; Apr. 10, 1885; June 9, 1889.

Jackson *Whig*, June 1884–July 1888.

Knoxville *Chronicle*, Jan. 1880–Sept. 1886.

Knoxville *Journal*, Feb. 1885–Dec. 1891.

Knoxville *Negro World*, Nov. 19, 1887.

Knoxville *Tribune*, Apr. 1881–July 1883; 1887–1891.

Maryville *Republican*, Oct. 23, 1869; Apr. 25, 1874; Nov. 4, 1876.

Maryville *Times*, Oct. 11, 1884–June 3, 1891.

Memphis *Appeal*, 1880–90.

Memphis *Appeal-Avalanche*, 1890–91.

Memphis *Avalanche*, 1880–90.

Milan *Exchange*, 1880–84.

Morristown *Gazette*, 1880–86.

Nashville *American*, 1880–91.

Nashville *Banner*, 1880–91.

Nashville *Dispatch*, 1866.

Nashville *Republican–Banner*, Apr. 1867.

Nashville *Tennessean*, Feb. 13, 1971.

Nashville *Union and American*, 1874.

New York *Age*, 1887–91.

New York *Freeman*, 1884–87.

New York *Globe*, 1883–84.

New York *Times*, 1880–91.

Pulaski *Citizen*, 1880–86.

Washington *Bee*, June 10, 1882–Dec. 1890.

Weekly Toiler (Published by the Tennessee Farmers' Alliance), June 1888–Aug. 1890.

Periodical Articles

Bishop, Joseph B. "The Secret Ballot in Thirty-Three States." *Forum* 12 (Jan. 1892), 589–98.

Clark, E. P. "The Negro in Southern Politics." *Nation* 41 (July 23, 1885), 67.

Keating, John M. "Twenty Years of Negro Education." *Popular Science Monthly* 27 (Nov. 1885), 24–37.

Kirke, Edmund. "How Shall the Negro Be Educated?" *North American Review* 360 (Nov. 1886), 421–26.

Poe, Clarence H. "Suffrage Restrictions in the South; Its Causes and Consequences." *North American Review* 175 (Oct. 1902), 534–63.

Tillet, Wilber Fisk. "The White Man of the New South." *Century Magazine* 33 (Mar. 1887), 769–76.

Weeks, Stephen Beauregard. "The History of Negro Suffrage in the South." *Political Science Quarterly* 9 (Dec. 1894), 671–703.

Contemporary Reports and Pamphlets

Key, David M. "Legal and Political Status of the Negro." *Tennessee Bar Association Proceedings, 1885*. Nashville, 1885.

Phelan, James. *The New South*. Memphis: S. C. Toof, 1886.

Proceedings of the Eighth Republican National Convention, 1884. Chicago: Rand, McNally, 1884.

Proceedings of the Ninth Republican National Convention, 1888. Chicago: Blakely Printing, 1888.

Proceedings of the Republican National Convention, 1880. Chicago: Jeffrey Printing & Pub. House, 1881.

Twenty-first Annual Report of the Freedmen's Aid and Southern Education Society of the Methodist Episcopal Church, 1888. Cincinnati: Western Methodist Bk. Concern Printer, 1888.

Twenty-fifth Annual Report of the Freedmen's Aid and Southern Education Society of the Methodist Episcopal Church, 1891. Cincinnati: Western Methodist Bk. Concern Printer, 1891.

Contemporary Books

Clayton, W. W. *History of Davidson County, Tennessee, with Illustrations and Biographical Sketches of Its Prominent Men and Pioneers*. Philadelphia: J. W. Lewis, 1880.

Du Bois, W. E. B. *The Philadelphia Negro: A Social Study*. Philadelphia: Univ. of Pennsylvania, 1899.

Fortune, T. Thomas. *Black and White: Land, Labor and Politics in the South*. New York: Fords, Howard, & Hulbert, 1884.

Fuller, Thomas O. *Twenty Years in Public Life, 1890–1910.* Nashville: National Baptist Pub. Bd., 1910.

Goodspeed, Weston A., *et al.*, eds. *History of Tennessee, from the Earliest Time to the Present* . . . Chicago & Nashville: Goodspeed Pub., 1887.

Haley, James T., comp. *Afro-American Encyclopedia.* Nashville: Haley & Florida, 1895.

————., ed. *Sparkling Gems of Race Knowledge and Worth Reading.* Nashville: J. T. Haley, 1897.

Hamilton, Green Polonius. *Beacon Lights of the Race.* Memphis: E. H. Clarke & Bro., 1911.

Haygood, Atticus G. *Our Brother in Black: His Freedom and His Future.* New York: Phillips & Hunt, 1881.

Hubbard, G. W. *A History of the Colored Schools of Nashville, Tennessee.* Nashville: Wheeler, Marshall & Bruce, 1874.

Keating, John M. *History of Memphis and Shelby County, Tennessee.* 2 vols. Syracuse: D. Mason, 1888.

Lane, Isaac. *Autobiography of Bishop Isaac Lane.* Nashville: Pub. House of the Methodist Episcopal Church, South, 1916.

Payne, Daniel Alexander. *History of the African Methodist Episcopal Church.* Nashville: Pub. House of the A. M. E. Sunday School Union, 1891.

————. *Recollections of Seventy Years.* 1888; rpt. New York: Arno Press, 1968.

Penn, Garland I. *The Afro-American Press.* Springfield, Mass.: Wiley, 1892.

Prentis, Noble L. *Southern Letters.* Topeka: George W. Martin, 1881.

Simmons, William J. *Men of Mark: Eminent, Progressive and Rising.* Cleveland, Ohio: George M. Rowell, 1887.

Speer, William S., comp. and ed. *Sketches of Prominent Tennesseans.* Nashville: Albert B. Tavel, 1888.

Straker, D. Augustus. *The New South Investigated.* Detroit: Ferguson, 1888.

————. *Negro Suffrage in the South.* Detroit: Straker, 1906.

Taylor, Charles Henry James. *White and Black, or, The Question Settled.* Atlanta: Jas. P. Harrison, 1889.

Vertrees, John J. *The Negro Problem.* Nashville: Marshall & Bruce, 1905.

Warner, Charles D. *On Horseback: A Tour in Virginia, North Carolina, and Tennessee.* Boston and New York: Houghton, 1888.

White, J. Bliss, comp. *Biography and Achievements of the Colored Citizens of Chattanooga.* N. p.: n. p., 1904.

Whitson, Mrs. L. D. *Personal Sketches of Members of the Forty-fourth General Assembly of Tennessee.* Nashville: Southern Methodist Pub. House, 1885.

Woolridge, J., ed. *History of Nashville, Tennessee.* Nashville: Methodist Pub. House, 1890.

Contemporary Almanacs and Directories

Cumberland Almanac for the Year 1881. Nashville: American Pub., 1881.

Cumberland Almanac for the Year 1885. Nashville: American Pub., 1885.

Directory of Chattanooga, Tennessee. 1880–90.

Memphis City Directory. 1880–90.

Nashville City Directory. 1880–90.

Tennessee State Gazetter and Business Directory. 1876–77, 1881–82, 1887, 1891.

SECONDARY SOURCES

Books

Abshire, David. *The South Rejects a Prophet: The Life of Senator David M. Key, 1824–1900.* New York: Praeger, 1967.

Alexander, Thomas B. *Political Reconstruction in Tennessee.* Nashville: Vanderbilt Univ. Press, 1950.

————. "Political Reconstruction in Tennessee." In *Radicalism, Racism, and Party Realignment,* ed. Richard O. Curry. Baltimore: Johns Hopkins Univ. Press, 1970.

Allison, John, ed. *Notable Men of Tennessee.* Atlanta: Southern Historical Assoc., 1905.

Baker, Thomas Harrison. *The Memphis Commercial Appeal: The History of a Southern Newspaper.* Baton Rouge: Louisiana State Univ. Press, 1971.

Berghe, van den, Pierre L. *Race and Racism: A Comparative Perspective.* New York: Wiley, 1967.

Blassingame, John W. *The Slave Community: Plantation Life in the Ante-Bellum South.* New York: Oxford Univ. Press, 1972.

Bond, Horace Mann. *Negro Education in Alabama: A Study in Cotton and Steel.* 1939; rpt. New York: Atheneum, 1969.

Botkin, B. A., ed. *Lay My Burden Down: A Folk History of Slavery.* Chicago: Univ. of Chicago Press, 1945.

Brock, W. R. *An American Crisis: Congress and Reconstruction, 1865–1867.* New York: Harper, 1966.

Bullock, Henry Allen. *A History of Negro Education in the South: From 1619 to the Present.* Cambridge, Mass.: Harvard Univ. Press, 1967.

Burnham, W. Dean. *Presidential Ballots, 1836–1892.* Baltimore: Johns Hopkins Univ. Press, 1955.

Callcott, Margaret Law. *The Negro in Maryland Politics, 1870–1912.* Baltimore: Johns Hopkins Univ. Press, 1969.

Capers, Gerald M., Jr. *The Biography of a River Town; Memphis: Its Heroic Age.* Chapel Hill: Univ. of North Carolina Press, 1939.

Corlew, Robert Ewing. *A History of Dickson County, Tennessee.* Nashville: Tennessee Historical Commission, 1956.

Coulter, E. Merton. *William G. Brownlow: Fighting Parson of the Southern Highlands.* Chapel Hill: Univ. of North Carolina Press, 1937; rpt. Knoxville: Univ. of Tennessee Press, 1971.

Davis, Kingsley, and Wilbert Moore. "Some Principles of Stratification: A Critical Analysis." In *Class, Status, and Power: Social Stratification in Comparative Perspective,* ed. Reinhard Bendix and Seymour Martin Lipset. 2d ed. New York: Free Press, 1966.

De Santis, Vincent P. *Republicans Face the Southern Question–The New Departure Years, 1877–1897.* Baltimore: Johns Hopkins Univ. Press, 1959.

Duster, Alfreda M., ed. *Crusade for Justice: The Autobiography of Ida B. Wells.* Chicago: Univ. of Chicago Press, 1970.

Edmonds, Helen G. *The Negro and Fusion Politics in North Carolina.* Chapel Hill: Univ. of North Carolina Press, 1951.

Folmsbee, Stanley J., Robert E. Corlew, and Enoch L. Mitchell. *History of Tennessee.* 4 vols. New York: Lewis Historical Pub., 1960.

Foner, Philip S., ed. *The Life and Writings of Frederick Douglass*, IV: *Reconstruction and After.* New York: International Pub., 1955.

Fredman, L. E. *The Australian Ballot: The Story of an American Reform.* East Lansing: Michigan State Univ. Press, 1968.

Fredrickson, George M. *The Black Image in the White Mind: The Debate on Afro-American Character and Destiny, 1817–1914.* New York: Harper, 1971.

Fuller, Thomas O. *History of the Negro Baptists of Tennessee.* Memphis: Haskins, 1939.

Gaston, Paul M. *The New South Creed: A Study in Southern Mythmaking.* New York: Knopf, 1970.

Gillette, William. *The Right to Vote: Politics and the Passage of the Fifteenth Amendment.* Baltimore: Johns Hopkins Univ. Press, 1965.

Going, Allen Johnston. *Bourbon Democracy in Alabama, 1874–1890.* University: Univ. of Alabama Press, 1951.

Govan, Gilbert E., and James W. Livingood. *The Chattanooga Country, 1540–1951.* New York: Dutton, 1952.

———. *The University of Chattanooga: Sixty Years.* Chattanooga: Univ. of Chattanooga Press, 1947.

Green, Constance McLaughlin. *The Secret City: A History of Race Relations in the Nation's Capital.* Princeton: Princeton Univ. Press, 1967.

Hair, William Ivy. *Bourbonism and Agrarian Protest: Louisiana Politics, 1877–1900.* Baton Rouge: Louisiana State Univ. Press, 1969.

Hale, William T., and L. Merritt Dixon. *A History of Tennessee and Tennesseans.* 8 vols. Chicago: Lewis Pub., 1913.

Hamer, Philip M., ed. *Tennessee: A History, 1673–1932.* 4 vols. New York: American Historical Soc., 1933.

Harlan, Louis R. *Booker T. Washington: The Making of a Black Leader, 1856–1901.* New York: Oxford Univ. Press, 1972.

Hirshson, Stanley P. *Farewell to the Bloody Shirt: Northern Republicans and the Southern Negro, 1877–1893.* Bloomington: Indiana Univ. Press, 1962.

Horn, Stanley F. *Invisible Empire, the Story of the Ku Klux Klan, 1886–1871.* Boston: Houghton, 1939.

Isaac, Paul E. *Prohibition and Politics: Turbulent Decades in Tennessee, 1885–1920.* Knoxville: Univ. of Tennessee Press, 1965.

Johnson, Guion G. "The Ideology of White Supremacy, 1876–1910." In *Essays in Southern History,* ed. Fletcher M. Green. Chapel Hill: Univ. of North Carolina Press, 1949.

Key, V. O., Jr., with Alexander Heard. *Southern Politics in State and Nation.* New York: Knopf, 1949.

Kirwan, Albert D. *Revolt of the Rednecks, Mississippi Politics: 1876–1925.* Lexington: Univ. of Kentucky Press, 1951.

Kousser, *The Shaping of Southern Politics: Suffrage Restriction and the Establishment of the One-Party South, 1880–1910.* New Haven and London: Yale Univ. Press, 1974.

Lewinson, Paul. *Race, Class, and Party: A History of Negro Suffrage and White Politics in the South.* London: Oxford Univ. Press, 1932.

Logan, Frenise A. *The Negro in North Carolina, 1876–1894.* Chapel Hill: Univ. of North Carolina Press, 1964.

Logan, Rayford W. *The Betrayal of the Negro: From Rutherford B. Hayes to Woodrow Wilson.* new enl. ed., New York: Collier-Macmillan, 1965.

Mabry, William Alexander. *The Negro in North Carolina Politics since Reconstruction.* Durham: Duke Univ. Press, 1940.

McGuffey, Charles D., ed. *Standard History of Chattanooga, Tennessee.* Knoxville: Crew & Dorey, 1911.

McKitrick, Eric L. *Andrew Johnson and Reconstruction.* Chicago: Univ. of Chicago Press, 1960.

McPherson, James M. *The Negro's Civil War: How American Negroes Felt and Acted during the War for the Union.* New York: Knopf, 1965.

Mangum, Charles Staples, Jr. *The Legal Status of the Negro.* Chapel Hill: Univ. of North Carolina Press, 1940.

Marszalek, John F., Jr. *Court Martial: A Black Man in America.* New York: Scribners, 1972.

Mason, Philip. *Race Relations.* London: Oxford Univ. Press, 1970.

Meier, August. *Negro Thought in America, 1880–1915.* Ann Arbor: Univ. of Michigan Press, 1963.

Miller, Zane L. *The Urbanization of Modern America: A Brief History.* New York: Harcourt, 1973.

Mooney, Chase C. *Slavery in Tennessee.* Bloomington: Indiana Univ. Press, 1957.

Morgan, H. Wayne. *From Hayes to McKinley: National Party Politics, 1877–1896.* Syracuse: Syracuse Univ. Press, 1969.

Myrdal, Gunnar. *An American Dilemma: The Negro Problem and Modern Democracy.* 2 vols. New York: Harper, 1944.

Olbrich, Emil. *The Development of Sentiment on Negro Suffrage to 1860.* Madison: Univ. of Wisconsin, 1912.

Olsen, Otto H., ed. *The Negro Question: From Slavery to Caste, 1863–1910. Major Issues in American History.* New York: Pitman, 1971.

Parsons, Talcott, ed. *Essays in Sociological Theory.* rev. ed. Glencoe, Ill.: Free Press, 1949.

Patterson, Caleb P. *The Negro in Tennessee, 1790–1865.* Austin: Univ. of Texas Press, 1922.

Patton, James Welch. *Unionism and Reconstruction in Tennessee, 1860–1869.* Chapel Hill: Univ. of North Carolina Press, 1934.

Phillips, Ulrich B. *American Negro Slavery.* 1918; rpt. Baton Rouge: Louisiana State Univ. Press, 1966.

Porter, Kirk H. *A History of Suffrage in the United States.* Chicago: Univ. of Chicago Press, 1918.

————, and Donald B. Johnson, eds. *National Party Platforms, 1840–1956.* Urbana: Univ. of Illinois Press, 1956.

Randall, J. G., and David Donald. *The Civil War and Reconstruction.* 2d ed., rev. Lexington, Mass.: Heath, 1969.

Redkey, Edwin S. *Black Exodus: Black Nationalist and Back-to-Africa Movements, 1890–1910.* New Haven: Yale Univ. Press, 1969.

Rice, Lawrence D. *The Negro in Texas, 1874–1900.* Baton Rouge: Louisiana State Univ. Press, 1971.

Robison, Daniel Merritt. *Bob Taylor and the Agrarian Revolt in Tennessee.* Chapel Hill: Univ. of North Carolina Press, 1935.

Rothrock, Mary U., ed. *The French Broad-Holston Country: A History of Knox County, Tennessee.* Knoxville: East Tennessee Historical Soc., 1946.

Rule, William. *Standard History of Knoxville, Tennessee.* Chicago: Lewis Pub., 1900.

Savage, Horace C. *Life and Times of Bishop Isaac Lane.* Nashville: National, 1958.

Scott, Mingo. *The Negro in Tennessee Politics and Governmental Affairs, 1865–1965: "The Hundred Years Story."* Nashville: Rich, 1964.

Shadgett, Olive H. *The Republican Party in Georgia from Reconstruction through 1900.* Athens: Univ. of Georgia Press, 1964.

Sproat, John G. *"The Best Men": Liberal Reformers in the Gilded Age.* New York: Oxford Univ. Press, 1968.

Stampp, Kenneth M. *The Era of Reconstruction, 1865–1877.* New York: Knopf, 1965.

Stephenson, Gilbert Thomas. *Race Distinctions in American Law.* New York: Appleton, 1910.

Talley, Robert. *One Hundred Years of the Commercial Appeal, 1840–1940.* Memphis: Memphis Pub., 1940.

Tatum, Elbert Lee. *The Changed Political Thought of the Negro, 1915–1940.* New York: Exposition, 1951.

Taylor, Alrutheus Ambush. *The Negro in Tennessee, 1865–1880.* Washington, D.C.: Associated Pub., 1941.

271

Temple, Oliver P. *Notable Men of Tennessee from 1833 to 1875.* New York: Cosmopolitan Press, 1912.

Thornbrough, Emma Lou. *T. Thomas Fortune: Militant Journalist.* Chicago: Univ. of Chicago Press, 1972.

Tindall, George B. *South Carolina Negroes, 1877–1900.* Columbia: Univ. of South Carolina Press, 1952.

———. "Southern Negroes since Reconstruction: Dissolving the Static Image." In *Writing Southern History: Essays in Historiography in Honor of Fletcher M. Green,* ed. Arthur S. Link and Rembert W. Patrick. Baton Rouge: Louisiana State Univ. Press, 1965.

Turner, Arlin. *George W. Cable: A Biography.* Durham: Duke Univ. Press, 1956.

Wharton, Vernon Lane. *The Negro in Mississippi, 1865–1890.* Chapel Hill: Univ. of North Carolina Press, 1947.

White, Robert H. *Development of the Tennessee State Educational Organization, 1796–1929.* Nashville: George Peabody Coll. for Teachers, 1929.

Wiley, Bell Irvin. *Southern Negroes, 1861–1865.* New Haven: Yale Univ. Press, 1938.

Woodward, C. Vann. *American Counterpoint: Slavery and Racism in the North-South Dialogue.* Boston: Little, 1971.

———. *Origins of the New South, 1877–1913.* Baton Rouge: Louisiana State Univ. Press, 1951.

———. *The Strange Career of Jim Crow.* 2d rev. ed. New York: Oxford Univ. Press, 1966.

———. *Tom Watson: Agrarian Rebel.* New York: Macmillan, 1938.

Wynes, Charles E., ed. *The Negro in the South since 1865: Selected Essays in American Negro History.* University: Univ. of Alabama Press, 1965.

———. *Race Relations in Virginia, 1870–1902.* Charlottesville: Univ. of Virginia Press, 1961.

Young, John Preston. *Standard History of Memphis, Tennessee.* Knoxville: H. W. Crew, 1912.

Periodical Articles

Alexander, Thomas B. "Kukluxism in Tennessee, 1865–69." *Tennessee Historical Quarterly* 8 (Sept. 1949), 195–219.

Alilunas, Leo. "Legal Restrictions on the Negro in Politics." *Journal of Negro History* 25 (Apr. 1940), 152–202.

Andrews, Norman P. "The Negro in Politics." *Jour. Negro Hist.* 5 (Oct. 1920), 420–36.

Ball, Clyde. "The Public Career of Colonel A. S. Colyar, 1870–1877." *Tenn. Hist. Quar.* 12 (Mar. 1953), 23–47 (June 1953), 106–28 (Sept. 1953), 213–38.

Bejack, L. D. "The Taxing District of Shelby County." West Tennessee Historical Society *Papers* 4 (1950), 5–27.

Belissary, Constantine G. "The Rise of Industry and the Industrial Spirit in Tennessee, 1865–1885." *Jour. of Southern Hist.* 19 (May 1953), 193–215.

———. "Tennessee and Immigration, 1865–1880." *Tenn. Hist. Quar.* 7 (Sept. 1948), 229–48.

Bowen, David W. "Andrew Johnson and the Negro." East Tennessee Historical Society's *Publications*, No. 40 (1968), 28–49.

Brewer, W. M. "The Poll Tax and the Poll Taxers." *Jour. Negro Hist.* 29 (July 1944), 260–99.

Bunche, Ralph J. "The Negro in the Political Life of the U.S." *Journal of Negro Education* 10 (July 1941), 507–84.

Cook, Samuel DuBois. "A Tragic Conception of Negro History." *Jour. Negro Hist.* 45 (Oct. 1960), 219–40.

Crofts, Daniel W. "The Black Response to the Blair Education Bill." *Jour. Southern Hist.* 37 (Feb. 1971), 41–65.

"Death of Honorable J. H. Dortch." *Tennessee Historical Magazine* 7 (July 1921), 142.

Dethloff, Henry C., and Robert R. Jones. "Race Relations in Louisiana, 1877–98." *Louisiana History* 9 (Fall 1968), 301–23.

Ellis, John H. "Businessmen and Public Health in the Urban South during the Nineteenth Century: New Orleans, Memphis, and Atlanta." *Bulletin of the History of Medicine* 44 (July-Aug. 1970), 346–71.

———. "Memphis Sanitary Revolution, 1880–1890." *Tenn. Hist. Quar.* 23 (Mar. 1964), 59–72.

———. "Business Leadership in Memphis Public Health Reform, 1880–1900." WTHS *Papers* 19 (1965), 94–100.

Feistman, Eugene G. "Radical Disfranchisement and the Restoration of Tennessee, 1865–66." *Tenn. Hist. Quar.* 12 (Mar.-Dec. 1953), 135–51.

Folmsbee, Stanley J. "The Origins of the First 'Jim Crow' Law." *Jour. Southern Hist.* 15 (May 1949), 235–47.

273

Frazer, Walter J., Jr. "John Eaton, Jr., Radical Republican: Champion of the Negro and Federal Aid to Southern Education, 1869–1882." *Tenn. Hist. Quar.* 25 (Fall 1966), 239–60.

Genovese, Eugene D. "Rebelliousness and Docility in the Negro Slave: A Critique of the Elkins Thesis." *Civil War History* 13 (Dec. 1967), 293–314.

Going, Allen J. "The South and the Blair Education Bill." *Mississippi Valley Historical Review* 44 (Sept. 1957), 267–90.

Goodwin, Lawrence C. "Populist Dreams and Negro Rights: East Texas as A Case Study." *American Historical Review* 76 (Dec. 1971), 1435–56.

Grantham, Dewey, W., Jr. "Georgia Politics and the Disfranchisement of the Negro." *Georgia Historical Quarterly* 32 (Mar. 1948), 1–21.

Hays, Samuel P. "The Politics of Reform in Municipal Government in the Progressive Era." *Pacific Northwest Quarterly* 55 (Oct. 1964), 157–69.

Henry, H. M. "The Slave Laws of Tennessee." *Tenn. Hist. Mag.* 2 (Sept. 1916), 175–203.

Howell, Sarah M. "The Editorials of Arthur S. Colyar, Nashville Prophet of the New South." *Tenn. Hist. Quar.* 27 (Fall 1968), 262–76.

Imes, William Lloyd. "The Legal Status of Free Negroes and Slaves in Tennessee." *Jour. Negro Hist.* 4 (July 1919), 254–72.

"James C. Napier" (obituary). *Jour. Negro Hist.* 25 (July 1940), 400–401.

Johnson, Guion Griffis. "Southern Paternalism toward Negroes after Emancipation." *Jour. Southern Hist.* 23 (Nov. 1957), 483–509.

Jones, Robert B. "Tennessee Gubernatorial Elections, II, 1880—The Collapse of the Democratic Party." *Tenn. Hist. Quar.* (Spring 1974), 49–61.

Jordan, Weymouth T. "Negro Enfranchisement in Reconstruction Tennessee: An Interpretation." *Essays in the Social Sciences.* Florida State University *Studies*, No. 10 (1953), 63–69.

Kiger, Joseph C. "Social Thought as Voiced in Rural Middle Tennessee Newspapers, 1878–1898." *Tenn. Hist. Quar.* 9 (June 1950), 131–54.

Kousser, J. Morgan. "Post-Reconstruction Suffrage Restrictions in Tennessee: A New Look at the V. O. Key Thesis." *Political Science Quarterly* 88 (Dec. 1973), 655–83.

Matthews, Linda M. "Keeping Down Jim Crow: The Railroads and the Separate Coach Bills in South Carolina." *South Atlantic Quarterly* 73 (Winter 1974), 117–29.

Meier, August. "The Negro and the Democratic Party, 1875–1915." *Phylon* 17 (2d Quarter 1956), 173–91.

Mooney, Chase C. "The Question of Slavery and the Free Negro in the Tennessee Constitutional Convention of 1834." *Jour. Southern Hist.* 12 (Nov. 1946), 487–509.

Moore, John Hammond. "Jim Crow in Georgia." *South Atlantic Quarterly* 66 (1967), 554–65.

Patton, James W. "The Progress of Emancipation in Tennessee." *Jour. Negro Hist.* 17 (Jan. 1932), 67–102.

Phillips, Paul David. "White Reaction to the Freedmen's Bureau in Tennessee." *Tenn. Hist. Quar.* 25 (Spring 1966), 50–62.

Qualls, J. Winfield. "The Beginnings and Early History of the LeMoyne School at Memphis, 1871–1874." WTHS *Publications* 7 (1953), 5–37.

Queener, Verton M. "A Decade of East Tennessee Republicanism, 1867–1876." ETHS *Publications*, No. 14 (1943), 59–85.

———. "The East Tennessee Republicans as a Minority Party, 1870–1896." ETHS *Publications*, No. 15 (1943), 49–73.

———. "The East Tennessee Republicans in State and Nation, 1870–1900." *Tenn. Hist. Quar.* 2 (June 1943), 99–128.

———. "East Tennessee Sentiment and the Secession Movement, November, 1860–June, 1861." ETHS *Publications*, No. 20 (1948), 59–83.

———. "Origin of the Republican Party in East Tennessee." ETHS *Publications*, No. 13 (1941), 66–90.

Richardson, Joe M. "A Negro Success Story: James Dallas Burrus." *Jour. Negro Hist.* 50 (Oct. 1965), 274–82.

Robison, Dan M. "Governor Robert L. Taylor and the Blair Educational Bill in Tennessee." *Tenn. Hist. Mag.* 12d Ser., II (Oct. 1931), 28–49.

Sharp, James A. "The Downfall of the Radicals in Tennessee." ETHS *Publications*, No. 5 (1933), 105–24.

———. "The Entrance of the Farmers' Alliance into Tennessee Politics." ETHS *Publications*, No. 9 (1937), 77–92.

———. "The Farmers' Alliance and the People's Party in Tennessee." ETHS *Publications*, No. 10 (1938), 91–113.

Sheeler, Reuben J. "The Development of Unionism in East Tennessee." *Jour. Negro Hist.* 29 (Apr. 1944), 166–203.

Smith, Samuel Boyd. "Joseph Buckner Killebrew and the New South Movement in Tennessee." ETHS *Publications*, No. 37 (1967), 5–22.

275

Taylor, Alrutheus A. "Fisk University and the Nashville Community, 1866–1900." *Jour. Negro Hist.* 39 (Apr. 1954), 111–26.

Trabue, Charles C. "The Voluntary Emancipation of Slaves in Tennessee as Reflected in the State's Legislation and Judicial Decisions." *Tenn. Hist. Mag.* 4 (Mar. 1918), 50–68.

Tucker, David M. "Black Politics in Memphis, 1867–1875." WTHS *Publications* 26 (1972), 13–19.

Van Deusen, John G. "The Negro in Politics." *Jour. Negro Hist.* 21 (July 1936), 256–74.

Walton, Hanes, Jr. "Another Force for Disfranchisement: Blacks and the Prohibitionist in Tennessee." *Journal of Human Relations* 18 (1970), 728–38.

Watts, Eugene J. "Black Political Progress in Atlanta: 1868–1895." *Jour. Negro Hist.* 59 (July 1974), 268–86.

Williams, Frank B. "The Poll Tax as a Suffrage Requirement in the South." *Jour. Southern Hist.* 18 (1952), 469-96.

Woodward, C. Vann. "The Political Legacy of Reconstruction." *Journal of Negro Education* 26 (Summer 1957), 231–40.

Work, Monroe N. "Some Negro Members of Reconstruction Conventions and Legislatures and of Congress." *Jour. Negro Hist.* (Jan. 1920), 63–125.

Unpublished Works

Abramowitz, Jack. "Accommodation and Militance in Negro Life, 1876–1916." Ph.D. diss., Columbia Univ., 1950.

Arendale, Marirose. "Political Viewpoints of the Chattanooga *Times*, 1878–1884." Honors thesis, Univ. of Chattanooga, 1952.

Bacote, Clarence Albert. "The Negro in Georgia Politics, 1880–1908." Ph.D. diss., Univ. of Chicago, 1955.

Ball, Clyde. "The Public Career of Colonel A. S. Colyar, 1870–1877." M.A. thesis, Vanderbilt Univ., 1937.

Belissary, Constantine G. "The Rise of the Industrial Spirit in Tennessee, 1865–1885." Ph.D. diss., Vanderbilt Univ., 1949.

Brinkley, Edwin. "History of the Chattanooga *Times*, 1869–1949." M.A. thesis, Univ. of Missouri, 1950.

Brown, Donald. "Southern Attitudes toward Negro Voting in the Bourbon Period, 1877–1890." Ph.D. diss., Univ. of Oklahoma, 1960.

Buggs, John Allen. "Racial Legislation in Tennessee." M.A. thesis, Fisk Univ., 1941.

Cartwright, Joseph H. "The Negro in Tennessee Politics, 1880–1891."M.A. thesis, Vanderbilt Univ., 1968.

Corlew, Robert E. "The Negro in Tennessee, 1870–1900." Ph.D. diss., Univ. of Alabama, 1954.

Crowe, Jesse Crawford. "Agitation for Penal Reform in Tennessee, 1870–1900." Ph.D. diss., Vanderbilt Univ., 1954.

Davis, Thomas Woodrow. "Arthur S. Colyar and the New South, 1860–1905." Ph.D. diss., Univ. of Missouri, 1962.

England, James Merton. "The Free Negro in Ante-Bellum Tennessee." Ph.D. diss., Vanderbilt Univ., 1941.

Gentry, Amos Lee. "The Public Career of Leonidas Campbell Houk." M.A. thesis, Univ. of Tennessee, 1939.

Hart, Roger Louis. "Bourbonism and Populism in Tennessee, 1875–1896." Ph.D. diss., Princeton Univ., 1970.

Holloway, Margaret Endsley. "The Reaction in Tennessee to the Federal Elections Bill of 1890." M.A. thesis, Univ. of Tennessee, 1970.

Jones, Robert B. "The State Debt Controversy in Tennessee, 1865–1883." Ph.D. diss., Vanderbilt Univ., 1972.

Jordan, Weymouth T. "The Negro in Tennessee during Reconstruction." M.A. thesis, Vanderbilt Univ., 1934.

Kousser, J. Morgan. "Tennessee Politics and the Negro: 1948–1964." Senior thesis, Princeton Univ., 1965.

————. "The Shaping of Southern Politics: Suffrage Restriction and the Establishment of the One-Party South, 1880–1910." Ph.D. diss., Yale Univ., 1971.

Looney, John Thomas. "Isham G. Harris of Tennessee: Bourbon Senator, 1877–1897." M.A. thesis, Univ. of Tennessee, 1970.

McKinney, Gordon B. "Mountain Republicanism, 1876–1900." Ph.D. diss., Northwestern Univ., 1971.

Phillips, Paul D. "A History of the Freedmen's Bureau in Tennessee." Ph.D. diss., Vanderbilt Univ., 1964.

Queener, Verton Madison. "The Republican Party in East Tennessee, 1865–1900." Ph.D. diss., Indiana Univ., 1940.

Robison, Daniel M. "Preliminary Sketches, Biographical Directory, Tennessee General Assembly." State Library and Archives, Nashville, Tennessee.

Roitman, Joel M. "Race Relations in Memphis, Tennessee—1880–1905." M.A. thesis, Memphis State Univ., 1964.

Rose, Stanley Frazer. "Nashville and Its Leadership Elite, 1861–69." M.A. thesis, Univ. of Virginia, 1965.

Sallis, William Charles. "The Color Line in Mississippi Politics, 1865–1915." Ph.D. diss., Univ. of Kentucky, 1967.

Samples, Ralph. "The Development of Public Education in Tennessee during the Bourbon Era, 1870–1900." Ph.D. diss., Univ. of Tennessee, 1965.

Seehorn, John B. "The Life and Public Career of Henry Clay Evans." M.A. thesis, Univ. of Tennessee, 1970.

Stanton, William A. "The State Debt in Tennessee Politics," M.A. thesis, Vanderbilt Univ., 1939.

Walker, Joseph Alexander. "The Negro in Tennessee Politics, 1865–1880." M.A. thesis, Fisk Univ., 1941.

Walker, Joseph E. "The Negro in Tennessee during the Reconstruction Period." M.A. thesis, Univ. of Tennessee, 1933.

Webb, Allie Baine. "A History of Negro Voting in Louisiana, 1877–1906." Ph.D. diss., Louisiana State Univ., 1962.

Williams, Frank B. "The Poll Tax as a Suffrage Requirement in the South, 1870–1901." Ph.D. diss., Vanderbilt Univ., 1950.

Index

279